HARLEY AND THE HOLY MOUNTAIN

Through the heart of
Greece to its soul

John Mole

For Alfie, Catherine, Elizabeth,
Emily, Harrison, Ruth and William
who also love Greece.

First published 2020

Fortune
241
95 Wilton Road
London SW1V 1BZ

CONTENTS

TIMELINE

Helladic - Homeric - Archaic - Classical - Hellenistic - Roman - Byzantine - Frankish - Ottoman - Modern

Greece has such a long and eventful history that when you wander round museums or archaeological sites it can merge into a hotchpotch of Greekery from different ages and places. Do you know your Minoans from your Mycenaeans, your Helladic from your Hellenistic? If you do or you don't care, please skip this. They are labels invented in the Nineteenth Century and unknown to the people who lived through them.

Helladic 1600-1100 BC

The Bronze Age so-called 'Palace' culture, communities centralised around an aristocratic power base. Famous for bull-leaping Minoans on Crete, Mycenaeans on the mainland and Cycladic people on the Aegean islands making shovel-faced white statues. Minoans used 'Linear A' script which has not yet been deciphered. Minoans used 'Linear B' script which has.

Homeric 1100-800 BC

The age that Homer looked back to of Gods and Heroes and The Trojan War which allegedly took place around 1100 BC. It was a time of economic and social collapse, famine and invasion but also the stirrings of a new Greek culture.

Archaic 800-480 BC

The emergence of City States with systematised political systems and religion centred on temples. The first Olympic Games were held along with athletic and cultural festivals in other places. Coinage facilitated trade. Sculpture and pottery flourished. Greek script was developed based on Phoenician. In around 700 BC the *Iliad* and *Odyssey* were written down allegedly by Homer. Greeks battled Persians at Marathon and Thermopylae.

Classical 480 - 323BC

The Golden Age and the foundation of European Civilisation. Democracy was developed. The Parthenon and other famous buildings were created. Most of the Greek writers, playwrights and philosophers you have heard of flourished from Aeschylus to Zeno. Alexander the Great conquered the known world. He died in 323 BC

Hellenistic 323-140 BC

The peak of Greek power and influence throughout Alexander's conquests. Greek became the lingua franca from Italy to India. Alexandria was the leading city, where Euclid fathered geometry. In Sicily Archimedes applied maths to physics. In Athens Stoics, Epicureans, and Cynics disputed moral philosophy.

Roman 140 BC - AD 400

Romans completed the conquest of Greece. Augustus took Alexandria in AD 30 after defeating Antony and Cleopatra at the battle of Actium. Christ was born and initiated another kind of conquest. In AD 70 Romans destroyed the Temple of Jerusalem.

Byzantine AD 400 - AD 1453

The thousand year Eastern Roman empire based in Constantinople. Constantine the Great converted to Christianity in AD 312. Mohamed was born in about AD 570. The Great Schism divided Orthodox and Catholic in 1054. Flowering of art, architecture and gastronomy.

Frankish AD 1204 - AD 1450

In 1204 Western Europeans of the Fourth Crusade, collectively known as Franks, captured Constantinople. They installed a Latin Emperor and divided Greece into several Latin states. The Byzantines recovered Constantinople and much lost territory but not their previous dominance. Muslim ascendancy accelerated.

Ottoman AD 1453 - AD 1830

In AD 1453 Mehmed the Conqueror took Constantinople and installed himself as the Emperor of Rome. Greeks continued to dominate trade. In Constantinople the Patriarchate administered Orthodoxy while Greek nobility was influential in Ottoman governance.

Independent Greece

1821 The Revolution
1830 Independent Greek State
1923 Exchange of Populations with Turkey
1940 Oxi!, Greece defeated Italy, Occupation
1946-1949 Civil War
1967-1974 Military dictatorship
1981 Greece joined the EU
2010 The Crisis

John Mole

INTRODUCTION

For some of us 'Greece' means marble ruins and muscly heroes in crested helmets. Or we think of boxy whitewashed houses huddled round a church with a blue roof and a gnarly old fisherman mending a net. Between the pagan temple and the Christian church, the Spartan 300 and *Mama Mia!* are more than three millennia that have created Greece.

Greeks are brought up to believe they are descendants of Ancient Greeks. When they feel Greece is undervalued they trot out the mantra 'two thousand years ago we gave you civilisation, law, democracy, philosophy, culture, medicine…' They also believe they are custodians of the one true religion, Orthodox Christianity, the defining characteristic of Greekness for over a thousand years.

The state of Greece is two hundred years old. Since their bloody revolution against the Ottomans, Greeks have resisted British, French, Russian, German, Italian, Bulgarian and American invasion or domination. The struggle continues for independence from Brussels, Frankfurt and Washington that control its finances. Through turbulence and disaster Greeks have created a vibrant, enterprising, European democracy with a unique identity. It is an extraordinary story of an extraordinary people.

This is the account of a road trip on Harley, a twenty-five year old 50cc motorcycle, through the history and geography that give Greeks the sense of who they are. We pass sites and sights from the Bronze Age to the present: a beehive tomb, 3500 years old; the shrine of a Russian saint, who teleported pilaff; a refugee camp in a chicken factory; and many other extraordinary places. Having travelled through time and space I abandon Harley for a spiritual dimension among the monks of the Holy Mountain of Athos.

Welcome to Greece.

MAP OF GREECE

MAP OF THE JOURNEY

'Ithaca gave you the marvellous journey.

Without her you wouldn't have set out.

She has nothing left to give you now.

And if you find her poor, Ithaca won't have fooled you.

Wise as you will have become, so full of experience,

you'll have understood by then what these Ithacas mean.'

from 'Ithaca' by Constantine Cavafy translated by Edmund Keeley

'Last night I saw a friend
wandering around
like a gnome
on his motorcycle
and dogs were chasing him.'

from 'Zeybekiko', a song by Dionysis Savvopoulos

1 READY FOR THE ROAD

"Arfa, what would you say to me biking up to Mount Athos?"

"The Holy Mountain? All those monks? Have you been drinking ouzo?"

"Me?"

"It sounds like one of your ouzo ideas. Breathe out. Yup."

"I'm serious."

"How far is it?"

"Not sure. Five hundred miles?"

"You'll fall off. What about poor Harley? He's as decrepit as you."

"Nonsense. It'll do us both good. The open road."

"You're too old for a mid-life crisis."

"An end-life crisis then."

I take this wifely encouragement on the chin, one of them anyway, light the lamps and lay the table on the terrace under the vine. Arfa is her nickname. When offered wine she used to say a modest 'just arfa glass' until she decided it was too much trouble refilling it twice as often as everyone else. I fetch a bottle of Shed from the fridge. Instead of a chateau on the label it has a photo of the concrete shed where it was made. €2.50 for a litre and a half, cheaper than water. A couple of glasses and I hope Arfa will come round to the Athos idea. She brings out plates of green beans, creamy feta, octopus stew, a salad of cucumber and tomatoes still warm from the vine where they had been growing an hour ago. We watch the moon come up, applauding when it clears the hilltop, our tradition since the children were little. I fill our glasses.

"About my idea."

"Which one?"

"Biking up to Athos."

"The ouzo idea. Why would you want to do that?"

"To take Father Makarios his books."

"Hmm. That's a flimsy reason. Why don't you mail them?"

"They might get lost in the post."

"Getting flimsier."

I try another tack.

"To explore the Greece I don't know while I can still remember where I've been."

"What do you expect to find?"

"Dunno until I find it."

"Hmm. It sounds like one of your frolics."

"I might climb Mount Athos."

"You? With your knees?"

She laughs. The moon smirks. Crickets snicker. I should never have asked. I should have just gone.

"Hmm. Promise me you'll wear a helmet."

If you look at a map of Greece you will see in the north what looks like a stunted hand with three fingers sticking out into the sea. The top finger is the peninsula of Mount Athos. It is a ridge fifty kilometres long and ten kilometres wide rising to the bare summit of the Holy Mountain before plunging down to the sea. The 'Autonomous Monastic State of the Holy Mountain' is a self-governing state within the Republic of Greece. It has been famous as the spiritual home of Orthodoxy for a thousand years and notorious for banning women.

I have been to Athos before. The first time was out of curiosity. The second out of fascination with a community that is glibly described as a throwback to medieval Byzantium. It is more accurate to say that the monks live in the modern world but according to a philosophy that predates modernity. I have been twice more in search of understanding, of what I haven't yet discovered. The strange beauty of the place promises mystery, in the ancient sense of truth beyond comprehension.

And the books for Father Makarios? I met him on Athos last year. He is from Moldova and spent two years in college in America, so speaks fluent English. We got on well for the short time I was at his monastery. He gave me a crucifix that he carved himself.

"Father, what can I send you from London?"

"Thank you. I got everything I need."

"Please. There must be something."

"Well, I guess there's one thing. My favourite author is English. I have some of his books. I'm missing a few."

The mind flipped through the canon from Shakespeare to Dickens as he was a favourite in Socialist countries along with Jack London and Rabbie Burns.

"I'd be delighted to get them. Who is it?"

"Pelham Grenville Wodehouse."

I felt my eyes pop and my jaw drop.

"My mom was corresponding member of the Russian Wodehouse Society. I like Jeeves and Wooster best. Top hole. Real funny and not a tad of wickedness in them."

Harley

Harley is a twenty-year-old Yamaha 50cc step-through. In motorcycle years that would make him about my age. Why don't I get a bigger bike? 50cc is the most I can drive on my ordinary licence and I'm too wimpish to get a motorcycle licence. Besides, Harley matches my temperament. Happiest on the flat, coasts downhill, weak and wheezy uphill. We rarely go faster than 40kph/25mph. Sometimes we are overtaken by bicyclists. On steep hills a brisk walker would leave us behind. Greek slang for such a bike is *papaki,* a little duck.

It's a good idea to give him a check-up before we go. Zervas's motorcycle workshop is on the main road into Aliveri, the closest town to our village. A row of bikes line up against a rail outside like horses outside a cowboy saloon, a couple of fancy thoroughbreds but mostly old hacks like mine. Inside is a knacker's shed of wrecks and parts, tackles and jacks, pipes and cables, tins and drums, fragrant with rancid oil, petrol, rubber and grease, and in the middle of it a mahogany desk with a penholder, calendar and a clickety-clackety Newton's cradle made of steel nuts.

Zervas is getting on for fifty, wiry and cheerful. A shock of salt-and-pepper hair and a week's worth of salt-and-pepper beard meld into the salt-and-pepper complexion of men who work with machinery. His overalls match the workshop floor. His hands are surprisingly clean. He must wear gloves to work.

"Hello. What do you want?"

"Full service. Brakes, spark plug, everything." My automotive vocabulary runs out at this point but he gets the message.

"When was the last service?"

I am thrown back to childhood and a creepy confessional, peering through mesh at the shadowy cheek of one-legged Father Mallarkey asking how long it has been since my last confession.

"Fifteen years…"

Zervas stares at me, a damned soul.

"…but I only use it in the summers so it's half that really."

As mitigation goes, it doesn't travel far. Zervas winces and grunts and shrugs and tells me to come back in the afternoon.

Harley's colours are Byzantine blue and cream, picked out with chrome and rust. It's called a step-through because, like a scooter, you don't have to cock your leg over the saddle to get on. It's not a moped as it does not have pedals. The engine is a four stroke, I know because they don't put oil in with the petrol like my two stroke weed-whacker. They put it in a separate hole - I say 'they' because I leave technical things to specialists. That's all I can say about the inner workings of the machinery as the rest is a mystery.

The grip on the right handlebar turns to work the throttle. In front of it is the front brake lever. Underneath is a yellow thumb switch for the indicator. The thumb switch for the lights is on the left handlebar. I get them mixed up so that when I come to a turning I flash the headlight. Next to the choke stuck permanently open is a black button for the horn. With age, like Shakespeare's big manly voice, it now pipes and whistles in his sound. More of a squeak-squeak than a toot-toot. The top of the left handlebar sports a side mirror that automatically adjusts within minutes to a view of the driver's left elbow.

These are all the manual controls. Now for the feet. The left foot operates a heel-and-toe gear shift. You change up by pressing the front of the lever with your toe and down by bending your ankle and pressing down with your heel. Except in my case it's a toe-and-toe as I'm too stiff to get my heel down. There are three gears, all forward, no reverse, unless I haven't found it yet. The gear pedal under the left foot is not to be confused with the lever under the right foot that operates the enthusiastic rear wheel brake. In careless moments trying to change up results in a slithering rear wheel skid. A kickstarter is also under the right foot but folds away once its job is done and has led to no mishaps. Yet.

A blue plastic vegetable crate is wired to the luggage rack behind the saddle. It is a standard accessory on village bikes for trips to the market and the vegetable plot and the chicken house. My crate is the smaller runabout version so I need to upgrade to a touring model with higher sides for a backpack and other stuff. A lockable trunk would keep things safer and a crate detracts from the glamour of the bike but is practical and cheap.

On main roads I put on a helmet bought in the Harley Davidson store in Glendale California. I got it partly as a tribute to Harley, partly because it was the only helmet I could find that fits my big head. I regret I didn't get the model with flames or Pegasus wings stencilled on the sides. For pottering round the village the helmet stays in the vegetable crate upside down for carrying eggs.

Time to find out what Zervas has done. He sits behind his executive desk chatting with a middle-aged man in the visitor's chair. The visitor has a facial tic that repeatedly winks one eye as if signalling a left turn. He stands up to let me sit down and I grit my teeth to stop winking back. He perches on the saddle of a venerable Suzuki 500cc. Laid out on the desk on a copy of *Avgi,* the left-wing newspaper, are Harley's former entrails. The oil filters are turned to putty, the air filter is packed with sludge, I won't go on, it was shaming. Zervas changed all the bits you can change, tightened nuts and spokes and other things, replaced the broken indicator from when I fell off avoiding a sheep, straightened the gear lever from when I fell off avoiding a different sheep, pumped the tyres, wiped years of dirt off the bodywork.

I ask about the juddering when we speed up or slow down. Zervas launches into technical jargon. As far as I can tell the cure would involve the motorcycle equivalent of a heart transplant and not worth the expense for a machine so old. I pat Harley's saddle in a spasm of fellow feeling.

Getting your hair cut or the toilet mended or your bike serviced in Greece is to start a relationship. Zervas phones for coffee from the café next door. He opens with the usual gambit - where are you from, where do you live, how come you speak Greek? Greeks are overly impressed if foreigners string two ungrammatical sentences together. I tell him I keep my Greek up by playing in a band in London.

I play the baglama, a miniature bouzouki, with a neck eighteen inches long and a body shaped like a tear drop. It sounds sweet, muddy, jangling, resonant, clear, silvery, brassy, leaden, depending on whether you pluck, stroke, caress or ham-fistedly strum it. We play rebetiko, urban blues from the first half of the last century, which is why my Greek is seasoned with 1930's lowlife Athenian slang.

"What? Rebetiko? Do you hear that Mitso? What do you play?"

"Baglama. I'm not very good. I like to sing."

"Sing something. Come on. I want to hear a foreigner sing rebetiko."

"I don't know many."

"One is enough."

"By Markos?"

"The master."

I launch into a standard rebetiko number, *Frangosiriani*, the Catholic girl from Syros. Zervas and Mitsos grin and wink and make one-handed flicking gestures as if they'd burnt their fingers on hot chestnuts. The workshop resounds with three gravelly voices accompanied by percussion on an exhaust pipe, a petrol can, a pair of spanners. We finish with applause and handshakes but I'm not taken in. I feel like Doctor Johnson's dog *'walking on his hind legs. It is not done well; but you are surprised to find it done at all.'*

Zervas thumps his chest.

"I'm a bouzoukist. And Mitsos is a guitarist. We play together."

This explains the pampered hands. It is mixed news. I like my mechanics to be mechanics and my musicians to be musicians. I don't take my bike to a luthier or my guitar to the garage.

We discuss weighty matters like the respective merits of the three string and the four string bouzouki, of amplified and acoustic, of Smyrna style and Piraeus style, until I run out of vocabulary and ask for Harley's bill. 30 euros. Surely he missed out a zero.

"Special price for baglamists."

Boy, is Harley frisky now, like I felt when I had my hernia done. 0-25 in half a minute, uphill in second not first. The good thing on a road trip is I can get repairs in villages anywhere I'm likely to go. Harley I mean, not hernias.

Franks

Frangosyriani is a well-known song recorded by Markos Vamvakaris in 1935. He was one of the founders of rebetiko, famous enough now and in his lifetime to be known simply as Markos. *Frangosyriani* means Catholic girl from Syros. It is a sweet love song to the girl and also to the Catholic landmarks, where he wants to snog her. Markos was a Catholic, a *Frangos*, a Frank, the medieval name for western Europeans. If he went to church he probably heard mass in Latin and heard the organ, which Orthodox churches do not have. This was his musical heritage along with the folk music of the island his father played on the bagpipes.

There are about 50,000 Greek Roman Catholics, some of them on Syros, Tinos and Corfu and most of them in Athens. The mass is usually said in Modern Greek now, not Latin, and the congregation joins in the singing of western-style hymns, unlike the Biblical Greek and oriental chanting of the Orthodox. In Catholic villages you are likely to see the priest clean shaven and barbered in a black suit and dog collar, unlike his Orthodox counterpart in a cassock and stovepipe hat with a bushy beard and long hair in a bun. Greek Catholics are outnumbered by about 300,000 immigrants, notably from Poland and the Philippines, and smaller numbers from Africa, Ukraine and Iraq.

How did Greeks become Roman Catholic? In 1204 the valiant knights of the Fourth Crusade diverted their mission from the Holy Land to the easier pickings of Constantinople, capital of the Byzantine Empire. It was a disaster for the Orthodox. Even Pope Innocent III was shocked, although he was happy to take his share of the loot. The crusaders carted off or wrecked its treasures, massacred fellow Christians and deposed the emperor. They replaced him with one of their own as the Catholic emperor of a new Latin Empire. The Patriarch of Constantinople was replaced by a Latin Archbishop and throughout the empire the Orthodox clergy were subject to Catholic bishops. Franciscans, Cistercians and Dominicans founded monasteries, built churches and tried to convert the Greeks. Catholic Lords from Italy and Spain and France divvied up Greece into statelets, making it easier for Turkish invaders to pick them off over the years that followed. Whisper it quietly but if it wasn't for the Turks a lot more of Greece might be Catholic today. They threw out the Catholic clergy and restored Orthodoxy. There were a few exceptions, like Syros which was under French protection.

Catholic, Muslim and Jewish are the main minorities in Greece. Among other 'recognised religions,' allowed to have their own places of worship and conduct marriages, is 'Hellenism', worship of the ancient Gods of Olympus. One Sunday morning Arfa and I came across a liturgy on the Philopappou Hill looking over to the Parthenon. Dressed in white they chanted hymns and spilled libations before statuettes of Olympian gods adorned with flowers. It felt like a Druidic solstice ceremony, daft but touching.

Ready For The Road

Before setting off there are rat-shitty things to do. Road tax is optional for pottering round dirt roads and nipping to the village and the beach but I don't want to take to the highways in trepidation of every policeman I see. Besides, it is illegal, a concept that doesn't have the same force in Greece as in some countries but still weighs on the civic conscience.

I shall spare you the bureaucratic rigmarole and repeated visits to the insurance brokers, bank and police station that I endured to get the paperwork. I frittered away €70 for insurance, €15 for tax and four days of my diminishing life span. Is time wasting pettifoggery for countless minor transactions a cure or a cause of dire unemployment? I don't care. Harley is legal. I tuck his authenticated logbook and insurance certificate into a plastic sandwich bag and stash it under the saddle on top of the fuel tank.

What about me? Adventures begin with a haircut. Yannis throttles me with a strip of elasticated paper and gets on with a classic villager's bullet-head. He learned the business from his grandfather seventy years ago. An old 5 lepta coin with a hole in the middle hangs on a nail by the mirror, the first he was ever given, he says.

Little has changed since those days, except for dust and decay. A saggy chair sprouting horsehair, neatly barbered of course, psoriatic walls, piebald linoleum, liver-spotted mirror, a counter arranged with venerable tools of his ancient trade steeped in opaque tumblers of murky green liquid. Modern innovations include a hair dryer and half a dozen black and white posters of young men sporting 1970's quiffs, bobs and flat-tops. Tucked in a corner of the mirror is a price list from 1987, the drachma symbols inked over with the euro, the prices whited out and pencilled in. I have contemplated these timeless things for forty years while snippets fell onto the black cape, brown bleaching over the years to white.

We chat about his pension cut in half by the Crisis, his dead wife, the grandchildren in Australia, his career sweeping floors in a plywood factory, his life at sea waiting at the officers' table, the sights of San Francisco and Montevideo, Yokohama and Cardiff that he never saw, as he stayed inside the port gates for fear of foreign food and venereal disease. After finishing touches with the cut-throat - I wish it wasn't called that when he scrapes over the jugular - and the sting of whatever chemical he pats on afterwards, he takes off the cape and I stand up from the chair in an aura I can best describe as toilet freshener. I hand over the ten-euro note. *"Me yia"* he says, "with health," and slaps me on the shoulder like a shorn sheep chased out of the pen.

His bike is outside. A burnished gunmetal and gold vintage Yamaha Virago, the name stencilled on the fuel tank. In a spasm of disloyalty to Harley, I wish I was going on that instead, much cooler. I'm happy for Yannis there is something in his life that I envy.

Time to pack. I'm wearing a cotton shirt and adventure trousers with legs you can unzip for fording torrents or scaling cliffs or otherwise baring the knees to danger. My sunglasses are clip-on-flip-up-and-down. I used to laugh at my mother's but now I like to think they are stylish. On a bike they have a disconcerting habit of flipping up in the slipstreams of trucks breezing past. I have a cheap Indian smartphone I don't mind losing and the ten year old Toshiba mobile I am writing this on, which is useless as a phone but brilliant at handwriting recognition. I would use old fashioned notebooks, Moleskines of course, if I could read my own writing. Driving licence and passport are in a sandwich bag secreted in an inside zip pocket of the trousers. I am a Plastic Paddy, born in England to an Irish mother, so have an Irish passport. It means I don't have to explain Brexit to incredulous foreigners.

This is what else I take: floppy hat doubling as towel and hankie and saddle wipe and glasses cleaner; Opinel knife; plastic bottle for toilet water (from toilet taps and other opportunistic sources); multipurpose three metres of string and four clothes pegs; hiking poles; boxers; T-shirt; bathers; sandals; toothbrush and paste; torch; camera; chargers; plastic rain jacket and trousers; map; Makarios's books.

Arfa catches me slipping a tin into my pack.

"What's that?" she asks.

"Zwan. For emergency luncheons."

"A few times in the last fifty years you have appalled me, John Mole. This is one of them. You are taking Spam to Mount Athos. I hope they excommunicate or exorcise or excoriate you or whatever they do. I will say no more."

And she doesn't, which is a rare blessing.

I'm a Sixties re-enactor. I have the clothes, the bike, the map, the Spam, the girlfriend - subsequently wife - some of the teeth, less of the hair. Hit the road on clapped-out wheels without TripAdvisor, Booking.com, Expedia, Airbnb, GoogleMaps, the nanny technology infantilising us as we suck on the teat of Silicon Valley. Turn off the smartphone, put the helmet on your elbow and let's just drive somewhere, anywhere, and see what happens. Man and machine are ready for the road.

2 SETTING OFF

It's so pleasant sitting here under under the mulberry tree. A good place for second thoughts.

"I wish I hadn't told so many people about my trip. I've got to go now. It sounded amusing after a half a litre of Chateau Shed. Actually doing it seems pointless."

"I'm going to Strasbourg. You've got nothing else to do except sit round here."

"What's wrong with that?"

You've ordered your dia-whatsit anyway."

"Diamonitirion." This is the visa you need to get into Athos. I plan to stay the permitted three days with the possibility of getting permission for longer when I am there.

"How long will you be gone?"

"A couple of weeks."

"Is that all? Not so much the trip of a lifetime as a fortnight's holiday."

"If Harley doesn't break down. Or me."

"Get the bus. You'll be there in a day."

"I'd rather stay here."

Forty years ago we bought a tumbledown goat shed and mule stable in a deserted hillside hamlet on the island of Evia. The idea was to do it up like the house it used to be, no electricity or running water, oil lamps and a well, the simple life as it was lived for generations. A toilet was the only concession to modernity. We would leave the garden as it might have looked a hundred years before, barely distinguishable from the rest of the hillside.

'Garden' flatters our patch of wild-grassed mountain turned golden in the summer's drought. The mulberry tree was planted sixty years ago by the father of the last child born in the house. It has pink mulberries and I have just eaten a few. They taste sweetish and bland, no tang of acidity, a fruit for an invalid diet. The tree is noisy with chirpy little birds looking like the wren on the coin I took to the sweet shop for a farthing chew seventy years ago. Others squabbling in the tree are black but I don't know if they are technically blackbirds. Bigger birds grub around on the ground wagging their tails so I hazard a guess they are wagtails. They all come for the mulberries or the insects that come for the mulberries. A score of butterflies, white, yellow, brown, red, scarlet, flutter round the fruit above me and are picked off on the wing by darting black and white jobs. The Greek for butterfly is the charming *petalouda*, little flying thing, which sounds like Greek for flying flower. They compensate for the paucity of the earthbound variety.

I sometimes think I should find out the names of the birds. Our Greek neighbours are no help. They classify birds according to whether you can eat them. Flocks of slender things fly past, caramel and cream with a harsh, skittering call, doves I think. A rowdy magpie sits on the roof. I can just make out a stork's nest on the bell tower of the village church down in the valley. They feed on frogs from nearby Lake Dystos, an assumption I base on Aesop's fables. The predatory lord of the birds, a fat buzzard, wheels high over us all.

A village cat stalks a cricket in the grass. A weasel runs along the boundary wall, a red-brown body creamy white underneath. It comes to share the drips from our leaking water tank with birds and wasps. I wish it would make a nest on the premises as they are partial to snakes and mice.

A second mulberry tree is a runt I must have planted on solid bedrock so it can't get to water. Thin, stunted, bent by the wind, it doesn't bear mulberries and has trouble making leaves. I don't have the heart to put it down. We have two olives and an almond. This denotes both the number of trees and the number of fruit they produce. The fig beside the house compensates with abundance in August. Oh the decadence of waking up, sticking a hand out of the window, plucking a sun-warmed fig and eating it in bed. A dishevelled cypress completes the arboretum.

In our neglectful hands perennials become annuals, annuals become seasonals. The shrubs and flowers still with us have survived careless planting, random pruning, overwatering when we're here and drought when we're not. Lavender, thyme, oregano, sage, oleander, geraniums, iris, and a couple of other very pretty, delicate things smelling of garlic, whose name I can never remember, thrive on neglect, exposure, drought, flood, sun and snow, as do the bully weeds and spiky grass covering most of the patch. I whack them at Easter, making a golden carpet to set off the colours of the rest of the stuff until next spring when it comes back luscious green with bright flowers.

Let's not forget the annoying things. Steely burrs and thorns in the grass, big yellow wasps, stingy little wasps living in the oregano flowers, the hornets' nest over the back window, biting ants and spiders, poisonous centipedes called *sarandapodarousa,* meaning forty not a hundred feet, tickly flies, mosquitoes, snakes, mice, rats.

You get peace but not much quiet in the garden. Along with bird chirruping there's sheep bleating, bell clanking, bee humming, wasp buzzing, hornet droning, fly whining, leaf rustling, cicada tymbaling, and the church clock striking seven when it means nine. At least it's on the hour this year. Last year it chimed when it felt like it. On Saturday evening and Sunday morning a different bell calls us to church, bi-dong bi-dong bi-dong / bi-dong bi-dong bi-dong / bi-dong bi-dong bi-dong bi-dong bi-dong bi-dong bi-dong. A shepherdess passes by calling her sheep. Picture if you will Bo-peep or a Fragonard Amaryllis. Then reverse the image. An old lady in thick support stockings, corset outside her black dress, leaning on a staff, chivvying her sheep in a gruff troll's bellow. On weekdays at three o'clock the marble quarry on the shores of Dystos signals the end of the working day with a booming explosion as they prepare for tomorrow with dynamite. If the jets from the Skyros airforce base are patrolling at the same time it sounds like war.

We are in a cicada boom this year. They make a tremendous din. Ancient Greeks and Romans thought their noise was melodious, and so it is, compared with bagpipes or tinnitus. They produce it by vibrating a sound box called a 'tymbal' or kettle drum. Swarms take off from trees as you walk past, spattering you with pee, sap from the bark of trees they feed on. It tastes vaguely vegetal and is more pure than rain. Aristotle, a cicadic gastronome, thought the females were tastiest when they were full of eggs and the grubs even tastier. If they are not scoffed by philosophers the females lay their eggs in the bark of trees. They hatch and the grubs drop down into the soil where they burrow deep and feed on the sap of roots. After a year or two or more, up to seven, they burrow up again and climb trees or bushes or flower stalks or garden chairs, anything vertical. Metamorphosed into adults they take about twenty minutes to shed their skins. They spread their wings in the sun to dry and fly away, the males to add to the din and the females to admire them before choosing a mate. The sinister exoskeletons remain, still clinging to their perches. If you wake up in the night and find a live one crawling over your face it can give you a start but apart from that they are harmless to man or tree.

In the evening at the time the French call *entre chien et loup*, between dog and wolf, a little Athenian owl perches on the chimney. Wolves haven't been round here for a hundred years or so. *Entre mouche et moustique*, between fly and mosquito, would be more topical. Or *between bird and bat*, which would preserve the alliteration. This is the time to break out the ouzo and toast the setting sun in its splendour. Greek for set is *vasilevi*, to reign, an odd analogy for a dying light but understandable in its glorious pomp of reds and golds.

During the week the garden is quieter after nightfall. A bright moon casts tree shadows or in her absence a glittering sky sheds shooting stars. Athena's owl coo-coos before the terminal shriek of its victim, mosquitoes whine, leaves rustle in the night breeze, unseen creatures slither and creep in the dry grass. At weekends these sounds are drowned by the amplified racket of weddings and baptisms.

We love to sit under the mulberry tree in this scruffy patch of hillside for the memories it bears of our family over the years; noisy breakfasts with the table biblically dripping with milk and honey; dinners under the stars with the smoke-sweet smell of mosquito coils and the hiss of a gas lamp; children in pyjamas turning a grinning Easter lamb on his spit; ropes strung from the trees for swinging on and climbing up and falling off; racketing round and song and tears and laughter; flowers flown.

Leaving Home

Homes are for leaving, homes are for going back to. Travel is about coming from as well as going to, about what you leave behind and what you lug around inside you. Now I must leave the garden behind, like Odysseus. His home was Ithaca, an island on the other side of the mainland, near Corfu. In Homer's *Iliad* he was a hero in the Trojan war, tough as the others but clever too. He invented the enormous wooden horse that the Greeks hid inside. The *Odyssey* is about the twenty years he spent trying to get home to his wife and son and his kingdom. Happy ever after.

Or not. On his journey Odysseus learns that he will abandon Ithaca again and wander with an oar on his shoulder until he meets someone who admires his winnowing fan, used for tossing up grain from the threshing floor so the breeze blows the chaff away. There, where nobody knows what the sea is, he will sacrifice to Poseidon and his trials will be truly over. Ithaca, a byword for journey's end, is in fact another stop on the way.

Does Odysseus keep his oar over the fireplace like a Varsity rowing man and think of who he was then, a stranger now to himself? Does his past feel like it belongs to someone else? And my journey? What will I become? I'm kidding myself. This isn't a true journey. A true journey is one-way. A return journey is tourism.

My love of travel for its own sake was kindled by John Steinbeck's *Travels With Charley*. It came out when I was a teenager. Charley was the name of a poodle John Steinbeck took on a journey round the borders of the USA in 1960 in a camper he called Rocinante, after Don Quixote's horse. He wanted to find out what the Americans he wrote about were really like and had insightful encounters on the way. Turns out he made a lot of it up, he was a novelist after all. He stayed with friends, in hotels, in his own Californian country cottage and half the time his wife was with him. It doesn't make it a bad book, possibly a better one, and not the only example in the travel writing genre.

I didn't know this when I read it. I wanted to hit the road and live the hobo life with the amenities of a camper and have adventures and conversations but with more girls than Steinbeck met. I failed my driving test, which was a drawback, but we had a poodle, a fluffy white miniature called Suki. *Travels with Suki* didn't strike the right note but I did my best under the circumstances to live the Steinbeck life, like taking Suki on the bus into Birmingham and sitting on a bench in Chamberlain Square hoping for meaningful encounters and fending off propositions from fragrant middle-aged men. I soon learned not to recreate other people's escapism but to make my own. Suki's ghost rides on the pillion behind me, ears back, sniffing the breeze.

On a sunny Sunday evening I pack. It doesn't take long. A canvas rucksack is enough for clothes and toiletries and Father Makarios's books. A shoulder bag takes camera, map, chargers. A fleece tucks behind the saddle.

"Is that all you've got?" says Arfa.

"Travel light. Live free. Cast off the trammels."

"Have you got your blood pressure pills?"

"Ah. Good thinking."

"Have you got your statins? Ibuprofen? Paracetamol? Cod liver oil? Anusol? Multivitamins? Rehydration powders? Hydrocortisone? Antihistamine? Indigestion tablets? Athlete's foot powder? Rosacea cream? Sunscreen? Sunburn cream? Insect repellent? Dental floss? Interdental thingies? Mouth guard? Steradent? Ulcer gel? Ear drops? Eye drops? Blister pads? Cotton buds? Elastoplast? Knee bandages? Ankle supports? Stuff you rub on your knees? The five year old antibiotics you refuse to throw away? The tin of vaseline I don't know what it's for?"

"Neither do I. It's rusted shut."

"If you forget anything I can always come after you in the car."

"I'll need another bag."

Man and machine and medicines ready for the road.

We go for an au-revoir meal to our favourite meat taverna on the way to the beach. To get us in the mood is a foreigners' menu, a mirror image of how my Greek must sound to Greeks. It includes such delicacies as:

Appetiser
Slice. Pumpkins. Courgette beetles. Frying pan. Roundabout.
Meats
Boiled sheep. Boiled goat. Boiled calf. Jackets.
Salad
Bruise. Wild grass.
Creams
Cucumber sauce. Garlic sauce. Cheesecake (hot).

Arfa knows better than to ask what my plan is, the places on the way, where I am going to stay, but she does anyway. On the paper tablecloth I sketch as detailed an itinerary as I can, which is not very detailed. My idea is to head north to the tip of Evia and take a ferry to the mainland; follow the east coast past Volos up through Thessaly past Mount Olympus and into Macedonia; pass by Thessaloniki and head east through the Halkidiki to Athos; and back again. All on minor roads and staying in cheap lodgings. Arfa covers up her lack of attention with redundant imperatives - instructions that nobody in their right mind would think of doing the opposite.

"Be careful."

"Don't fall off."

"Don't have an accident."

"Don't get mugged."

"Mind how you go."

"Take care."

"Have a nice time."

What I really want Arfa to do is plead with me not to go. And then I can be heroic like Hector leaving his wife Andromache to go back to the Trojan war, Gary Cooper leaving Grace Kelly for a high noon shootout, Luke Skywalker defying Yoda to go off and duel with his dad. I suspect that in such tests of courage I would say 'oh alright then' and hang up my sword /six gun/ light sabre. But she doesn't try to dissuade me, leaving me wondering if she is tired of listening to my big talk and glad to see me get it out of my system.

"Will you call me?"

"Every night. I'll tell you how much and in how many ways I love you."

"I'll think you've been at the ouzo. Just say good night."

That night there is a storm. The rain comes in waves, cresting over the mountains and crashing over the valley, drumming on the roof, cascading down walls and windows, rushing downhill over terrace and garden, turning paths into rivers. We put chairs in front of the window and watch the show. A barrage of thundercracks shakes the floor, sheets of lightning surround us. The *son et lumière* lasts half an hour followed by distant lightning on the horizon, like the flashers you get inside your eye when the retina calves viscous floaters to bob around in your vision. I ask you, how many original similes for lightning are there?

I hope it's not an omen.

On The Road

The next day I creep out of bed into the dawn. It is chilly, cloudy and windy and I fight the instinct to creep back into bed. The gentle snores of the other occupant seem full of reproach. I pull on the clothes laid out the night before, blow a kiss, and heft my backpack down to Harley. I pat his saddle and wish him good morning. So I don't wake Arfa and have to endure the pain of parting and its redundant imperatives, we coast downhill from the house for fifty yards before I kick him into gear and he jolts into action. We are on the road.

I'll start my journey with one of the island's most ancient monuments, a Bronze Age Mycenaean beehive tomb half an hour from the house. The Mycenaean civilisation flourished three and a half thousand years ago. It takes its name from the city of Mycenae on the mainland of southern Greece, famous for its king Agamemnon, who led the Greeks in the Trojan War and was murdered in the bath by his wife Clytemnestra when he got home. The Evian tomb is a smaller version of the cavernous one in Mycenae but still the genuine article, a bronze age relic from the age of Odysseus on our doorstep. It is more or less on the way and will set my jaunt in the context of history and time.

Arfa and I fell in love with Greece at Mycenae over forty years ago on a weekend break from London. We admired the Lion gate, brushed against the walls, imagined axe-murderer Clytemnestra whacking her old man, ogled the grave pit where Heinrich Schliemann unearthed a gold death mask he claimed was Agamemnon's.

Escaping from the tour we sat by the roadside under a tree eating pistachios. A battered blue bus chugged towards us through groves of silver green olives shimmering in the brilliant light. In the window above the driver, faded white on a torn black canvas was the destination ΣΠΑΡΤΑ. It grumbled to a halt beside us. An old woman dressed from scarf to slippers in faded black got down holding a live chicken upside down by the ankles. The bus drove off in a cloud of dust and diesel. The old lady hobbled over to us and cackled and waved the spreadeagled chicken up and down in our faces before shuffling away.

"Is it a traditional greeting?" I said.

"I hope it's not a spell."

"I've just worked out where that bus is going."

"I think she was trying to sell us the chicken."

"It's going to Sparta."

Until that day on a lonely country road Mycenae and Thebes and Sparta belonged in books and films. That you could hop on a bus to Sparta should have come as no surprise any more than Camelot or Sherwood Forest. But seeing mythic places on the front of a bus brings them into the present, where the real and the imagined worlds collide. Whether it was that excitement or the old lady waving a chicken in our faces the spell was cast.

Stopping at the junction with the asphalt road to the cemetery I look back at the house with a pang, not at the ghostly figure at the bedroom window waving goodbye but the piling pitch black clouds of Mordor streaming from the north behind her, an image lost on Arfa as she can't stand

Tolkien. By instinct and experience a fair weather biker, I know it's not only the wet up the trouser legs, the visibility through misty spectacles, the dust-lubricated asphalt to fear but also the filthy wake of overtaking traffic. Never one to rise to a challenge if I can avoid it I am in two minds whether to turn back. Bah. Pull yourself together.

The village is deserted. Only the baker's is lit up, Thanassis putting a new batch of cheese pies out on the counter at the end of his day. His son loads their white van with the night's production for village shops in a twenty mile radius. He shouts *kalo taxidi*, bon voyage. Everyone knows where I am going and thinks I am nuts. I dare to take my hand off the handlebar, wave quickly, wobble and clutch the grip again. With extra weight on the back Harley feels unbalanced.

At the junction with the main road from Kymi to Halkida I go straight ahead and uphill at a steady 30kph/20mph, through the village of Lepoura, still sensibly asleep. The paved road winds through orchards and olive groves into the back country. Little birds flutter and sing, big birds flap and complain. The asphalt stops but the dirt road is smooth so I carry on, up and down hills and round bends. Harley and I are properly awake and enjoying ourselves until the road gets gradually worse. The rain has made it rocky and gullied on the inclines, muddy and slippery on the flat. Hand on the brake and feet on the rocks we inch down, rock by rock, gulley by gulley, past the point of no return. The reward is at a T-junction at the bottom, a big brown sign pointing right to Tholos Mycenaean Tomb. My heart lifts as the road improves then sinks again as we slide and grumble down another rocky cleft to another T-junction. But where is the sign? Right or left?

I have no idea where I am. I have lost interest in dead Mycenaeans. For no good reason I turn left. Close on either side maquis and trees hem me in. The road is covered with red-brown silt rutted with parallel tyre marks dipping in and

31

out of murky pools of water. In the puddles I put my feet down to stop slithering into ruts, leaving my legs booted to the knees in mud. Just as nerve-wracking are potholes filled with sharp gravel, puncture traps. No choice but to carry on to where tracks from right and left empty their run-off into a pond twenty yards wide. I daren't stop in case I get stuck or mud gets sucked into the engine so rev up and forge ahead, reliving the frisson of driving through a ford on a country road, nervous that it is not the promised shallows but a deep pit. It is hard to tell if this pond is mud or water as it is covered from edge to edge by an army of tiny frogs. Hundreds of them. By the time I realise what they are we are in among them, squelching them under the wheels and eviscerating them among the spokes and trampling them underfoot. We surge through with a bow wave of mud and mashed frogs, wobbling and veering in a spray of brown and green and red.

The road comes out of the froggy slough onto hard ground. I stop, trembling and nauseous. Harley and I are spray-painted with mud and frog juice in the gamut of ochres, yellow to brown to red to purple to burnt and shades in between. Amphibian body parts stucco the wheels. The appetising smell is viscera frying on the hot exhaust pipe. I look up to curse the Heavens in despair. Actually despair is a bit strong, more fed-upness. But hope is at hand. Etched on the skyline is a telephone pole and the wires it bears cross our route. Telephone wires lead to telephones and human habitation and proper roads. Thank you, Heavens.

I sidle through the front door. Arfa is still in her nightie, concentrating on frying eggs.

"That was quick. Have you given up already?"

"I ran into a bit of trouble."

"Have you got separation anxiety? Why don't I just take you to Athos in the car? We'll be there by evening."

She turns round and sees a golem, a man created from clay. Or, if you aren't into Jewish folklore, her husband enacting Flanders' and Swann's Hippopotamus Song, which she kindly performs.

"Mud, mud, glorious mud..."

"I'm touched."

"Get those things off. I'll do your eggs."

After a naked hose-down on the terrace and breakfast I restore Harley to his Byzantine blue and cream and rust and go back to bed until lunchtime.

That evening we go for an au-revoir-but-not-so-soon meal to our favourite fish taverna at Klimaki, overlooking the moonlit sea, to eat sweet red mullet and boiled greens with mashed garlic washed down with lemony wine from vines growing on the hillside below. We have no more to say about my trip. We discuss the little things of life, like the nest of hairy hunting spiders, big as saucers, that have moved into the crack in the wall behind our bed. I argue against extermination on the grounds that they keep down the other creepy-crawlies. She argues that if I don't evict them, she won't tell me where she's hidden Harley's key.

Driving back home over the hills through the starless night I brake to avoid a white donkey, bathed in headlight, crossing the road into blackness. Arfa and I hold hands as it is swallowed by the dark, a reminder of the mystery that breathes behind things. We go to bed. Athena's owl coo-coos. Bigfoot geckos squeak for mates. Lizards scamper across the roof and mice beneath. A beetle scrunches in a rafter. Snakes and spiders and armoured centipedes creep and slither out of sight and hearing.

On The Road Again

On the second attempt to get more than 10km from home I creep out of bed and into the dawn. The weather is bright and clear, a brisk wind scouring the sky of clouds. What the hell. I get back into bed and go to sleep until Arfa nudges me at 8 o'clock. After a nutritious breakfast of fried eggs and fried tomatoes and fried bread, and a lecture about the implications of Brexit on the legal standing of British expatriates - anything is better than redundant imperatives - I pull on the clothes laid out last night, we exchange fond au-revoirs, and I heft my backpack downstairs.

We drive through the streets of the village of Krieza. I risk raising a finger off the handlebar to salute the bust of the local hero Nikolaos Kriezotis, who supervises the children's playground in front of the town hall. He was a warlord in the War of Independence in 1821 when Greeks threw off the Cruel Yoke of Turkish Slavery (it's what you say in Greek for Ottoman rule). Krieza is an odd name in Greek, and that's because it is Albanian. It means Black Head. There are a couple of villages called Kryezi in central Albania but there's no talk of twinning. There are many such place names on Evia and many have been changed to more patriotic Greek ones. The inhabitants are mostly of Albanian origin, whose first language until the middle of the twentieth century was Arvanitika, an old dialect of Southern Albania.

How did they get here? Albanians had a long tradition of fighting for the Venetian, Byzantine, Ottoman and Latin empires throughout the Middle Ages. They may have settled in Greece as early as the tenth century. Other accounts have them invited by Ottoman pashas to underpopulated areas to create wealth. Or they simply walked south to greener pastures.

Large tracts of the region of Attica, neighbouring Boeotia (pronounced Vee-ow-tia), Southern Evia, the north-east corner of the Peloponnese, were predominantly Arvanitika-speaking until the middle of the twentieth century. Arvanites (Arvan-eetes) cultivated the agricultural plain to the east of Athens, where the airport is today or kept flocks in the mountains that ring the city. Plaka at the foot of the Acropolis, was predominantly Arvanitic until the beginning of the twentieth century. The islanders of Hydra, Andros, Spetses, Salamina, Poros were mostly Arvanites. When Bavarian Otto, the first king of Greece, landed on Greek soil in 1832 to a tumultuous welcome he is said to have asked "where are all the Greeks?" Before the influx of two million refugees from Asia Minor in the 1920's, half the population of Greece may have been Arvanites.

Since then they have self-identified as Greek speaking. Assimilation has sometimes been forced. In the Metaxas dictatorship between 1936 and 1941 it was officially forbidden to speak Arvanitika in public and punished in schools. After the Second World War, radio and then television snuffed out what survived. Arvanitika is a spoken language with little written down to preserve it. There is a modest revival of Arvanitic culture, primarily in music, but in general Arvanites keep a low profile.

Recently we were haggling with a neighbour my age about buying a scrap of land next to us. She said something we did not understand and laughed. "We are Arvanites. We are not from here," she said. Yet her family had been in the village for well over a century.

Albanians came back to Greece in 1990 when their communist regime collapsed. Within a few weeks over half a million undocumented migrants flooded over the mountains into Greece looking for work. Taxis and minibuses waited for them in the foothills and distributed them around the country. In our village they slept in stables and ruins and the local landfill. They skulked in fear of the police, who made periodic roundups for shipment back over the border. Within a couple of weeks they were back, grateful for the free transport to visit their families.

Albanians were exploited and swapped and lent out like a commodity. Building sites mushroomed with the influx of cheap labour. We had a stone terrace built with traditional skills that had been lost among our neighbours. One of the shopkeepers became their bank, looking after their money in case they were robbed by other migrants or the police and sending it back to their families. Villagers in their fifties and older spoke Arvanitika with them. At the same time they were feared and resented. Badmouthing fed on sensationalist media reports of Albanian gangs in the cities stealing cars and stripping houses. 'My Alvanos' was a good man but the rest were godless communists and scroungers.

Over time enterprising incomers set up as independent contractors, traders, bought land. They brought wives and families from Albania. Their children saved the primary school from closing and, spurred on by their parents, excelled. And then the Eurocrisis hit and those who were not settled in houses or jobs or graves went back to Albania.

With the rising sun at my back and wind in my face we drive the long mile to Lepoura, an Arvanitika word meaning hare. This time I find the Mycenaean tomb along a narrow dirt road skirting a valley. It is marked by two rusty metal poles on the verge. A short path between stone walls leads to a wicket gate guarding a tunnel into the hillside. Undo a couple of turns of wire to open it, stoop, and by the light of your phone creep down a narrow passage into the musty dark. After 20 feet or so it opens up into a stone clad beehive chamber 15 feet wide and 15 tall at its apex. A flittering storm of bats fans your face and ruffles your hair. You drop the phone, lens down, and scrabble in the dark and bat guano. Homer sings in the *Odyssey* about gibbering souls of the dead like bats sped by Hermes into hell. You see what he means as you flee the realm of death into the light.

I wipe bat shit off my phone on the grass and look out over a rumpled landscape of fields and olive orchards to the gleam of the narrow sea. People who once stood here might have watched Agamemnon's invasion fleet cruising up the gulf on their way to Troy. Or imagined it. As I do.

Mycenaean ship from ancient Kynos
1200 BCE

3 ALIVERI TO HALKIDA

I saddle up and navigate dirt roads to Aliveri. The name is Turkish, possibly after the first Pasha to rule the area after Mehmed the Conqueror took Evia off the Venetians in 1470. It is built on the shores of Karavos, a deepwater bay dominated by the ruins of a 12th century castle, a cement plant and Greece's first steam power station, fed by a lignite mine a few kilometres inland. Lignite is crumbly brown, half way between peat and black coal, the most polluting of all the fossil fuels. Greece is the third biggest producer in the EU after Germany and Poland. Over 40 percent of Greece's energy is generated from the stuff. A narrow gauge railway took it to Karavos until the mine closed in 1990, leaving slag heaps, old locomotives, an open geological scar and a sinister bright green lake. A lignite brown statue of a miner with his pick, helmet and lantern directs traffic at a roundabout in the town. We call him Zorba, after Greece's most famous dancing miner. Da-dum. Di-di-di-dum.

When we bought our house forty years ago many of our neighbours worked shifts at the mine in-between cultivating their fields. The power station now uses natural gas. Greece's biggest cement factory was built next to it. At night floodlights on the massive plant, blinking red lights on the chimneys, swirling plumes of cloud, bring a taste of Gotham to the bay. As dawn tinctures pink the towers across the steely water, nightclubs empty. Couples leave to consummate their evening, underage ravers stagger home to puke cheap vodka and ecstasy, gaggles of giggling women and braying men mob empty taxi ranks, abandoning the dance floor to *palikaria*, young Greek men. The music changes from western rock to traditional Greek, updated with drum machines and electric bouzoukis but resonating still the quarter tones and tangled rhythms of old songs. They put their arms around each others' shoulders and dance in circles as the sun comes up, complex steps, skips, and jumps like generations before them. It's as if the last to leave clubs in England round off the night with Strip-The-Willow.

Vehicles hog the winding two-lane road from Aliveri to Eretria. I concentrate on not wobbling when overtaken, dodging potholes, not closing my eyes when trucks come towards me, braking with the correct foot when cars draw out from side roads, not accidentally indicating right or left when I use the front brake, keeping my mouth shut against airborne wildlife, ignoring the tickle under my left eye as I daren't take my hand off the handlebars, and all the other minutiae of nervous driving. When I assemble a cortège of trucks, buses and cars behind me I pull over onto the verge and let it past.

The road shakes off the town and clings to the edge of the long sweep of a bay aptly, if unimaginatively, called Blue Waters, green pocked ochre hills to the right, sea to the left. Fish farms breeding bream flourish in the sheltered waters. Tanks on the roadside shoal with fish and advertise *zondonas*. Ordering them in a taverna caused puzzlement until I discovered that *zondonas* means 'live'.

Amarinthos has excellent tavernas by the sea supplied by waiters dodging through the traffic with overloaded trays from restaurants and kebab joints on the other side of the road. Amarinthos was famous in antiquity for its shrine to Artemis, Diana, Apollo's twin sister, virgin goddess of hunting and childbirth. A couple of weeks ago the discovery of the shrine hit the headlines but there is no point in looking at an archaeologists' gazebo over a trench. A turnoff is signposted to a fourth century BC Macedonian tomb, which I've never managed to find and I'm not going to try now. I've had enough tombs for one day.

I may be inventing a novel form of travel journal listing places I haven't seen. The scope is endless and there's less looking up to do on Wikipedia.

Eretria

We come to the port, resort and classical site of Eretria, where I stop to shake the pins and needles out of my arms from gripping the handlebars too tight. I have an Eretrian silver coin from 100 BC with an octopus, the city's emblem, on the reverse. Recently caught specimens are hanging out to dry outside an *ouzeri*, a café specialising in ouzo and *meze*, tasty dishes like Spanish tapas. Since we read that octopuses are intelligent and a fascinating alien life form we steel ourselves against the guilt, as with pork, and avoid reading about squid, just in case.

It's too early for that treat, so to celebrate surviving the first hour and a half of our journey I let Harley cool off and order a cheese pirogi and a hot Nescafé at the Polish café near the waterfront, a meeting point for local Poles. It has the improvised charm of a pop-up, with a tiny kitchen and some plastic chairs squeezed into a corner of the pavement. A plump middle-aged couple on cycles unload a tiny terrier from a plastic basket on the handlebars and sit at the next table. They are dressed the same in white shirts, shorts, socks and peaked caps. They order *kawa* and *pączki* and nod and smile in my direction. The woman says something slavic I assume is Polish.

"Sorry?"

"Mmm you are English? Not Greek because you eat pirogi. Frankly speaking Greeks do not eat Polish food."

The man feeds ginger biscuits to the toy dog nestled under his stomach while she informs me without encouragement or pause for breath that they have a house here and a flat in

Athens where they are teachers at the Polish school and they love Greece and Greeks are so hospitable except frankly speaking they grumble all the time about their country and you should not join in or they will be offended and and and... Eyes glazed like the doughnuts she stuffs, I wave goodbye and waddle to Harley, already stiff.

On the waterfront you can browse souvenir shops for resin statuettes of gods, heroes and philosophers, snow-globes of the Parthenon, spooky helmets with long noses and cavernous eyes, novelty T-shirts, diaphanous dresses, plastic trinkets, postcards for every taste from kittens on lobster pots to viagric satyrs, and the rest of the imported tat you find throughout the Aegean. Some shops, where we go for presents and take-homes, have a better class of merchandise. Crockery hand-painted with dribbles round the edges, chisel-marked busts of bearded baldies hand-sculpted in local marble, olive-wood boxes hand-crafted by refugees, wooden spoons for stirring pulses whittled by vegans, trinkets engineered from marginally-precious stones and discarded cutlery by ecological arts graduates, everything slightly wonky so they don't look factory made. The delightful owner of one shop, a beautiful, smiling East African woman, speaks the fluent Greek, English, French, German, Italian, Polish and Russian necessary to her trade. Two thousand years ago traders also came to Eretria from Africa bringing their Egyptian goddess Isis with them. In about 300 BC they built her a temple at the edge of the port.

The ferry comes in, the bow grumbling down to meet the quay. It comes from Scala Oropou on the mainland. It is only two kilometres or so but the feeling of release, absolution, transition from one state to another as you cross the water has never diminished. We have made the crossing on the ferry many times over the past forty years, or multiple times if you are American. I watch it come in this morning with a pang of happiness and loss at the memories of slurping ice creams, crunching crisps, mental arithmetic, the alphabet game, the improvised escapades of nefarious Master-Criminal-at-Large 'Fingers' Bumcrusty, his incompetent sidekick 'Soapy' Flannel, and his nemesis Dilly Dewdrop.

An unmissable treat in Scala Oropou on the way back to Athens is a tasty spinach pie, *spanakopita*, from the bakery opposite the quay. The baker is Myrto Stamiri, a cheerful young woman who got a BA in Home Economics in London and then an MBA. She taught in English schools before bringing to an unsuspecting Greece the Great British Christmas Cake. In October she chops dried fruit and leaves it to fester in black treacle before baking with eggs and flour into digestive dynamite. She sozzles it daily with brandy until December when she glazes, seals with marzipan, camouflages with innocent-looking icing, and decorates with Santas and snowmen the rich, sweet, moist, diet-shredding, laxative Bowel Trembler. Delicious. And available from her website.

I am proud of this rare British contribution to Hellenic cuisine but it is not the first I know of. Kyria Voula, the cleaning lady of a friend in Athens, watched her making a Christmas pudding. Her jaw dropped when she saw the pudding put on to boil for three hours. "So that's what it is," she said. She was a hungry child on wartime Ikaria when British planes bombed them with Christmas puddings. With no cooking instructions the children used raw pudding as chewing gum, masticating until the taste was gone and then spitting it out.

Rebetiko

Another reason to linger in Scala Oropou is to visit the old prison. You can see it from the ferry, at the edge of the beach a few hundred yards from the jetty. It looks like an army camp ringed by wire fencing with a two storey main building, a few long concrete huts and a parade ground. Its most famous inmate was the composer Mikis Theodorakis, jailed by the military junta in 1969. You could be arrested for whistling his tunes or even listening to them. The jail is abandoned now, a haven for squatters and homeless holiday-makers. I once drove in with Harley and my baglama. I looked through the fence at the sea and the mountains, as Theodorakis and countless other political prisoners did, unable to decide if I was grateful or regretful that my pale convictions have never been put to the test and wondering whether they would pass. I tried a verse or so of the Theodorakis songs I know but they don't sound good on the baglama, not the way I play it anyway. The most appropriate would have been *You People Who Have Suffered, Don't Forget Oropos* but I couldn't remember the words. Theodorakis sang it to a rapturous audience in Athens after the Junta fell in 1974.

Penned behind barbed wire, but our hearts sound
Always the same vow, freedom and progress.
And you, tortured people, don't forget Oropos.

I was on firmer ground with rebetiko. Or rebetika. Experts can't agree how to spell it or where the name comes from. It first appeared on gramophone records in New York before the First World War. In his autobiography Markos Vamvakaris, never mentions the word. He calls his music *laika*, popular. The name stuck on records and posters outside night clubs.

Rebetiko grew out of the docks, squats, hash dens and ouzo boozers of Piraeus at the turn of the twentieth century. It was the theme music of the low-brow lower-class and shunned by the bourgeoisie. It sings of criminality, drugs and sex, simple songs about lovelorn stoners and spivs, sharp dressers strutting the streets and hash dens in search of an easy lay and an easy drachma to feed their habit, as ready to break into a dance as a knife fight. Such a tough guy was called a *mangas*, another word of unknown origin.

In the 1920's the 'Café Aman' tradition arrived with refugees from Smyrna and Constantinople. *Aman* is Greek and Turkish for Alas! and sighed in songs lamenting lost love and exile and misfortune. There are also more cheerful love songs and dance tunes and the lively *Tsifteteli*, the Anatolian belly dance. The two genres, the Piraeus and the Smyrna, competed in the clubs of Athens until they merged to capture each other's patrons under the rebetiko umbrella, creating a mixed repertoire enlarged over the years by songs from Aegean, Balkan and American traditions. Rebetiko became not so much a genre as a brand.

In 1936 the dour dictator Metaxas seized power. He outlawed Rebetiko and decreed that all songs had to pass through the government censor, a law that was finally repealed in 1976. Police smashed bouzoukis and baglamas on sight and arrested their owners for a beating and a few weeks in Oropos jail. Rebetiko was detested by many, leftists as well as rightists, until the 1960's when it was absorbed into the black hole of popular culture with TV specials and a spot in the Athens Olympics opening pageant.

We went to live in Athens fifty years ago. A friend played us a Vamvakaris record and we were hooked. When we went back to London I jumped at the chance to join the Famous SOAS Rebetiko Band that rehearsed in the School of Oriental and African Studies and played in pubs.

The baglama was the mangas instrument of choice because it could be hidden inside a coat. It's my instrument of choice because it's easy to carry round on buses and bikes. The musicians of Oropos would not have had a neat factory-made baglama like mine. Usually they were improvised out of tins and sticks and bits of wire.

In 1934 George Batis recorded *I Filakes tou Oropou, The Warders of Oropos*. When I first went to the jail I tried to mimic his ouzo-hash-tobacco-fuelled gravelly voice.

At Oropos we get by just fine
Much better than Athens
Tuesdays, Thursdays macaroni
A lad can do his time
And on Sundays meat
Even the barber's free
I'll tell you how bad the cells are
In the first go the cold turkeys
In the second the stoned
in the third the hard men ...

And so on through the hierarchy of the underworld. I should have relished playing it more inside Oropos than I did. I'm an elderly, law-abiding, non-smoking, monogamous, middle-class, mild-mannered numpty of moderate habits. Playing these raw songs of hash-heads, tarts and wide-boys gives a safe little frisson of a life that might have been. But here, in this place of brutality and misery, it felt silly and pretentious and I stopped half way through.

Lefkandi

We are not crossing over to mainland but taking the road to Northern Evia. Fortified by Polish refreshments I take the ribbon sprawl road to the island's capital Halkida, skulking along the gravel-strewn verge in a haze and stink and rumble of diesel. We scoot past the vestigial amenities of classical Eretria - acropolis, ruined temples, theatre, villas with mosaics. The excellent museum is a favourite, especially with children and others with a short attention span. The history of Ancient Greece over a thousand years from the Bronze Age to the Romans is encapsulated in two rooms. Choice exhibits date from the oldest centaur statue in existence, made in 900 BC, to gravestones of Roman colonisation in AD 100. We are fond of a little terracotta man in a pointy hat riding a duck authoritatively identified by scholars of the Swiss Archaeological School as *man in a pointy hat riding a duck date unknown*. But the museum is closed today and we can add it to The List of unvisited places with an easy conscience.

The road to Halkida goes through the busy village of Vasiliko, with its handsome tower from the late 14th century dating from the time Evia was occupied by feudal lords of the crusaders' Latin Empire. A banner over the road points left to Lefkandi. Two kilometres down the road is a narrow beach along a shallow bay lined with holiday apartments and houses. At one end is a flat promontory, about five hundred yards long and a hundred yards wide that the concrete has spared. Park the bike and puff up the path onto a low flat treeless hill fifty feet above the narrow shore. The view is nothing much, a narrow stretch of water a few hundred yards across to the mainland. Welcome to one of my favourite sites in Greece.

The immediate attraction is there is nothing to look at. You can see everything there is to see in fifteen minutes. There are no ruins, excavations, pits, nothing to tax the imagination in trying to re-erect a town in the mind's eye on a grid of abandoned damp courses; no information panels to study and forget; no stumbling round with a guidebook; no marble torsos, fallen pillars, stones in a jumble; no ticket kiosk; no postcards; just a flat field on a hill beside the sea where the Great Greek Adventure began.

Four thousand years ago, when Troy still stood, ships set off from here to explore, plunder and pillage, trade, settle and colonise. They were the Vikings of the early Bronze Age, before Homer and Hesiod, before history. They traded pottery, wine and olive oil for precious stones, metals and ivory as far west as the pillars of Hercules, as far east as

Mesopotamia. They founded cities in southern Italy, Sicily and the Balkans. Some of the earliest examples of Greek alphabetic writing, from around 750BC, were found here. It's possible that the *Iliad* and the *Odyssey* were first written down in Lefkandi by the poet or poets we call Homer. The evidence for all this has been found in graves, notably that of a cremated warrior buried with a woman and horses to keep him company. The necklace she wore was Babylonian and already a thousand years old when she was buried. Some of the finds, including the terracotta centaur, are in the Eretria museum while the rest are in Athens. None are more evocative than that narrow stretch of water.

Next to the site is a harbour and beyond that the beach. I go into a café in search of an espresso. I sit down and the waitress gives me the traditional welcome - *'Kapnizete?'* Do you smoke? I raise my eyebrows to signal no and she whips away the ashtray. This is as far as anti-smoking legislation goes. I was hoping to find someone who I can engagingly describe. But the only patron is engrossed in his newspaper and the waitress is from Belorussia. The coffee is watery and bitter.

The Pageant Of History

Greece actively cultivates the relevance of ancient sites like Eretria and Lefkandi to its present. In 2004 Athens hosted the summer Olympic Games. The opening spectacle was an opportunity to celebrate the achievements of the ancients that Greeks weave into their national identity. A dream-like pageant put at the heart of human progress the march of Greek civilisation from its mythical beginnings. The stage was a massive lake covering the floor of the spectacular Olympic stadium. A boy sailed across the water in a giant paper boat waving the Greek flag. A woman in a black dress holding a marble head recited a poem. A centaur, half man, half pantomime horse, threw a spear at a massive shovel-faced Cycladic head rising out of the depths that burst into statues. A man in a loin-cloth balanced on a gigantic sugar lump dangling from the roof. Winged Eros egged on a sprightly young couple having it off in the water before guiding us over a procession of carnival floats evoking historical periods of art and culture from the earliest human realisation of self in myth to the mystery of the DNA double helix. The closing ceremony of the Games was the apotheosis of the holiday hotel floor show, a joyful celebration in dance, costume and song of the living diversity of Greek popular culture. The spectacular pageantry of 3000 years of Hellenism reaffirmed a national narrative that is the thread of our journey.

Halkida

Halkida, otherwise written Halkis or Chalkida or Chalkis or Khalkis, is the capital of Evia. Nineteenth century pictures show one of the prettiest towns in Greece, ringed by ancient walls and towers and with a fairy-tale castle in the middle of the Euripos, a narrow strait dividing it from the mainland. They were demolished at the beginning of the twentieth century by an administration heady with modernity and progress, casting off the dead weight of the past. With the railway linking it to Athens and Piraeus it became a busy city.

Dodging potholes, trying not to breathe the fumes too deep, nervous of trucks and buses thundering past, I am caught in a one-way maze and end up at the old bridge across the Euripos, famous for currents that reverse direction four times a day and often flow both ways at once. This so flummoxed Aristotle that he reputedly jumped in and drowned. Except that it is a myth and he died at home of a stomach complaint.

Washed up by the tide of traffic onto a quiet road along the shore, I stop at the Karagiozis Traditional Café. I'm not sure which tradition it alludes to, millennial hipster circa 2010 perhaps, awash with Greek rock. It has a nice garden looking over the bay of Aulis, where the Greeks mustered before setting off for Troy. Homer says there were 1186 ships, taking about 140,000 men, a similar number to the D-Day army of 1944. Feeding and watering them must have been a commissary's nightmare and you wouldn't want to take a dip in the sewage sea. They were trapped for weeks by storms sent by the goddess Artemis because Agamemnon had killed a sacred deer. He appeased her by sacrificing his daughter Iphigeneia on a hill behind the cement plant. Clytemnestra had her revenge when he got home.

The waitress comes to take my order. She could double for Iphigeneia, classic Greek looks, pitch dark hair, melting dark eyes, pale skin, straight nose. She picks up the vowels in my 'espressow parakalow' and breaks into lilting English.

"Is that with milk, love?"

"No thanks. Where are you from?"

"Swansea."

"Do you like it here?"

"I wouldn't be here if I didn't would I now?"

Classic Welsh looks, pitch dark hair, melting dark eyes, pale skin, straight nose. She saunters back inside tapping her tray on her knee in time with the music. So far today I have been served by Polish, Belorussian and Welsh. Like King Otto I ask where are the Greeks? In a couple of decades Greece has become a land of inward as well as outward migration. Africans sell trinkets in the street and labour unseen in factories. North Africans man the fishing boats in our local port. Bangladeshis work in the fields. Aliveri has a Chinese shop. Riding Harley down a winding lane in Horio the other day I narrowly avoided three men wielding a cricket bat and juggling a red ball.

A few Greeks are outside with me in the subaqueous light of a green awning. Two young women made up for Instagram flick through their screens, sharing with two straws a latte with soya cream and sprinkles. They ostentatiously ignore the glances of two sporty lads in track suits, engrossed in men's talk of sport or cars or, these days, hair gels and moisturisers.

The Karagiozis Café (pronounced Kara-yow-zis) evokes the hero of shadow theatre popular throughout the Ottoman Empire - a sheet for a screen, a light behind it, articulated cut-outs in profile, pressed against the screen and worked with a couple of sticks. In northern Greece in 1809 Lord Byron and his crony Cam Hobhouse saw a play in a café with an audience of raucous boys.

'*The hero of the piece was a kind of Punch called Cara-Keus, who had, as a traveller has well expressed it, the equipage of the God of the Gardens supported by a string from his neck... the action was too horribly gross to be described. Those who have seen the morrice-dancing in some counties of England may have a faint idea of it*'.

Eighteenth century Morris Dancing must have been saucier than today's jingly hankie-waving.

By the 1880's Karagiozis' enormous phallus became an enormous, family-friendly arm, a tool of his mischief. He survives in live performance as children's entertainment and in cartoons on TV. His world is a caricature of Ottoman society, including the Vizir, his Albanian guard, Solomon a Jewish merchant, Giorgos a mountain shepherd, impecunious Sir Dionysos from Italian Zakinthos, ugly Morphonios, a greedy Frank with a big head, who thinks highly of himself.

In the heroic plays Karagiozis is a comic foil to a hero, for example Alexander battling with the devil or the leaders of the Revolution against the Ottomans. In the comedies Karagiozis struggles to feed his family. Unlike violent, wife-beating, infanticidal Punch, Karagiozis is fond of his wife and three sons and wields cunning rather than the slapstick. Poor, hunchback, ragged, barefoot, hungry, he is anarchic, slippery, tricksy, anti-authoritarian, quick witted and witty, full of humour. He is an anti-hero and ever popular because Greeks see an archetype of themselves. He is the tax-dodger, the man who builds a house without a permit, the one who comes off best in a bargain, and at the same time the doting father, the soul of generosity, the graceful dancer, the free spirit.

In Athens the ground floor of the Melina Mercouri Cultural Centre is given over to Karagiozis and the Haridimos family of players. Sotiris is nearly eighty and still performs. White-haired and bearded he bursts with energy and humour. Last year he invited me into his sanctum and showed me puppets he and his father and uncle had made over the last hundred years, versions of the stock cast alongside guest appearances from topical plays - a motorcyclist with coal-scuttle helmet and rifle, a sheikh and his camel, a cowboy, a parade of politicians from Venizelos to Papandreou, Churchill to Merkel. Tired of being pumped about his art he tells me to shut up and show my profile so he can snip a silhouette of me out of a sheet of A4. He scribbles in some details with a pencil and hands it to me.

"Oh! Marvellous!" I say. It bears an uncanny lack of resemblance. What he has captured is the character I play: big-headed Morphonios the Frank, deluded and smug.

In the Karagiozis Café it's time to get back in the saddle. I bat away the hope that Harley won't start, that he has broken down in this convenient place, that I'll have to call Zervas to come and fetch him while I catch the bus. No such luck.

Google says I should go up the street past the Italian Gothic basilica of Agia Paraskevi, patron of the island. In the land grab after the crusaders captured Constantinople in 1204, Evia was divvied up between three gentlemen of Verona. Their church was built by Dominican monks and not radically altered since. In their day the city and the island were called Negropont, nothing to do with a black bridge but a corruption of Euripos via Egripos. From the Veronese it passed to the Venetians. In 1470 Mehmed the Conqueror brought up his army and one of the Hungarian superguns that battered the walls of Constantinople. The Governor Paulo Erizzo vowed that he would be cut in half before he surrendered. Mehmed respected his word. He sawed Erizzo in half and sent the top to Venice and the bottom to Crete, his next target. Evia remained Turkish until 1830, by which time their rule had long become oppressive.

After the basilica Google sends me past the mosque and the synagogue. Halkida claims to have the most ancient Jewish community in Europe, in residence for over 2,000 years. The story is that after he spared Jerusalem in 332 BC, Alexander the Great was so impressed with the industry of Jews that he invited them to settle here. Greek Jews are known as Romaniotes and are distinct from their Ashkenazi and Sephardic cousins. Many of their scriptures and prayers are in Greek and to my cloth ears the hymns sound like their Orthodox counterparts. About twenty Halkida Jews died in the holocaust while three hundred or so survived, sheltered by neighbours or in the mountains with the resistance. The Archbishop hid their sacred scrolls and objects in his church. After the war most Romaniotes left for the USA or Israel, but there are said to be about fifty still in Halkida.

The next half hour is a sensory labyrinth, a blur of streets, a honking, yelling cacophony. Ancient Halkidians, Athenians, Macedonians, Romans, Byzantines, Lombards, Venetians, Ottomans, Bavarians, liberated Greeks and property developers all left traces and stories in this exhaust-hazy maze of narrow streets beside the conflicted waters. I buzz at random through the murk of the past like a fly trapped in a jar, passing the synagogue twice before being sucked over the Euripos by the one way system to the mainland side and the hulking Karababa castle, built by the Ottomans. An illegal U-turn takes me back into the maze. At last there is a sign to Northern Evia.

Morphonios
Mole
by Haridimos

4 NEA ARTAKI TO KLEISOURA

Keep The Shiny Side Up is the motto of us knights of the road. It means keeping the bike upright. Not so easy. I fall off. I have near misses. It has never been anyone else's fault. I'm not a good driver. Sometimes I am admiring the scenery or myself in the mirror or a leggy girl on the pillion of a fellow knight or otherwise not paying proper attention, so I go into a ditch or the back of a parked car or a pothole. Fortunately I have not yet tumbled into the path of a moving vehicle or broken a bone. I have escaped with bruises, cuts, grazes and quiet evenings at home picking gravel out of my skin with tweezers.

I panic in the face of danger in a way that I don't in a car or on a bicycle. I bang down on the heel-and-toe instead of the rear brake or accelerate and brake at the same time or brake too hard or freeze and do nothing and all this on a dry, quiet, sunny, secondary road at 30kph/20mph.

The reward is to feel in touch with the world, senses heightened not dulled in the isolation bubble of a car. I take three times longer to get anywhere but feel I've done something worthwhile. There doesn't need to be much of a view. A bird, a tree, the grass at the side of the road, brought to life by the breeze of going past, give a sense of witnessing something. And by witnessing the world I witness myself.

A lot of the time I watch the tarmac for potholes, debris and roadkill but even this can be enthralling on different shades and patterns of grey, like travelling along an unending abstract painting. I am a connoisseur of road surfaces and get a thrill when they are unusual or beautiful. I once went out of my way to follow a tractor pulling a trailer-full of fresh slaughtered sheep because of the blood-red splashes in the white dust. I recently lay on the asphalt with Harley pinning down my left leg, entranced by the close-up of pearly gravel scattered in mother-of-pearly oil glistening in the sunlight. Aesthetic enjoyment may have had something to do with the elation of not being dead but this is true of many pleasures.

A hazard on the back roads is tortoises. I have yet to see one among the road kill. Perhaps it is because they are not built for darting out in front of you. There is plenty of time to see them, like rocks in the middle of the road. Another possibility is that they sleep at night, when most road killing happens. The hazard is more for drivers, who brake, pull over, get out to carry the tortoise out of danger and are hit by passing vehicles. I like to enhance the tortoise's flight, soaring up and plummeting down, banking and weaving, making aeroplane noises. The aerophobic shrink into their shells, others crane their necks to enjoy the view or paddle their legs under the illusion that they are responsible. Or dreaming. Or a shaman among tortoises.

It seems odd that the tortoise is one of the symbols of speedy Hermes in sun hat and seven league sandals, the messenger of the gods. The reason is that he invented the lyre with a tortoiseshell as the soundbox, the first baglamist.

We pass under the arches of a Roman aqueduct and into the subtopia that lines the North Evian Gulf. I struggle to find anything else to say about this stretch as we chug over it in a state of numb resignation. It is flat ex-marsh, with only the prospect of leaving it an incentive to continue.

Feeling peckish in the village of Nea Artaki I stop beneath the sign of a laughing chicken beside a bakery. His rakish comb flops over his forehead, his manic eyes look down a leering beak. What is he laughing at? I'll soon find out. With sensible misgivings I order the speciality of the house, a deep fried two egg omelette wrapped round a salty cod's roe filling, an eggy surf and turf. It is an excellent choice for a diet. Even I, famous among my familiars as indiscriminatingly greedy, can manage only a couple of bites. The mangy black cat in the car park, an habitué of bins and dumps, is just as finicky.

Eggs are big in Nea Artaki. They come from the chicken factories in the hills rising steeply to the right on a plateau between Mount Olympus and Mount Dirfis. Not Olympus Home of the Gods but one of three Greek impostors, the other two being in Lesbos and Attica. It is rolling, fertile, well watered country, good for the grains that feed the chicken batteries, cattle barns and piggeries that bring prosperity to the area. It is also the home of Dirfis Mushrooms, celebrated growers, pickers and driers of the shroom, producers of an excellent risotto mix and mycological chocolate.

As we get to Psachna roadworks, deviations, emergency lanes, temporary signs, angioplasty of the arterial highway, shunt me this way and that. On a road sclerotic with fruit and vegetable trucks, I ask for directions beside a pick-up sagging on its suspension under the combined weight of its load of tomatoes and its driver, a bald middle-aged man looking as if he had been poured like jelly into his cab with plenty left over to bulge out of the side window. He asks where I am going. With the modesty of a sanctimonious pilgrim I tell him St John The Russian, Prokópi. He looks at Harley as an affront to decency and sneers.

"On that *papaki*? You will never get up the mountain."

For a moment I see Harley through his eyes, a heap of junk. The guilt of betrayal is swamped by the rancour of resentment. Tomato man is twice my girth so I suspect he talks from bitter experience. For a man who can't remember when he last saw his knees it's four wheels good, two wheels bad. Harley would disappear up his fundament. Wheels protruding from between his arse cheeks under his rippling belly, he would scutter along like some human-mechanical chimera.

On the main road out of Psachna a battered sign points left to Vrysakia beach. A dip would be refreshing after a morning in the saddle. Besides, in July 1821 it was the site of one of the first battles of the Greek Revolution, in which our friend Nikolaos Kriezotis first distinguished himself. I'm sure there will be nothing to see but I can tread the blood-soaked earth and imagine flag-waving janissaries and mounted spahis, fierce Balkan mercenaries and conscripts, foot-sloggers and bombardiers marching to the beat of great mehter drums and wailing *zurnas* against a raggle-taggle band of Evian *klephts* waving makeshift flags embroidered with crosses and their battle cry 'Freedom or Death'.

Klephts

Klepht means robber. The word is at the root of kleptomania in English. They came down from mountain villages and hide-outs to rob and extort. In old folk songs they have an ambivalent reputation, sometimes a scourge to honest folk, sometimes symbols of resistance to Turkish oppression. Occasionally the Ottomans sent troops into the mountains to hunt them down but this was expensive and impractical. So they hired other bands of klephts to keep the peace, called *armatoles,* armed men. It was a kind of protection racket. A klepht in one pasha's territory was often an armatole in another. They became heroes in the Revolution, a vital if volatile element of the Greek forces.

They give their name to *klephtiko,* a dish of lamb on the bone slow-cooked in a parcel with garlic, lemon, potato slices and wild mountain oregano. We do sheepshanks in foil, one per person, very tasty and with the Christmassy thrill of unwrapping presents.

The traditional dress of the klepht was the *fustanella*. It became the Greek national costume. You can see it in national parades and on the guards honouring the tomb of the unknown soldier in front of the Parliament building in Syntagma Square. What looks like a pleated gym skirt is the bottom of a long shirt worn over woollen trousers. Whenever I see them I think of William Leake, a British army surveyor who explored Greece before the Revolution. His escort wore the fustanella.

'Among the soldiers it is sometimes worn without ever being washed, though occasionally taken off and held over the fire, that the animals contained in it, intoxicated by the smoke, may fall into the fire, when a crackling announces the success of the operation.'

Friendly Societies

As he screwed up his courage to face the Turk, it would have been of little concern to Nikolaos Kriezotis that the Revolution he was fighting for was rooted in radical ideas seeded in the European Enlightenment and flowering in the revolutions of America and France. In Vienna in 1797 the poet and pamphleteer Rigas Feraios published a Greek version of the French Revolutionary Constitution with the snappy title *New Civil Government of the Inhabitants of European Turkey, Asia Minor, and the Mediterranean Islands and Wallachia and Moldavia*. While its heritage and official language would derive from Ancient Greece, the Hellenic Republic of Rigas's imagination embraced all the inhabitants of Ottoman Europe and Anatolia without exception for religion or language: Hellenes, Bulgarians, Albanians, Aromanians, Turks and every other race, enjoying religious plurality and tolerance. Women would have full equality, to the extent of joining the army. It ended with the *Thourios*, the war song, inspired by the Marseillaise. Stirring stuff ends with the lines *Better one hour of free life, Than forty years of slavery and prison* that became a rallying cry for the Revolution and is still sung with gusto.

Rigas created a visual aid to go with his tract, a 2m x 2m map of his republic from Belgrade in the north to Crete in the south, Constantinople in the east to Corfu in the west. The cartography is eccentric and most of the place names are medieval precursors of the classical Greek they adopted after independence. You wouldn't use the map to plan a road trip but that's not the point. It is a political construct based on independent territory, a common language and a cultural line of descent from the Ancient Greeks. I love his brilliant, crazy map, a Greater Greece that includes all the languages and musics and peoples and religions and cultures of the Aegean and the Balkans. The Great Idea that Greece's birthright is Greek-speaking Europe and Asia, with Constantinople at its heart, inspired politicians for a century.

Not all Greeks believed in revolution. One of them betrayed Rigas to the Austrians who handed him over to the Ottomans for secret execution. He became a national hero and the first martyr of the Revolution.

Among those with different ideas, Adamantios Korais moved from Smyrna to Paris at the time of the French revolution. If Rigas's blueprint was an inclusive republic based on shared values. Korais's vision was the 'nation', the *ethnos,* the regeneration of Ancient Greece by its direct descendants. His practical contribution was adding classical texts in modern Greek to the tide of literature flooding into Ottoman Greece. He began 'purifying' popular Greek to look like the Athenian version of Ancient Greek that was later called *Katherevousa,* Purified, the language of officialdom and education for most of the succeeding hundred and fifty years. Adamantios Korais was the first to be called 'Father of the Nation'. The fatherland of his imagination was a sketch of the monocultural, monolingual, monoreligious Greece of today. His portrait in the National History Museum is appropriately adamantine, stern and waspish. Rigas's portrait shows a tubby lad with curly hair, handlebar moustaches, and an endearingly wistful expression. I know whose vision I prefer and who I would rather go to the taverna with.

In the cafés and counting houses of the trading cities of Europe and Russia, Greek merchants, intellectuals and functionaries absorbed ideas of nations, nation states, national regeneration, self determination, constitutional government, rule of law, freedom from Turkish governors and Orthodox bishops. Edicts and fatwas condemned them. The Orthodox arm of the Sultanate, the Patriarchate, joined in with sermons and anathemas. Such ideas were equally unwelcome in the chancelleries of European empires, afraid of subversion among their subjects. Many Greeks joined one of the half-baked conspiracies for implementing them. The most surprising, because it was successful, was the Friendly Society, the *Philiki Etaireia*. Founded in 1814 in Odessa by three young Greek merchants, it was modelled on Freemasonry with secret signs, elaborate rituals, oaths of secrecy and lodges, which they called temples, whose members knew only each other. By 1821 it numbered as many as ten thousand, spread throughout the Greek communities of Constantinople and the commercial centres of Europe, from modest merchants to princes and courtiers of the Sultan. Above all it fomented a new sense of identity. Two hundred years ago Greeks identified as Christian and Roman, subjects of the Sultan. The language they spoke, a dialect of Greek mixed with Turkish, French and Italian, they also called Roman. They had no concept of being citizens of a state. If they needed officialdom, for example in marriage or property affairs they went to their priest or their kadi or their rabbi. Within a generation they would be Hellenes, citizens of an independent republic. A driving force of independence, the Philiki Etaireia melted away on the outbreak of revolution, its work of conspiracy over, leaving its motto, 'Freedom or Death', fluttering over Vrysakia beach and battles to come.

Hesiod

Three hundred outnumbered rebels including Kriezotis defeated the Turkish army at Vrysakia. There is nothing to see but a flat shore and a narrow pebble beach beside a puckered sea. Reinvigorated by a paddle and a lie down, I meander back with Harley through the labyrinth of roadworks to the road north. The winding climb into the pine forests of Kandili Mountain begins, not the gloomy forests of northern countries, light-forbidding dead places, nurseries of newsprint and bog roll, but Mediterranean pine, shades of luminous, bright green, feathering branches, long soft needles, twisting trunks hopeless for ships' spars and telegraph poles and paper mills but kind to birds and insects, sunlight glinting through them. Through zoetropic gaps are glimpses of the Gulf of Evia and the mountains of the mainland beyond. Patient Harley chuffchuffs up the winding road in second, the hot sour smell of his engine deodorised by the sharp sweet scent of the trees on either side. In a Proustian sponge finger moment I am whisked back to an Uber to Heathrow and a fragrant cardboard Christmas tree dangling from the rear-view mirror. In a couple of places the road dips down to cross a stream or a ravine by an ancient bridge of crafted stones and a keystoned arch. I stop to give Harley a breather under spreading plane trees, on a carpet of dead leaves, a gentle breeze stirring living leaves with gentle susurration, punctuated by the ticking of Harley's recuperating engine and the crack of my joints.

I think they are plane trees. My guidebook says there are also several varieties of pine, plus oak and elm and arbutus. I learned to identify trees in the school cadet force when we aimed our rifles at German coal-scuttle helmets hiding behind Christmas trees and Bushy-tops and I haven't added much to my arboreal lexicon since. The bit of my brain where such data is supposed to stick, along with wine vintages, dishes on an Indian menu and the names of people I meet at parties, has never been up to the job.

Onwards and still upwards to a pass over the mountains. There was a fire here recently. It came over the mountain from the north, dragon's breath of doom. In our warming climate it is becoming more common to see the blackened skin of the earth, naked, its shapes, folds, cracks, rocks like cysts, charred bones of shrubs, black dust, the acrid smell of burn and damp. Dead leaves on bronze-headed trees rattle in the breeze. Word on the street used to be that people started fires in forests so they would be re-zoned for housing. Now the rumour is that they want re-zoning to collect EU subsidies for putting up wind turbines.

At the summit is the appropriately named Summit Restaurant and a good excuse for a coffee and a restorative baklava. From a clearing in the trees are glimpses of the panorama, the forest, the valley, the villages, the sea, the silhouettes on the northern horizon of the Sporades Islands, Alonissos, Skiathos, Skopelos. From the balcony of the restaurant I squint west over the Gulf of Evia to the mountains of the mainland, straining into the past to see Mount Helikon, where Narcissus in the time of myth wasted away over his reflection and the farmer-poet Hesiod scratched a living on soil and wax about the same time as Homer.

Hesiod is known for the Theogony, a pioneering attempt to cram the confused and contradictory genealogy of the gods into a systematic family tree. He is first in a line through Homer and Ovid and Robert Graves and Stephen Fry to bring down to earth the terrible and unknowable godheads and mysteries men fear and worship and placate, to give them names and squeeze them into superhero costumes, folk like us with magic powers. Hesiod's follow-up was Works and Days, an instruction manual, almanac and inspirational fiction for farmers, packed with useful information such as how to forecast the weather, read the stars and domesticate a wife. When we bought our house in Horio I had no idea how to look after the trees that came with it so I turned to Hesiod for advice. He lived a hundred miles away so in more or less the same climate. It can't have changed that much in two and a half thousand years. For example he advises pruning vines in February, which I do.

He was a harder sell to the four children than the wonderful tales of Homer.

"What's that book Dad?" said Harry.

"Shuddup Titch. It's Greek. He'll start reading it to us," hissed Jack.

"An old geezer called Hesiod. He lived over two and a half thousand years ago. He had a farm the other side of the Halkida bridge."

"We're on holiday," groaned Jim, clapping his hands over his ears.

"*Avoid the month of Lenaeon when the frosts are cruel and the north wind blows over the earth. The animals shiver and tuck their tails under their private parts. Even those who are covered in fur...*"

"Bo-ring" said Kate.

"Lenaeon was the month of January. In ancient Greece..." But they all had their hands over their ears and were humming tuneless hums to shut out cultural indoctrination. I persevered.

"He said you should never pee facing the sun or into a river. Or have a poo in the middle of the road."

There's nothing like violence and bodily functions to arouse an interest in the Classics. Having got their attention we compared and contrasted personal hygiene and taboo in the late Bronze age as evidenced by Hesiod and Homer with the contemporary era as evidenced by lavatorial jokes. Arfa sighed and went to the sink to cut up a cucumber for lunch and stick the peelings on her forehead.

"I bring them up, you bring them down," she said.

I did not pass on Hesiod's advice about not drying your privates in front of the fire after sex. It would be their reward if any of them picked it up to read for themselves.

Kleisoura Castle

We start the winding descent down through the pines into the valley of the Kireas river. The road follows the river into the Derveni Gorge, a tautology as the former is Turkish for the latter, hugging a reassuring concrete wall on the left, dropping unnervingly down to the river bed on the right. Mysterious pools reflect crevices and caves on the tree-matted mountainsides, crags jagging a bright blue ribbon of sky. A hundred years ago I might have burbled about gods and nymphs frolicking in the streams and dappled shade. Today I try to decipher graffiti on the concrete wall.

On top of the precipitous hillside on the left is one of Evia's finest castles, appropriately named Kleisoura, meaning defile, that dominates the gorge and marked the boundary of the Frankish central barony of Evia. The Gentlemen of Verona held the castle until 1281, followed by Venetian *stradioti* and Albanian *arnauts*. Ottoman *armatoles* didn't have much use for it, as the island was pacified into somnolence, until klephts made it their stronghold in 1821. The latest occupants were *andartes*, communist guerrillas in the Civil War of 1946-1949.

The excellent website www.square.gr has a history of the castle by Giorgos Lons. It is in Greek but Google Translate gets the gist and exudes its own charm. It ends with the gripping story of Evia's entry into the War of Independence. Here is an excerpt:

> *The revolutionary effervescence has begun, focusing on Lagoon, where a small flotilla of four Limniotic pots and two equipped pancakes from Magnesia was set up... spreading anxiety among the beekeepers and lovers of Halkida... In the medieval castle of Kleisoura they met the Prototype of Barlaam...*

I like *pots and pancakes* for schooners and brigantines; *beekeepers and lovers* for Beys and Agas. (A Bey is a governor, an Aga is a military commander). Prototype is the best Google can do for the ecclesiastical title of Protosyncellos, what Anglicans and Catholics call a Vicar General. I'd be wary of Google's translation of Greek Wikipedia: *prototype means the first of the syncals, the homosexuals of the diocese.* Google translates Greek like I speak it.

The castle lies in ruins from earthquake and neglect. The spectacular view from the top takes in the sea on both sides, the island south beyond Halkida to Mount Dirfis, north to Mount Pilion over the waters of the Evian Gulf and the Sporades islands. On the horizon is my journey's destination, Mount Athos. I am content to take Giorgos Lons' word for all this as he says that the steep track is overgrown with trees and vegetation and not for the faint-hearted, among whom I count myself. I wander instead into a delightful ravine for a sit-down on a rock, wallowing in the silence and scoffing restorative peanuts. It's getting to be lunchtime and it's already been a long day.

The nuts make me thirsty so I trudge along a path into the ravine in hope of a stream but it turns up along the side of the cliff. I hurry past a noisy colony of beehives, blue and white, numbers stencilled on the sides, but I'm not wearing white or yellow so they are not interested. It looks at first like a goat trail, narrow and rocky, but, as it gets steeper, boards have been fixed across to make steps, so it must be for people. It's an easy climb with only a few stops for breath on the pretext of admiring the exquisite ochre-striated silvers and greys of the precipice below the castle on the other side of the ravine. Just as I'm about to give up and turn round and leave the rest of the path to my imagination it widens into a ledge in front of a cave in the hillside gentrified with a stone facade, a round arched doorway and a matching window. A wooden door is unlocked. It opens into a cave, ochre with minerals and green with lichen, dressed as a church with a flat stone altar, waist high ledges for an iconostasis, stone ledges for benches, a couple of pendants, a floor candle-stand, a lectern. The main items of worship are four icons about 40cm tall on the iconostasis. From the right are John the Baptist, Christ, the Blessed Virgin and on the extreme left, the usual place for the saint to whom a church is dedicated, St John Chrysostom, Golden Mouth. He was a fourth century Saint and Doctor of the Church in Orthodox and Catholic calendars, intellectual, writer and preacher, creator of the divine liturgy, or mass if you are Catholic. He seems an odd choice for a rustic chapel, usually dedicated to miracle workers, holy helpers, martyrs, myth-makers and other celebrities. Perhaps it was once a hermitage for a theologically minded anchorite. I am personally acquainted with Chrysostom. On Mount Athos I have kissed his bald head, albeit through protective glass. One of his heads anyway. There are others in Florence, Pisa and Moscow, sacred relics of much veneration.

For want of anyone else to talk to I share my thoughts with my companion.

"Harley, do relics like the various skulls of St John have intrinsic sanctity? Or only what we are deluded into giving them?"

"Vrroom vrroom"

"Come on Harley, what do you think? Shit, I might as well talk to myself."

"Vrroom vrroom"

Am I crazy talking to a machine? Ask Siri.

To go with The List of things I should see but didn't, I have another list of things I didn't expect to see but did, which is far more satisfying. Arfa and I have no bucket list of places to see and things to do before we die. We can leave the party without regret at missing out on the Taj Mahal or Machu Pichu or bungee jumping. In fact we have a slop bucket list of underwhelming places we'd rather not have bothered with like the Giant's Causeway or the Chelsea Flower Show or Hollywood. But we look forward to seeing wonderful things we are ignorant of until they sneak up and grab us, like the cave of John Golden Mouth.

Who Lost Greece?

The Greek Revolution of 1821 that shook off four hundred years of Turkish rule is a recurring motif in our journey. It was the foundation of the Greek state and an enduring element of Greeks' sense of identity. So what actually happened?

Mahmud II was Sultan at the time of the Greek Revolution. His tomb is inside a pretty cemetery on busy main street of Istanbul a few hundred yards from the Blue Mosque. He lies in a pitched roof sarcophagus, covered in green silk and topped with a fez - the egalitarian hat he ordered to replace the turban throughout his Empire. In front of his tomb is an epitaph in English and Turkish. The gist is that he was a moderniser. He reformed the army, bureaucracy, legal and taxation systems. The achievement that caught my eye was "the Grek (sic) rebellion was suppressed in 1826." I puzzled over the Turkish original to make sure. *1255/1821 de Yunan ihtilâli oldu.* 'Also in Greece there was a revolution'.

1242/1826 *Yılında Yunan ihtilâli bastırıldı.* 'During the year the
Greek revolution was suppressed.'

What? Suppressed? Fake history surely.

On 25 March 1821, the Feast of the Annunciation, Bishop
Germanos of Patras initiated the first Greek Independence
Day at the monastery of Agia Lavra in the Peloponnese. In
pictures his left hand brandishes the blue and white flag of
revolution and his right blesses the outstretched weapons of
klephts swearing Freedom or Death. Inspiring stuff. It has
resonated ever since, no matter that the incident was the
invention of a French journalist. The uprising had already
begun in Kalamata and Patras.

An improvised Greek navy led by the merchant captains
of Hydra, Spetses and other Arvanitic islands, including
Bouboulina, the first female admiral, prevented the Ottomans
from landing reinforcements. Uprisings in Macedonia, Crete
and Cyprus were ruthlessly suppressed but in the heartland
victories outnumbered defeats to leave the Peloponnese and
Central Greece as far north as Thessaly in Greek hands by
the end of the year.

Patriarch Grigorios and many of the Greek elite in
Constantinople were opposed to the rebellion.
Excommunications and encyclicals did not save him from
lynching on Easter Sunday 1822 or many of the bishops and
notables from public beheading. Their crime was that they
had not prevented rebellion among the Christians for whom
they were responsible. In Greece bishops were also opposed
at first, fearful for themselves and their flocks, but many local
priests and monks supported and sometimes actively
participated in the uprising. Meanwhile national assemblies
sketched the outline of a modern state with a constitution
and elected representatives. They called themselves Hellenes
to symbolise a connection with ancient pagan Greece and a
revolution against two tyrannies, the Ottoman state and its
arm the Orthodox Patriarchy.

The Revolution is also known as the 'Struggle', the *Agonas*, a bloody conflict in which Freedom and Death were everyday partners. The memoirs of warlords like Kolokotronis and Makriyannis, and the diaries of European Philhellenes who fought alongside them, evoke the chaos of bloodshed, betrayal, personal enmities and loyalties, cruelty, incompetence, defiance and heroism that filled those years. Victories were measured by the headcount, incontrovertible facts in the myths, deceptions, propaganda and lies that feed on war. Some heads were pickled in barrels and sent to Constantinople to be exhibited outside the Topkapi palace. In Greece most were heaped by both sides in their camps like apples on a market stall, cemented into towers and walls beside the roads, hung on saddles, catapulted into enemy encampments, strung on lines like dried figs. Battlefields were strewn with headless corpses. Kolokotronis, paid a silver dollar - a Maria Theresa Thaler - for every Turkish head his men brought him. Greek comrades pledged to cut off each others' heads if they were killed so they would not fall into enemy hands.

Non-combatants were no better off. The default treatment of women, children and the old was rape and murder. Survivors were sent to the slave market of Thessaloniki until a glut collapsed prices. In September 1821 the Greeks' first victory was the capture of Tripolitsa, main city of the central Peloponnese, now known as Tripoli. They massacred the Muslim and Jewish inhabitants. Kolokotronis writes that he rode from the gates to the centre over bodies without his horse touching the ground. In the following March Turkish troops on Chios massacred or enslaved three quarters of the island's population. These atrocities set the pattern of reprisal and killing for the rest of the war. Barbarism on both sides stoked fear and loathing. Greek klephts were impaled, Turkish sailors roasted alive. Those who escaped the yatagan and fled into the mountains were likely to starve to death. It was routine for troops to eat the livestock and stores, burn the houses and fields of the villages they pillaged. The exception was fruit trees, the lasting wealth of the countryside. Kolokotronis was incensed when Turks overstepped the conventions of war and deliberately destroyed groves of olive, mulberry and fig around Kalamata.

It was also a struggle to innovate and explore for the first time in Europe an independent, democratic, secular state. Greeks were divided between traditionalist warlords who wanted to carve out independent territories for themselves to rule as they saw fit, and modernisers schooled in the salons and courts of Europe and Russia, who believed in central government based on a constitution and the rule of law. In the middle of the Revolution the two sides took up arms against each other and for a time there were two governments of the new Hellas.

Weakened by civil war the new Greek state could not resist the return of the Ottomans. Sultan Mahmud's rebuilt army reconquered Central Greece, capturing all the main cities. He promised the Peloponnese, Crete, Cyprus and Syria to Muhammad Ali, the ruler of Egypt, in return for sending his son Ibrahim to crush the Greeks in the south. By 1826 Ibrahim had purged the Peloponnese of Christians, except for pockets of resistance in the Mani and Nafplion. It was said that he planned to repopulate it with Egyptians. The combined Turkish and Egyptian navy stationed off Navarino in the south of the Peloponnese controlled access to Southern Greece and a second fleet in Alexandria prepared to crush the rebellious islands of the Aegean.

Among the Great Powers, Russia, Britain and France competed for territory and influence in the weakened Ottoman empire. They did not want an Egyptian foothold in Europe but they did not want an independent Greece either. Autocratic, frightened by the ideas behind the American and French Revolutions and the Napoleonic adventure, they suppressed revolution at home and abroad. To curb each others' ambitions the three Powers agreed in 1827 to send envoys to the Sultan calling for an end to the war and the autonomy of Greece under his continued rule. He sent them packing. He had defeated the rebels and now he and Ibrahim would crush them.

The Powers sent a joint fleet to press their demands and keep Greeks and Turks apart. It was supposed to be neutral. At Navarino Bay, where the Egyptian and Turkish fleets were anchored, trigger happy sailors in the Egyptian fleet fired warning shots at a British boat on a recce. The Brits returned fire, things got out of hand, and within hours the Turkish-Egyptian fleet was sunk. They lost about 60 ships and 8000 men. The allies lost 176 men. Unable to supply his armies in the Peloponnese Ibrahim's days were numbered.

It was a hostile act against a friendly power. The Duke of Wellington and King George IV apologised to the Sultan. But the damage was done. The Revolution was internationalised. Russia and France jumped on the bandwagon of Greek independence in the hope of territorial gain. French troops evicted the Egyptians. Greeks broke out of their enclaves and took up the brutal war again. Russia declared war on Turkey in the Balkans and the Caucasus, pulling Turkish troops north.

In 1830 the Powers forced Sultan Mahmud to accept the full independence of Greece, roughly from the border of Thessaly south to the Peloponnese. It was formally recognised in 1832. Although Greeks themselves were not invited to the negotiations that gave them their independence it was an extraordinary achievement. The desire expressed in 'Freedom or Death' overcame the direst setbacks, a resilience to adversity that is celebrated to the present day.

25 March is the national holiday. The day starts off with prayers by priests and speeches by politicians and the laying of wreaths at local war memorials. The dignitaries then take

the salute at parades of military pomp and folkloric splendour. Children in traditional costumes, grown men in fustanella and fez, school-kids in best white shirts and blue scarves, police, firemen, coastguards, scouts, sailors, airmen, soldiers in uniform and battle dress, flag wavers and banner flaunters, schools, clubs, sodalities and sororities, shuffle and swagger and strut to the thump and blare of competing bands. My favourites over the years include frogmen with wetsuits and scuba tanks, alas not marching in flippers, teenage girls in folkloric dresses clumping on Doc Martens, primary school klephts marching undaunted in the pouring rain. It's a combination of Armistice Day, Armed Forces Day and St Patrick's Day, a time for Greeks to be justifiably proud.

The long arm of Karagiozis

5 PROKÓPI

I rouse Harley from his slumbers and carry on down into a spreading valley where I can take my nervous foot off the brake as we are on the flat and can resume our habitual 40kph/25mph. The river on the right widens out into a gravel bed and is lost among the pebbles. We follow its leisurely course through the plane trees and at latish lunchtime arrive in the village of Prokópi, the home of Saint John the Russian. I park Harley outside the courtyard of his massive white marble church and go inside to pay my respects.

In the narthex - the vestibule before you get into the main part of the church - I put a euro in the box for a toffee-coloured candle, light it from one of the many already flickering in a big round sand tray, and stick it in. It has a lovely smell and such a pretty flame. A friend died the other day and I give her a thought. I can't think of any pieties to utter. The sign of the cross will have to do, Orthodox style, first two fingers against the thumb, to the forehead, chest, right shoulder, left shoulder. Good luck, Jenny.

The church is almost empty and I have Saint John to myself. He sleeps in a glass case untroubled by prayers and sighs of the living, the chanting of a solitary cantor, the effluvium of incense and candle wax, the flash of my camera. He looks gorgeous. He lies on his back with his head turned to the left, dressed in a gold-embroidered, sky-blue robe and matching brimless hat. Round his waist is a broad gold belt with dangling gold tassels. A gold prosthesis replaces his missing right hand. His eyes and nose are covered with a gold wrap-around domino, like a carnival mask. His mouth is closed in a faint smile. The rest of his face and his left hand, are pitch-black skin and bone.

John was born in 1690 in Ukraine. At the age of nineteen he was conscripted into the army of Peter The Great for a war with Turkey. He was captured and sold to an Aga from Ürgüp, corruption of the Greek Prokopium, in Cappadocia. His sanctity was recognised when he teleported a copper pot of pilaf to his master on pilgrimage in Mecca. If faith can move mountains it can surely deliver a helping of savoury rice to the heart of Islam. It was the making of the holy man. Believers flocked to him and he performed many more miracles even after he died, mostly of the medical variety without clocking up food miles. The priests of Prokópi preserve the pot, complete with lid to keep the contents piping hot. Although it's nice that Deliveroo has a patron saint I struggle to see the spiritual utility in the trick.

In 1881 John appeared in a dream to a monk of the Russian monastery of Saint Panteleimon on Mount Athos and told him to fetch his right hand as he had always wanted to visit the Holy Mountain. Cash in hand for the hand financed a new church in Ürgüp to accommodate John's remaining remains. A hundred years later bits of the amputated hand ended up in the Holy Transfiguration monastery in Boston Massachusetts and in the high altar of The Nativity of the Virgin Mary, Madison Illinois.

After the defeat of the Greek army in Turkey in 1922, known to Greeks as the Asia Minor Catastrophe, two million Christians in Turkey were exchanged for half a million Muslims in Greece. Two hundred and twenty families from Ürgüp brought John's relics to a village on the estate of the Noel-Baker family called Ahmet Aga and re-named it Nea Prokópi. Most of them left for better prospects in Athens and Thessaloniki, leaving fifty families behind. Life was hard for the homeless, penniless and jobless refugees. Other than being Christian, Cappadocians had little in common with the Greeks they were foisted on. They spoke Karamanlidika, Turkish laced with Greek words, which they wrote in Greek script. In smaller villages people spoke Cappadocian, derived from Byzantine Greek and laced with Turkish, which was equally incomprehensible. Uprooted, isolated, impoverished, despised, displaced, a refugee, John the Russian shared their exile until 1950, when they built a final resting place for him.

Some pilgrims have deduced from his black skin that he was an African but there is an explanation. During the first Egyptian-Ottoman War in 1832, Turkish troops ransacked his church in Ürgüp. They threw his body on a fire. He stood up and shouted at them until they ran away. The next day, when it was safe to come back, the townspeople found him intact and unharmed in the ashes, except that his skin had turned black in the flames.

The face on his icon is that of a clean-shaven young man, winsome and gentle, not your usual glum old beardie. As an Ottoman slave he was obliged to shave but his iconographer may have been striving less for historical accuracy than to put over his essential qualities of humility and kindness, earth-inheriting meekness, his feminine side, if I may say this in our gender-neutral age. He comes to sick people in apparitions and dreams and makes them well; he warned a primary school class to get under the desks just before the roof fell in; he warns travellers to avoid dangers ahead; and many more miracles recorded this century and attested on the internet. Outside the church on the way out by a side door is a glassed-in kiosk displaying John's very own black leather belt and cap. I ask a devout young lady next to me what they are for. She says that pilgrims queue up on his feast day to put on the belt and cap and there are many miraculous cures. I leave her to her obeisance and go to an array of taps in the next kiosk for a drink of beneficent Holy Water.

Outside in the sunshine I think about relics and try not to be cynical. When you put on John's belt and cap and pray to be cured of cancer, is that veneration or superstition or desperation? I get out the phone and to my surprise I can get data. What better place to research relics than next to one?

Relics are integral to Roman Catholic and Orthodox practice. All altars have a holy relic beneath or inside them. The Orthodox eucharist must be celebrated on an *antimins,* a piece of cloth with a relic sewn into it. The belief is that saints achieve union with God on this earth and that sanctity permeates their bodies, their clothing, things they have touched. After death their relics remain imbued with sanctity and tangible links with the divine. Each particle encapsulates the sanctified essence of the departed Saint. A finger of John in an altar in Madison Illinois has as much sanctified essence as your man in the glass case. You don't worship a relic, a reverence due only to God, but venerate it, a demonstration of respect. If it works a miracle, it is because the Saint it once belonged to has interceded with God to make it happen. It has no wonder-working power of its own. Hmmm - internet speak for scepticism before the yellow-faced emoji was invented - this is the official line but it doesn't seem to coincide with the behaviour of ordinary believers.

The Catholic Church ranks the classes of relic. First Class are those associated with Christ's life or a body part of a Saint, for example the Sandals of Jesus Christ in Prüm, the Holy Girdle of the Virgin Mary in various places including Athos, the bones of St Andrew in Patras and elsewhere. Second Class is something a Saint wore or used. Sanctity is contagious - a Third Class, or Contact Relic, is something that has touched a First Class or Second Class Relic. Simony, the traffic in relics, is still rife. A fragment of the True Cross on eBay starts at around €100 going up to a few thousand, depending on the reliquary. Contact relics start at €1.50 They make nice Christmas presents for the right persons. I'm going to stop before I mention the Holy Foreskin, venerated in Italy until the last century and alas now lost.

Noel Baker

It's time to find a souvlaki and somewhere to stay the night. The first is easy. Pop-up grills in the street cater for the lunchtime trade. I munch on a staple of the Mediterranean diet, the *pita souvlaki*, cubes of fatty pork wrapped in flat bread with chips, tomato, onion, tzatziki, and mustard.

Somewhere to stay is harder. Opposite the church is a hotel-looking building but obviously way out of my budget, a grand four storey edifice wrapped in balconies with big glass windows on the ground floor, flags outside the marble steps to the door and a shiny black car parked outside. It might be an ecclesiastical palace. I don't bother to find out and in any case I feel too scruffy to go in the main door in case I am sent round the back to empty the bins. So Harley and I potter up and down the streets of the village looking for somewhere more my status, a room-to-rent or a one star hotel. Nothing. This is very odd. Where do humble pilgrims like me stay? At last, on the outskirts of the village, I come across my kind of flop house, a run-down two storey building with a wonky rooms-vacant sign dangling from a window sill. A café on the ground floor is a depository for decrepit furniture and men. As I step into the murky interior, the youngest of them, a wrinkled lad with twinkles in his blepharitic eyes, asks what I want. When I tell him, he rolls them upwards and his head arches back, not a seizure but body language for not a hope. Why don't I try the pilgrim hotel, the big place opposite the church, I can't miss it? *Vairy chip*, he says in English.

I go back to the grand hotel. The desk in the foyer is unmanned and has a typed notice: ask at the church shop. What? Where is the receptionist, the porter, the concierge?

They are subsumed in the person of the church repository manager, a kindly George Clooney look-alike, who breaks off from helping two Serbian ladies in widow's weeds choose between an icon of John painted on wood and one printed on gold plastic. He tells me to come back at six when he will be able to book me in over the road. Tentatively, for we are in a House of God after all, I ask how much the room is. Twenty-five euros! I leave him to the widows and skip outside, a spring in my step, cutting capers and heel clicks. Twenty-five euros! *Vairy chip* indeed.

There is plenty of time to call on Philip Noel-Baker. He is the grandson of Philip Noel-Baker, who helped the League of Nations engineer the Exchange of Populations between Greece and Turkey in 1923. Grandfather started life as single-barrelled Baker, a Quaker, who put pacifism into practice in a glittering career. In the Great War he set up an Ambulance Corps in France, commanded one in Italy and was decorated for bravery by three countries. He was an Olympic silver medallist, London University professor, Labour Member of Parliament, government minister, the first British delegate to the United Nations, Nobel Peace Prize winner. Note to quizmasters: he is the only Olympic medallist to win a Nobel.

During the War Philip married Irene Noel, a Red Cross nurse in France, whose energy and social conscience were a match for his. Her family owned an estate on Evia. To preserve the family name Philip changed his own to Noel-Baker. His work on the Exchange of Populations came back to bite them. In 1925 the Greek government expropriated 1200 hectares of Noel-Baker land to house refugees, leaving the family with a small farm and a forest.

The house is up a hill overlooking the village. I had sent Philip an email saying I was biking through and he expects to greet an ironman in lycra with a padded bum and protuberant calves on a sportive racing bike with proctological saddle. Instead he gets a beardy old scruff on a clapped out *papaki*.

Aghast, he quickly recovers and is utterly charming. He leads the way into a country house that oozes taste and comfort and understated elegance. If I had a cap I would doff it. We sit sipping lemony iced water on the terrace of an English country garden and look out on the mountains of Kandili, a surprisingly tasty combination, like tzatziki on a Bath Oliver.

Edward, the founder of the Noel dynasty, was twenty years old when he came here two years after Independence. Evia was underpopulated and impoverished by the brutal war. With a Swiss friend and finance from a cousin, Lady Byron, unhappily and briefly married to the (in)famous Lord Byron, he bought the estate of a repatriating Turk to make a philanthropic model farm. With extraordinary idealism and tenacity Edward overcame malaria, brigands, remoteness, natural disaster, jealous politicians, his partner's death. The attitude of the government and the locals to foreign investors fluctuated between gratitude and hostility. Then as now, Greeks found it hard to reconcile a desire for independence with dependence on outsiders to secure it. The Noel-Baker ownership of forest lands was still being contested in the courts until a few weeks before I arrived.

The family history through the generations to the present day is full of incident. Dramas and scandals, kidnap, murder, infidelity, profligacy, and mismanagement, took place against a backdrop of social change, wars, refugees, foreign invasion, civil war, dictatorship and austerity. The darker moments punctuated happier periods when the estate developed under a succession of strong-willed characters. Their history was written and published by Barbro, Philip's mother, in 2000. *An Isle of Greece: The Noels in Euboea* is an enthralling read.

Philip walks me to Harley, who is lowering the tone of the front courtyard. Philip is too polite to mention that his beautiful place is available for house parties to rent. It's on the web under Candili.

Philhellenes and Lord Byron

Edward Noel's determination to develop the Evia estate was founded on idealism and the financial necessity of repaying his debt to Lady Byron. He was also inspired by Philhellenism, the love of Greece, that flowered in the struggle for independence.

Two currents were at work. The first was an infatuation with an imaginary Greece fed by books written by and about the ancients. Probably more foreigners knew Classical Greek than Greeks. Generations of men had Latin and Greek beaten into them at school. Oxford and Cambridge undergraduates had to pass an exam in Greek before they could study anything else, including sciences. They saw the revolution as a war against Turks oppressing the descendants of Pericles, Socrates and Plato, Euclid and Pythagoras. Greek Committees in Europe sponsored volunteers and collected money for arms and equipment and ships. They raised loans on the London market for the Provisional Government.

The second current was the political ferment bubbling after the American and French Revolutions. Demands for change, such as parliamentary reform, curbing the power of aristocracy and monarchy, full male suffrage, were repressed by the autocratic governments of Kings and Emperors and Popes. Supporting the Greek Revolution was a proxy for radicalism at home. British and other European governments, tried to prevent volunteers from joining the struggle and put them under surveillance if they returned.

About a thousand or so Philhellenes made it to Greece and about a third died there. They included soldiers at a loose end after the Napoleonic wars, idealistic students, romantics, adventurers, misfits and fugitives from the law. Many claimed to be officers and accepted only assignments worthy of their rank. British, French and Germans competed for influence and fought among each other. Some of those who came back sang the praises of modern Greeks but many were disillusioned by the gulf between their imagined Greece and the reality. They could not reconcile Balkan peasants speaking incomprehensible Romaic or Arvanitika with descendants of their fantasy Greek heroes. Philhellenes were used to acting in a chain of command, obedience to superiors, regular pay, battle plans. What we now call guerrilla warfare, which they thought cowardly and dishonourable, was at odds with the pitched battles they had been trained to fight, standing in ranks opposite the enemy to shoot and be shot at, which klephts thought suicidal.

Both sides were shocked to find each other querulous, devious, money-grubbing, untrustworthy, ignorant. It was how Philhellenes interpreted constant renegotiation and improvisation under changing circumstances and shortage of money. Warlords like Kriezotis had no formal authority, no war chest other than what they could plunder or wheedle out of foreigners, no system of discipline other than charisma, family ties and traditional obligations.

The biggest source of misunderstanding was that they had different conceptions of the Liberty they were fighting for: Philhellenes for a nebulous recreation of their imagined Greece, modernisers for a dream of a centralised modern nation state, warlords to shuck off Turkish rule and replace it with their own fiefdoms. The confusion would persist for decades after independence.

The most famous Philhellene was Lord Byron, Poster Boy of the Revolution. His international best-seller *Childe Harold's Pilgrimage* and subsequent poems evoked a Greece yearning to be free. He devoted his celebrity to the Struggle. In December 1823 he was cheered ashore in Missolonghi, a port city built in malarial marshland on the west coast opposite Patras. He came with a trunk of fancy uniforms, crested helmets and money. He hired several hundred Albanian mercenaries and in the mornings loved to dress up in one of his gorgeous get-ups and ride out at their head. He dished out money to Greeks and foreign volunteers who joined him. He threw in his lot with the modernisers in the civil wars and donated large sums to the Government. The ignominy of being bled to death on a malarial sick bed was not what he would have wished. But it made the cause famous in Europe and his sacrifice honoured in statues and street names throughout Greece. Byron joined heroic names like Achilles and Odysseas and Jason at the baptismal font.

Kapodistrias

Promptly at six I loiter outside the church repository waiting for Clooney to complete the sale of a dangly St John Protector Of Travellers for a rear-view mirror to a Russian-speaking elderly gentleman camouflaged for hunting but for a red and white golfing cap. He has the shaking hands of a practising mixologist. I hope his purchase is a gift and not for his own vehicle. His transaction completed the hunter totters out agitating his stick and his purchase.

Clooney takes me to the hotel and swaps a key for my passport. The comfortable room on the third floor has a balcony overlooking the church, the village, the distant mountains glowing gold in the late evening light. John the Russian on the wall presides over the bedside table. After a nap I go out to look for the café where Barbro Noel-Baker says that heads of communist guerrillas were nailed up in the Civil War. There are four cafés but I don't like to ask which one. The famous guerrilla leader, Captain Anapodos was killed in his mountain hideout in 1949. He kept his head but his corpse was tied to a ladder on the back of a truck and paraded around the neighbourhood as far as Halkida.

The setting sun inflames the sky like an infected tonsil. I loiter on a bench in the square. Busy women run after kids, dogs, chickens, wandering grandfathers. I qualify but not theirs to worry about. The town lives on day-tripping pilgrims and the lunchtime trade. Only a couple of souvlaki joints are open. In one of them, on the pretext of a hard day, when all I've done is sit on the saddle and watch the scenery go by, I order a fatty pork chop with chips and cheese and a jug of white. I look for someone to engage in conversation but when the wine comes can't be bothered. I'd rather sit in the corner at a table for one and enjoy the anonymity of old age and shabbiness.

In honour of independent Greece I order an extra plate of chips. Potatoes were introduced by the first head of state, Governor Ioannis Kapodistrias. Born in Corfu, a former Russian foreign minister and designer of Switzerland's federal system, the Great Powers believed he could bring order into the chaos and in-fighting of the failing revolution.

For students of the moustache the National Historical Museum in Athens is a cornucopia. Leaders of the Revolution line the walls, striking manly poses in mountain warrior dress, tasselled caps and Hellenic helmets. Costumes are topped off with luxuriant moustaches, tended, teased and waxed into all manner of handlebars - drop, flat, riser, upright, cruiser. Byron grew one to go with his Albanian outfit, a wispy effort he wisely thought better of later. Archetypal is Kolokotronis's greying walrus and locks flowing over his shoulders under the iconic red helmet with a horsehair crest that he earned as a British officer in the Duke of York's 1st Greek Light Infantry in Zakynthos and wore throughout the Revolution. The moustache expressed Hellenic courage, defiance and freedom.

Kapodistrias, is instantly recognisable for his smooth chops and tidy haircut. Not for him the klephtic get-up but the black coat and white cravat of the European ruling classes. It signals a determination to build a modern nation state with a civil society based on centralised government, centralised taxation, the rule of law. He founded schools, a university, a national army to absorb the militias, a national bank to supervise the first currency he called the Phoenix. He instigated a land registry, a project still under way as I write these words. Like the potato these were alien things in a backward and lawless Balkan satrapy impoverished by Ottoman exploitation and a decade of war. Abrasive and peremptory, he antagonised warlords, who wanted to rule their own domains, independent and untaxed. In 1831, after four years of enlightened autocracy and festering rebellion he was assassinated in the capital, Nafplion. Civil war broke out again among the moustaches until 1832 when the troika of France, Russia and Britain imposed Bavarian Otto as King. His qualifications for the job were that his father King Ludwig I was a Hellenophile and substantial supporter of the Revolution and that he was not French, Russian or British.

The chop is excellent with plenty of juicy fat, the feta is creamy, the chips are firm and fresh, deserving another carafe. I get gently pissed until I ask myself what's the point of this ridiculous jaunt. This is what it has come to. A chop and chips, a jug of cheap wine, thumping disco music, a waitress in larded make-up. The entire history of the Universe since the Big Bang culminates in the very moment that I shovel in fries. I know from experience that this is the time to go to bed before I lapse into maudlin.

Pilgrims

I'm looking forward to a good night's sleep. Fat chance. In the middle of the night John the Russian stands beside me in the flashing green light of my toothbrush recharging on the bedside table, no eyes behind the gold mask, only plugholes

84

into cloaca of infinite dark. With his good hand he drags me out of the bedroom along a dark tunnel to a distant light. The anxiety is aggravated by forgetting the technical term for a guide of souls into the afterlife. John looks over his shoulder. PSYCHOPOMP he says in a weedy voice, mummification not being kind to vocal cords. We step onto a Strictly dance floor ringed by headless andartes…so the night wears on too chaotic and half-remembered to bore you with. Unless you are a Freudian other people's dreams are tedious. The climax is John's cyborganistic hand throttling me until I wake up in sweaty terror to a bell bonging in my skull. I bolt out of bed and tear open the curtains to brilliant light and the pealing campanile of the church over the road. Like Faust saved from damnation by the bells of Easter morning, I am flooded with contrition and a firm purpose of amendment never to eat pork and cheese twice on the same day.

Full of amorphous dread I shower and pack in a hurry, keen to get away. I keep lingering phantoms at bay with a breakfast of hot Nescafé and *bougatsa,* a pie of semolina custard in filo pastry, a bachelor pleasure as the very idea of it makes Arfa want to throw up. Other delicacies to make her clap her hands over her ears and hum include lumpy custard, the skin on hot milk, tapioca pudding, blancmange and other delights to squidge between the teeth. I make my daily phone call home, to say I am still alive and thinking of her and describe with malice the *bougatsa* I'm about to relish. She doesn't rise to this but asks if I'm going to see the plane tree.

"What plane tree?"

"The giant one. The oldest in Greece. By the river."

"You're thinking about somewhere else."

"It's past Prokópi."

"We've never been to Prokópi."

"Yes we have. The first time Harry fell in the river and the second Kate got stung by a wasp."

I don't remember. It was forty years ago. With four children, falling in rivers and getting stung by wasps is not enough of a clue. Still, it was troubling. Was I here before?

I enjoy the *bougatsa* at an outside table, surrounded by pyramids of local honey, Greek embroidery and Chinese crockery. A man older than me but fitter and dressed smartly casual brings out my coffee. The hand holding the mug is pale and liver-spotted. The other is encased or replaced by a glove. It's black not gold but still I bite my tongue, dribble custard down my shirt, struggle to wake up.

'Hi, where you from?' he says in a North American accent. Spraying him with filo flakes I mumble London. He sits down opposite me and I can't keep my eyes off his hand. He notices and thumps it down on the table.

"Mining accident. Got a good pension out of it. Thank God it happened in Canada not here."

His name is Jimmy and he left Prokópi in 1960 to mine gold in Manitoba at the age of nineteen. He rabbits on about his forty years underground, while I struggle to remember where Manitoba is. He tells me the temperature is under forty below in winter and over forty above in summer, which is why I have never taken much interest in the place. I try to steer the conversation to decorpitated andartes.

"Prokópi must have changed. What was it like when you were a child? In the war?"

"Folks came for the Saint. Like now."

By way of illustration a coach draws up and disgorges its cargo of pilgrims. Most hobble and shuffle and otherwise process to the church, some get in their way by lighting cigarettes the second they step onto solid ground, a few make a beeline for honey and souvenirs.

"The Catholics gotta shrine in Ontario. The Canadian Martyrs. Folks come from all over."

I put on the pontificatory voice of an authority. I grasp my lapels, figuratively as I am wearing a sweatshirt, and expound.

"Ah, there's a difference between Catholic and Orthodox pilgrimage. For Westerners the journey is important. The word pilgrim comes from the Latin peregrine, a traveller. The Greek word is *proskinitís*, someone who bows down. For Orthodox people worship is the main point and the journey is an inconvenience."

I pause to allow a respectful silence but in Greece nothing is said without contradiction. Jimmy shrugs his shoulders and sticks out his hands, palms up, one of them clenched.

"My friend, before you make the veneration you make your *tama*, that's what you guys call penance. On the Saint's feast here you walk over the mountain from Halkida. It's a hell of a hike and dangerous what with the cars on the road. On Tinos you walk up the hill on your knees to the Mother of God."

"So what are these people doing on a bus?"

"You think riding round in that shitty bus all day going to nine churches ain't a penance?"

Having made his point, the Church Triumphant goes back to his till, where a pilgrim waits with a devotional snow globe. I brush pastry flakes off my front and slouch back to Harley, digging into my trouser pocket for his key, with the habitual frisson of nervousness that I have lost it.

Lord Byron's Helmet

6 MANTOUDI TO LIMNI

I splash out €4 on filling Harley's tank, the first refuel since we set out. He might be slow but he's cheap to feed. I plan to drive to the north-east tip of the island and see where the sea battle of Artemision took place on the same day as the battle of Thermopylae that made movie stars of 300 Spartans.

I am troubled by the conversation with Arfa. Have I been here before? Under fifty, forgetting things is normal. Not remembering the names of colleagues, last year's cup final winners, the wives of Henry VIII never bothered me. But at my age you're afraid it might be a symptom. You lie awake at night trying to remember the names of the Rolling Stones or the actor who played Ben Hur. You go through the alphabet A-B-C and then again with the second letter AB-AC-AD... and the more you can't remember the more anxious you get until you get up for a drink of water and remind yourself you couldn't remember the Stones' names when you were thirty, except Mick Jagger of course. You fall asleep and wonder over breakfast why you can't get Charlton Heston out of your head.

The road winds gently between overarching plane trees. I pull over and fritter an exorbitant roaming charge on googling '*platanos evia*'. There are two pages of links about the oldest plane tree in the Balkans, 2,300 years, the days of Alexander the Great. It is a living historical monument, a metaphor for the survival of Greece through the ages. The trunk measures eighteen metres round and thirty metres high. Its shade covers two and a half thousand square metres. The photos look vaguely familiar, a massive trunk split down the middle and hollowed inside under a spreading crown but I can't be sure. An old tree is an old tree.

A few yards further on I spot a tourist panel beside a turn-off. In faded lettering it relays the information I have just paid for. Lips pursed in annoyance I follow a gravel road for a hundred yards through the trees until we come to a scene of desolation. A mountain of slag looms over a flat field penned by heaps of rubble. An excavator has been at work. At one side is a gigantic tree. Half of it has fallen, its massive branches amputated and cut into sections like the marble drums that litter the site of a temple. Lifeless roots are buried in waterless slag. If it's where we picnicked and played and consoled blubbing kids, river and tree are no more, like my memory of it. I leave Harley muttering to himself as I dismount only long enough to break off a lump of wood from the trunk, about as big as my hand, a relic older than the True Cross.

We are at the edge of a magnesite mine. It is called white-stone in Greek. It looks like limestone and is processed the same way by washing and calcination, in other words burning into a powder. In the old days this was done in open fields and nowadays by modern furnaces but the resulting slag is the same, to be dumped anywhere convenient, including near rivers and trees over two thousand years old. The powder, magnesia, is used to make linings for furnaces. It has nothing to do with the milk of magnesia I was dosed with as a child for a bilious attack.

Back on the road we get to Mantoudi. An unexpected attraction is a beehive house - the old fashioned conical skep that gave its name to bronze age tombs and a precarious sixties hairstyle. A wooden frame is thatched all the way to the ground. For light and ventilation it has only a door and a smoke hole at the top. It is the traditional winter home of the Sarakatsani, transhumant shepherds of northern Greece and southern Bulgaria. Fifty years ago they roamed the mountains of northern Evia. Transhumant means that they took their flocks into the mountains in summer and came back down to their beehive houses in winter. Until the suppression of minorities in the Metaxas dictatorship they spoke an ancient form of Greek but the origin of their race and their name is unknown. In my lifetime they have been settled and urbanised, working as farmers or miners, their way of life preserved in folklore museums and festivals.

Vlachs

We toddle along a winding road through the bucolic countryside of the Kireas valley, the gentle greens of river-fed trees turning a tinge of autumn. I stop for coffee and a bar of chocolate at a roadside minimarket on the outskirts of the village of Kirinthos, where old men sit outside waiting for oblivion or ouzo, whichever release comes first. I give them a collective *kalimera*. A couple look at me in puzzlement, should I know you? The rest pay no attention to me or each other, caught in the cusp between the disintegrating old and the repeatedly new. Their fractured conversation, repeated snippets of information about the weather, what they had for dinner, what day it is, breaks the silence into chunks. What is left to say? They have known each other all their lives, watched each other grow up and grow old. Now they keep company in confusions. The girl at the till also seems to live in another world, paying more attention to the Greek Hello! on the counter than to me. She has bewitchingly large eyes, hereditary or a thyroid condition I'm not sure.

According to the online newspaper *Mantoudi News* ancient Kirinthos has ruins and a bit of wall and Homer says it sent a ship to Troy. I distract the waitress from Hello! to pay what I owe and ask where I will find the *archaia,* the ancient stuff. She raises her eyebrows, shrugs her shoulders and jerks a thumb in the general direction of where I have come from. It's the best I can hope for. I add to my bill a packet of neon-yellow processed cheese slices for a picnic lunch to go with bread pocketed from last night's dinner.

I leave Harley in the care of the geriatric community and take a side street into the village. After a couple of hundred yards I come to a gate and a drive leading up to a pink-plastered mansion. I take a few steps inside until stopped in my tracks by an icy Greek "can I help you?", the universal greeting that means the opposite of what it says. It comes from an elegant blonde lady of middle height, middle age and middle class, coiffed and made up for a coffee morning, doing something horticultural with secateurs. I quickly explain what I'm looking for in case she assumes I'm a weary tramp looking for a glass of water please Ma'am.

"Where are you from?" she asks.

"I'm Irish," I say.

"Would you like a glass of water?"

Before I can touch my forelock she points the secateurs to a terrace in front of the house and invites me to sit down. Over refreshments she tells me that this is the Villa Averoff and has a similar history to the Noel-Baker's estate. Avgelinos Averoff, from Northern Greece, made a fortune in Odessa and bought the land from a Turkish owner in 1832. Avgelinos' brother George made a fortune in Alexandria. In 1910 his estate stumped up a third of the cost of a battleship named after him. The flagship of the Greek Navy throughout the first half of the twentieth century the *Averoff* is iconic to Greeks, not least because it remained out of Axis clutches in the Second World War and saw active service in the free

Greek navy. I ask my host if she is an Averoff. She giggles and tosses her head and tuts and puts a hand on her bosom.

"I am a neighbour. I love flowers. Flowers love me."

She takes me on a tour of the property, with swimming pool and a petting zoo with sheep and deer and rabbits. To save me lapsing into realtorese you can Google it for yourself.

Aromanian was the first language of the Averoffs. Aromanians are not Romanians, although their language and culture share common roots in the Latin of the late Roman empire. They lived in the Pindos mountains of Epirus in North-Western Greece. They had a similar lifestyle to the Greek-speaking Sarakatzani. They spread through Serbia, Albania, Bulgaria and Northern Greece. Many emigrated to the commercial centres of Europe and North Africa and made fortunes, like the Averoffs. Outsiders call them Vlachs, a corruption of Wallachians, from the principality of Wallachia, a part of present-day Romania. In a broader sense 'Vlach' is derogatory in Greek, 'ignorant peasant' being an equivalent in English, despite the part Vlachs played in the Greek Revolution and the worldly success of many since.

Shaking off the dust of the Villa Averoff, figuratively speaking, as there is not a speck to be found there, I return to Harley. The vestigial wall of ancient Kirinthos is several kilometres down a side road. As Doctor Johnson said about the Giant's Causeway, I suspect it is worth seeing but not worth going to see. Another one for The List.

With a splutter and a wave to the geriatrium we continue our journey to the north.

Limni

We come to a fork. I go left towards the seaside town of Limni where I have a friend, who lives in an old quarry. Feeling peckish I look for a pleasant place to stop for lunch.

Down a side road is an inviting clump of huge pines and cypresses shading an old stone building. It is a ruined two storey mansion, its doors and windows gone, the roof going. The rubble strewn rooms are covered in graffiti and smell of pee and worse. I sit outside on a stone bench against a wall and try to pretend that sweaty yellow cheese slices on last night's bread seasoned with pocket crud washed down with the lukewarm dregs of a plastic bottle filled from a toilet tap yesterday is a princely alfresco luncheon.

Limni is surrounded by hills with views across the water to the mainland. I stop at a rooms-for-rent at the end of the long promenade and phone for the proprietor, Costas, a nattily dressed pensioner. €35 for an excellent room next to a bakery and overlooking the sea.

"I have shaken the hand of Princess Diana," says Costas, radiant with celebrity.

"Gosh. In London?"

"In Limni. She came for the funeral of my cousin Yannis. It was her friend from the hospital in London."

Limni's fifteen minutes of fame.

I change into my bathers and hobble over the road to the stony beach, legs bandy, bum numb, arms sunburnt, spam fly-specked, ears drumming, sweaty all over. After two agonising yards inching out barefoot on the stones I come back for my all-weather hiking sandals, good for paddling into the water but buoyant when afloat, like having swimming rings round your ankles and inconvenient for the breaststroke as they force your head underwater. Backstroke is better but feels like trying to kick off the bedclothes. I make do with a starfish, drifting in the ripples as the rigours of the road melt away, sandalled feet bobbing out of the water like a couple of turds the other side of my beachball belly. Lying on my back, absorbed in the lymph of the sea, the sound of my breathing, the hoarse voice of anima, my spirit, intrudes in the world. Stop breathing and I am a foetus in a jar, dreaming the undreamt under a wan new moon floating bodiless in the blue, listening to its own old sighing. And other hallucinations brought on by fatigue, heat and the need for a drink. It's too early to get one from my friend Denise. There is a risk of being offered tea. Better wait until the yardarm signals wine.

In a side street a bazaar stretches through the town. Stalls offer many useful products from clothing to kitchen goods. Usually I gravitate to the tools and gadgets, cheap knock-offs that I know won't last, but habitually fall for the temptation of a pseudo-DeWalt or a mock-Stanley. This time I have business in the Men's Clothing Department. Pasty white arms is a reasonable trade-off for skin cancer and I am in the market for a long-sleeve shirt, XXL for preference to accommodate a midriff prone to further enlargement by sitting on Harley all day. It is after five o'clock and stall-holders emerge from afternoon sleep to pull dust sheets off their wares, switch on radios, check their phones, send boys for coffee. One stall specialises in shirts of all kinds, from summer Ts to unseasonal lumberjack flannels. Browsing among famous international brands like Hugo Buss, Tummy Hilfinger, Abercrumble and Flitch, I light on a dark green denim Levees. XXXL. €10. Perfect. I rouse the merchant from her slumber under the counter, a round young woman with startling blue eyes. I wait while she rubs them and remembers where she is. She stares at the note I'm offering her until her part in the world's work comes flooding back and she snatches it from me before subsiding under the counter again. I go back to my digs with a spring in my step, therapised by retail and congratulating myself on its cost.

Denise lives in a disused magnesite quarry a few kilometres outside town that her late husband, Philip Sherrard, bought in the late 1950's. His interest was not in the mine but the pretty houses above it built for the managers. With friends he restored them, planted trees, built a chapel. His book, the *Marble Threshing Floor* and his translations of

Cavafy and Seferis brought modern Greek poetry to many of us. He was a convert to Orthodoxy and became a respected theologian. *The Sacred In Life And Art,* is to my mind his most inspiring book. He was one of the translators of the *Philokalia,* Love of the Good, a collection of spiritual Greek texts from the 4th to the 19th century. I have it on Kindle and dip into it to get in the mood for Athos.

Denise carries on his mission as a publisher of books that are concerned, according to her website, "with modern Greek culture — its literature, history and music ... how Greek people see themselves and others, and how others see them, and the Orthodox Church that is the matrix, within which much of modern Greek culture has been formed." If this sounds heavy for the beach, her list includes books about rebetiko, Mediterranean gardening and a translation of the perennial Greek best-seller *Loxandra,* a tale of nineteenth century Ottoman Constantinople, the original Aga Saga.

The road into the mine winds through a man-made gorge hewn into the mountainside past rusted machinery and blocks of white rock, some of them sculpted, passing from the modern world through relics of a forgotten civilisation to an ancient wisdom. I stop to jot that whimsy down on my phone. At the end of the canyon the track turns steeply uphill to a couple of stone and wooden houses with marvellous views of forest and mountains and the sea. Andrew, a house guest and literary collaborator, joins us and we sit on a balcony illuminated by the sunset. Denise apologises that today is a fasting day, the vigil of the Feast of the Holy Cross. This means no meat, fish or cheese nibbles so we make do with olives from the trees below us, tapenade, and other vegan delicacies. Fortunately the Church only proscribes foods so they sip and I slurp an excellent dark yellow wine.

The Feast of the Exaltation of the Holy and Life Giving Cross commemorates the discovery of the True Cross in Jerusalem in 326 by Saint Helena, mother of the Emperor

Constantine. She found three crosses, the other two for the thieves. But which was which? A dead woman was sent for and laid on each cross in turn. The one she came back to life on was obviously Christ's. On the way back to Constantinople the cross of the Good Thief flew away to a monastery on Stavrovouni, Mountain of the Cross, in Cyprus, where it hovered unsupported in mid-air for a few centuries. I don't know what happened to the cross of the Bad Thief.

We exchange Athonite gossip and literary tittle-tattle. The moon is bright by the time I leave, hoping that I have not outstayed a generous welcome. We weave back through the quarry in the dark and along the shore, past pitch black mountains on one side, mercurial sea on the other. Harley carries me back over half a century to the thrill of gunning a Solex at 15mph on a summer night in Brittany. The Solex was a post-war bicycle with a half-horsepower petrol motor mounted in front of the handlebars. It powered a ceramic roller that sat on top of the front tyre to turn it. You started pedalling, lowered the motor and the engine started, if you were lucky. Solihull's James Dean on a Solex in desert boots, cavalry twills, nylon shirt, knitted tie, tweed sports jacket, clip-on sunglasses, prowled the mean streets of drizzly Plancoët in a see-through pac-a-mac with an erection thinking of the girl he snogged last night at a *surprise party* and the provocative way she whipped off her glasses so they didn't clash with his and her luscious lips and the steely taste of her brace. *Ah jeunesse!* I have never felt such heady freedom, and then I didn't need a drink, only youth. Is it why I'm doing this now, to recapture youth? Pathetic old fool.

The pathetic old fool is hungry. In the bazaar next to my digs a food truck is swathed in aromatic smoke. I sit down at a plastic table and opt for a hot dog with spicy country sausage, *loukaniko*, and a tumbler of rough red. A guitar-bouzouki duo belts out rebetiko, the rest of us joining in the bits we know. Bearded boys and busty girls dance in the street. The aroma of cannabis blends with the meat and tobacco smoke wafting up to the gods. Ancient Greeks called it '*thalassaelgi*', sea glow, a nicer name than weed or shit.

Feeling seedy and elated, thankful to be here, relishing the highbrow and the lowbrow and how they meet under a single brilliant moon, I go to bed and sleep solid until dawn.

Among the sinful passions St Peter of Damaskos, 12th Century, lists 'laughter, immodest dancing, clapping, improper songs, revelry, flute playing'.   The Philokalia

7 LOUTRA AIDIPSOU TO OREOI

Random glimpses of the past muscle into my journey through the present, landmarks on a mental map of half-remembered experience. Travelling the roads of Greece I also travel through seven decades of fragmented memories, the mind's eye watching my neural networks at play. We live simultaneously in so many moments from recent past back to childhood, to imaginary moments, hopes and desires. At the same time as Harley's handlebars I hold the handlebars of old bicycles I've owned and London rent-a-bikes and my Lambretta and my first tricycle and a scooter - layer upon layer of experience to make the lived-in moment like a painter putting layer upon layer of paint to make the final picture, all the layers underneath creating the texture and luminosity and depth of a single point of space and time.

One of the pleasures of life is putting on a new shirt for the first time. Being fashion unconscious I rarely do, which makes it more of an event. My Bangladeshi denim meets every expectation. XXXL in girth and M in length, sleeves long enough to protect the fingers from sunburn and superlative in one respect, the itchiest garment I have ever put on. It was even pricklier than the army shirts we were issued by the school CCF, the Combined Cadet Force. In a bid to escape horse blanket shirts I transferred to the RAF section which had more refined cotton.

A memory intrudes on my breakfast. At CCF camp on an RAF base I had my *baptême de l'air*, as the French put it, with my friend Prust, an avid historian with big glasses and small stature, weedy but full of derring-do. It was a blustery afternoon and touch-and-go whether we would fly. The Chipmunk was a tiny plane that to my nervous eyes seemed tossed about like a falling leaf as it took off and landed. I regretted putting myself through this for the sake of a comfy shirt. Nibbling a block of Battenberg marzipan sponge for the nerves we waited our turns on an iron bench, tightly strapped into the parachutes under our bottoms that would be our seats in the cockpit. The instruction was to step onto the wing if ordered, dive head first so you weren't decapitated by the tailplane and count to five before pulling the metal ring on your chest connected to the ripcord that passed under your legs. Prust sat at the end of the bench, his feet dangling off the ground. His turn came. He jumped off the bench, staggered and fell on his face. The ripcord caught on the corner of the bench. It did what it was supposed to do, pull out the pilot parachute. He struggled to his feet and shuffled off to the plane, the pilot 'chute fluttering behind him in the wind and pulling the main canopy after it. One minute he was trudging forwards like a cartoon tortoise, the next he was skipping backwards and trying to stay upright as the silk billowed out behind him. The parachute was half deployed now, dragging a screaming Prust in ever longer backwards bunny-hops pursued by two aircraftmen. Happily they caught him before he took off.

Plucky Prust. A mug of sweet tea and he tried again. After his premature baptism on wings of silk, aerobatics in the Chipmunk was a piece of cake, to be precise the Battenberg he puked up in the cockpit. Me, I opted for a gentler bird's eye tour of Lincoln Cathedral, which was nerve-wracking enough. Poor Prust. He went up to Cambridge and coxed his college boat. He jumped off a bridge to celebrate triumph in the Lent Bumps and drowned.

Having discovered a fear of flying, a handicap in budding aviators, I ended my CCF career in the band, sitting indoors on winter afternoons tootling the third clarinet part of Hearts Of Oak and other martial ditties while the cannon fodder toted leaden Lee Enfield rifles in the cold and wet.

Waiting for breakfast in the shade of a rustling mulberry by the sea, I mourn my friend and his fifty lost years. What have I done with the gift of my own half-century? Lived it. Done slightly more good than harm, I hope. When my time comes I look forward to hearing what the recording angel makes of it all. I can't make sense of it myself.

Breakfast is a warm *koulouri* from the bakery over the road, a ring of bread covered in sesame seeds, known as a Turkish bagel in America. To avoid confusion I avoid asking for them by name and point to one instead, as they share the same memory cells as *kourelou*, which means a rag rug. For the same reason I am careful if ever the conversation comes round to soft furnishings. A busy baker's boy brings a yellow mug of hot Nescafé. Squiggly red writing on the side asserts in English that "Happiness is not a destination - it is a way of life." Pure Epicureanism. Enjoy life, spend time with friends, avoid pain, be happy. And don't fret about recording angels, your soul dies with your body. It is a fine philosophy for the daytime. It does little for the terrors of the night.

Celery

We putput along the coast in the sunshine on a good road with only a few cars and trucks thundering past, pine-covered hills to the right, blue sea to the left. Every few hundred metres the Diocese of Chalkis puts me right with billboards advertising in big white letters on a blue background that

Jesus is the way, the truth and the life. I wish the secular authorities were as good with their signage.

We come to a turn-off for the village of Rovies, clustered around the remains of a Frankish tower. A few years ago an oracle of Apollo Selinaios was discovered on a hillside nearby. The west coast of Evia lies on a series of geological faults running from Mount Olympus to Corinth. In Classical times they exhaled fumes that fuelled the divine inspiration of local prophetesses called sybils or oracles. Selinaios means celery, not the stringy stalks for dipping in hummus but a wild herb with dark and spicy leaves, related to parsley, that seasoned ancient death cults. These days it's the key ingredient of a delicious stew, *hirino me selino*, pork with celery.

I need a walk to shake off the stiffness of riding. Celery is a good destination. I park Harley at the foot of a track uphill beside a fly tip of rubble and mattresses. I replace the itchy shirt with the T variety, the helmet with a sun-hat and pick up the bottle of toilet water. The track goes through lemon scented pine and then mountain oak and prickly scrub, kept open by hunters and barricaded by goatherds with piles of thorn, bleached white and sharp as needles. Goats watch me pass with cunning and malicious eyes, their tinny bells chiming complicated changes. A nanny bleats for her kid long since eaten. Squeezed for milk and killed for meat their revenge is to scourge the soil, leaf by leaf, blade by blade, flaying hills and valleys so that wind and rain can scour the earth down to bony rock.

The track peters out into a steep path zig-zagging through dusty scrub, desiccated until the rains, when it will come alive again with wild flowers and tender shoots of green to please the goats. In the hot sun, sweaty, breathless, stumbling on the stones, grateful to my long trousers for fending off calf-height thorns, it is a struggle on kapok legs. Keep going with The Grand Old Duke of York. Stop every 20 paces to take a breather, then 10, then 5. Be sensible, take care of yourself, don't overdo it, heart attack at your age, you're not so young any more, TURN BACK. I can't blame advancing age for sucking the strength out of my youth. I was always the wimp at the back of school mountain hikes and CCF route marches and avoided such exertion for decades afterwards.

I am unnerved by strange bird cries I don't recognise. Given where we are they could be the swans that pull Apollo's chariot - not the mutes we feed in the park but wild whoopers that honk until they warble a swan song when they die. Better candidates are Apollo's other birds, crows, white birds he burnt black when they told him his lover was unfaithful. Then I realise they are the squeaking of my sinuses, a let-down and a warning to get real.

A young hunter, fit and tanned comes down with a gun, a puppy and a wife laden with the dog's carry box. I ask if he's shot anything. He rummages in his shoulder bag to bring out a floppy mop of grey feathers. Dead partridges. Tasty I say and we continue on our ways with good wishes.

On a vindictive stretch of steep a church springs out of hiding, Agios Stavros, The Holy Cross. I totter through the gate of the enclosure, relief turning to smugness. It took me an hour to do what a fit person would do in half the time but I've made it with nothing worse than wobbly legs.

Giant rosemary and stunted mountain pine make shade. White church, green trees, blue sky, cool breeze, perfect quiet in a place made holy by generations of pious folk, who toil up the mountain on foot and mule every September on the feast of the Holy Cross, yesterday in fact. I sit against the wall beside the locked door, drink my tepid water and turn my soul to meditation. I focus on the kindness of strangers, the power of silence, the joy of being alive and let these notions mingle and fade to free the spirit and find communion with the infinity of creation. Not a hope. My untrammelled mind cannot rid itself of the flies that zip round my head and tickle my cheeks and hop around my trousers, rubbing their little hands. If I could speak fly language I would ask what they thought they were doing and why. I suspect they would say because it's what we do and it makes us happy. But then the flies might ask me the same question. My reply wouldn't be as glib as the one I put in their tiny mouths. I would find it hard to put it in terms they would understand. I find it hard enough to put it in terms that I understand. I have no idea, would be the honest answer. In that case just do what you do and enjoy it say the flies.

I feel bad about letting conversations with flies get in the way of meditation. I give up on Celery, which is half way down a dangerous cliff. I go down the safer path I came up, easier going except for the pain in the knees. I hardly notice the stunning view of the sea and distant Parnassus because I'm still puzzling over the bloody flies. The answer hits just as I arrive back at Harley beside the appropriately named fly tip. It's the maggots they come from that carry the burden of purpose. If it wasn't for them the world would be overwhelmed by rottenness. And when the maggots are done with their role in creation they metamorphose into buzzy things that have a good time in the sunshine. What am I for? Except one day to give their maggotty lives a purpose?

I hope for an answer on Athos. Meanwhile I have Harley.

"Harley, what are we here for?"

"Vrroom-vrroom."

"We're made of different stuff but we both transform energy for a purpose. Your mechanical purpose is to carry me around. What's my biological purpose? Survive and reproduce. Is there anything else? Apart from the stuff that dreams are made of?"

"Vrroom vrroom"

I wish I'd taken the trouble to find the Celery shrine. Another one for The List.

Loutra Aidipsou

On the same volcanic fault is the spa town of Loutra
Aidipsou. It has been a fashionable resort since ancient times
thanks to eighty or so hot springs, some of which bubble up
under the sea in a natural jacuzzi. I anticipated faded glory
and post-Crisis seediness but German and Russian investors
have done it up, the sweet stink of money wafting in the
aroma of volcanic fart. At the posh end of the promenade is
the Sylla Spa & Wellness Hotel, restored and remodelled. I
have time to take a picture of tone-lowering Harley posing
before the grand entrance before a flunkey shoos us away.
Through the iron bars of a double gate opening onto the
street I ogle arthritic fatties in white bathrobes waddling
around the hotel pool, as comical and sad as the penguin
enclosure at London zoo. Out of curiosity to try the waters I
think of joining them but, while I have the figure for it, am
too mean to pay. Instead I change into bathers under my
towel and go into the sea for free therapy among curious
rocks forged from lava, erosion and mineral accretion. The
restorative waters bubble up from the depths like an
elemental hot tub with the confusing sensation of hot and
cold taps running at the same time. It was ok but I've never
seen the point of these so-called cures, from hot springs to
saunas, mainly because of the discomfort and the flatulent
smell. A lie down and a couple of ibuprofen do me just as
well. I make an exception for a proper Turkish bath where
you get a jolly good wash into the bargain.

Redolent of wellness I cruise along the crowded
promenade, not tempted to stop. It is a popular place, not
only among hypochondriacs my age but also younger people
dressed in smart après-spa, the women cakily made-up and
fingernailed, the men glo-tanned and be-ringed. Seeing a jetty
and signs for a ferry I park in front of a café terrace and

cross the road to see where it goes - the other side of the gulf, so no interest to me.

Coming back I see my vegetable crate on the ground and two men piling my things back in. They parked their truck behind me, lowered the side to unload boxes of water and knocked the crate off, breaking the plastic ties. I go up to them and wave my arms but not a word of apology, just a laugh. I call the nearest one a fucker to his face. He stops laughing and stares at me and I am pleased to repeat it, louder. Oh so bold when I'm a yard away from a terrace full of spectators. He says something in Albanian to his mate and they carry on with their work, looking daggers at me now and then. Some vocabulary is universal.

I brought with me a spare packet of ties so I can fix the crate back on, glowering now and then at the Albanians. I pile everything back in, get on the saddle and kick the starter. And again. And again. Nothing. Have I flooded the carburettor? I jiggle the handlebars, kick the gear lever to make sure I'm in neutral, rock backwards and forward in case something's stuck. This exhausts my diagnostic skills. One of the Albanians comes over. Is he going to push us over in front of all these people? He reaches past me and before I can grab his arm turns the ignition key in the middle of the handlebars to the ON position. He goes back to his work. I spit out a grudging *falemenderit* and kick Harley into life.

I am happy to leave odorous Loutra Aidipsou.

Artemision

I want to put some distance between me and the Albanian watermen in case they are coming my way. I wouldn't be so brave on the open road. We putter along the coast to Cape Artemision in the north-east corner of the island, an hour and a half from Loutra Aidipsou.

In 480 BC the Persian emperor Xerxes led an army of 60,000 men from Asia Minor through mainland Greece. 800 ships sailed down the coast to support them. Some Greek cities joined the invaders, while most remained neutral, hoping to be spared. An alliance of the rest resisted, led by Athens and Sparta. A Greek force of a few thousand led by the Spartan King Leonidas held the pass of Thermopylae for a few days until they were outflanked over a mountain path and retreated. Leonidas with his famous 300 Spartans and the unfairly less famous 700 Thespians fought to the last man to protect the Greek retreat. Thespians were not there to entertain the troops but were citizens of Thespiai, a city near Thebes. They deserve to be better known for courage, patronage of the arts and their chief deity Eros.

At the same time, the Athenian general Themistocles confronted the Persian fleet with about 300 ships in the narrow straits between Artemision and the mainland to protect the flank of the Greek army. The battle lasted three days and both sides lost a similar number of ships. For the Greeks this was half their fleet, so when they heard that Thermopylae was lost they retreated down the Evian Gulf towards Athens. The Persian army continued its march south, followed by the remains of its fleet. Thespiai was razed. Athenians evacuated their city, which was also destroyed. Xerxes pursued them to the island of Salamis where the Greek ships were moored.

Thermopylae was a defeat and Artemision a draw. But they showed that the outnumbered Greeks could resist the Persians by land and sea and possibly defeat them. Like Dunkirk for the British two thousand years later, humiliating defeat turned into a moral victory. The two battles were the beginning of the end of the Persian invasion. A month after Artemision the Athenian fleet defeated the Persians at Salamis. The following year the Spartans led an army to victory at Plataea. For the next hundred and fifty years the

Greeks were still constantly at war but against each other not a foreign invader, until they were annexed by Macedonian King Philip II, Alexander the Great's father. Salamis and Plataea marked the beginning of the great flowering of Classical Greece on which our civilisation is built. If you want to know more about Artemision and Thermopylae I suggest you read the *Histories* of Herodotus. Everything written since about the Persian wars are paraphrases. And they omit entertaining bits that you can take with a pinch of salt but are light relief to politics and war.

I coax Harley up a rocky road to a bosky thicket of twisted Aleppo pine and scrub at the top of the headland of Artemision. Leaving Harley ticking to himself I struggle through the undergrowth to the cliff edge. Kindle open at Herodotus I look over the straits from the narrow sand and shingle beach below me, where the Greek fleet waited to do battle, to the mainland, where the Persian fleet anchored. There's not a lot to see, a square mile or so of empty sea, aquamarine in the shallows and ultramarine in the deep, imprinted with Herodotus's words and the cacophony of war from two hundred thousand men on a thousand ships.

At the end of the third day the Greek commander Themistocles hears that Thermopylae is lost. He decides to take what remains of the fleet back to Athens. Herodotus tells us

"Now it was the custom of the Evians to drive their flocks down to the sea there. He advised them to let everyone slay as many as he wanted. It was better that the fleet should have them, than the enemy."

As evening draws in, the survivors, twenty thousand men or more, have a barbie. Slit the throats of lambs, skin and gut them, spit them with spears, roast them on fires of driftwood and wreckage, meaty smoke swirling into the heavens; throw tough bits on the fire and splash wine on the ground for the gods; scoff kidneys and liver, sweetbreads and testicles, fat tail and belly skin, and then the meat, hacked onto shields and breastplates for platters, washed down with wine mixed in their helmets with seawater. This is how they honour catastrophe. They feed and carouse, throw up in the bushes and come back for more, unhinged from moderation by things they have seen and done that day. They know their cities will be razed, homes and temples destroyed, fathers and mothers slaughtered, wives and children raped and taken into slavery. In the early morning light they paddle among the bodies of the dead washed up in the shallows, stripping them of valuable things. They leave barbarians and enemy Greeks for the crabs and drag their own ashore, splash them with wine and put them on pyres stacked up on the fatty embers of the night before, more meaty smoke swirling into the heavens. In the reek of wine and death they push their ships out from the beach and bend to the oars, or hoist a sail if they are lucky, and head south through flotsam and corpses for Salamis and revenge.

Picturing the funeral feast makes me peckish. I struggle back to Harley for the water bottle and a 7-Days-Croissant-With-Chocolate-Cream-Filling I keep for emergencies. I scramble down the cliff to the beach. It's an ordinary beach with ordinary water lapping at ordinary sand and rocks. History is in books not here. I slump on the shingle, day-dreaming of the drowned, and doze off, nervous of nightmare, whose modern Greek name is *ephialtis,* the name of the man who betrayed the Greeks at Thermopylae by showing the Persians the path over the mountains.

A refreshing catnap later I climb back up the cliff and wake up Harley. We follow a different track along the headland in the hope that it will be easier than the one we came up. Round here somewhere is the site of a temple to Artemis, from which the place gets its name but I can't find it. Put it on The List.

Secret Police

The track turns downhill and we come to a chainlink fence, still shiny. The ground on the other side under half a dozen olive trees is covered with black plastic. A caravan on a concrete slab is extended by a canvas awning. A hut built of breeze blocks houses a lavatory. Rustic tables are strewn with cooking things and tools. A gas bottle, solar powered lights and a phone charger provide the utilities. A concrete patio shaded by a green awning is furnished with a yellow plastic chair and an office table on castors. The whole is functional, unpretentious, transitory, my kind of place.

A man in PT instructor's white T-shirt and blue shorts looks up from chopping wood. I wave and stop by the gate. He strides down the concrete, swinging the axe, so I don't turn the engine off. He waves it in a friendly way and we exchange *kalimeras*. I switch off Harley.

He is sixtyish, smiley round face, dyed black hair with white roots. He is keen to speak passable English. His name is Christos. I say I envy him the view from the cliff. In the days when he could afford data he used to take his morning coffee there and read the news on his phone. Now he gets it from the radio inside his compound. He asks if I know about the bronze statues discovered off the cape and mimes them, first a man standing sideways, feet apart, his arms outstretched, the right one throwing something, and second a man galloping on a horse. I enjoy the charades for a polite minute or so and let him tell me they are the famous bronzes of Zeus and a jockey on a horse in the Athens archaeological museum. He sighs and drops his arms to his sides.

"My friend, if it was not for the Ancient Greeks we would all be living in caves. We would not have art, language, science, poetry, theatre or medicine. You know, all scientific words come from Greek: biology, dermatology, cardiology, all

Greek. We would be nothing without the Ancient Greeks. We would be like everyone else."

He shows me his garden and I admire the black plastic. The idea is that instead of weeding and digging, the plastic does the job for you by depriving weeds of light and encouraging worms. In the spring you stick your veg straight into the ready-made tilth. A great theory. I'm all for no-gardening gardening. He fetches another yellow plastic chair and glasses and a jug of water chilled in an earthenware pot and we sit in the shade of the green awning. We admire the restless pines and ancient sea through chainlink diamonds.

Since before Homer strangers are expected to tell who they are and where they are going. My story is soon told: an old nutter chugging to Athos on a clapped-out bike. His turn.

"I am a secret policeman."

A gambit to activate the bullshit detector. Not so secret apparently. Is he in deep cover? Witness protection? A fantasy world? He joined the police in 1980. After a few years in uniform he was transferred to the anti-terrorist department. He is cagey about what he did, except that he was involved with Interpol. I try to imagine him storming a hide-out or infiltrating a cell or waterboarding suspects.

Christos bought 1500 square metres of olive orchard in the heady days of optimism, growth, liberal bank credit and inflated property prices after the 2004 Athens Olympics. He paid with a bank loan of €100,000 and spent what was left on a building permit, a septic tank, mains water, a fence and a caravan. He dreamed of bucolic weekends, his own tomatoes, a sylvan retirement. Oh happy days before greed, fraud, corruption, economic mismanagement, incompetence, irresponsible banking and other naughties of the noughties triggered the Eurocrisis and before a heart attack left Christos with a pacemaker, ventricular tachycardia and early retirement. His pension was cut by a third to €900 a month out of which he pays €750 to service his debt, not enough to stop it ballooning to €150,000.

"I have a hundred and fifty euros a month. My wife gave me cement for my birthday. A friend gave me the plastic."

"You're doing a great job."

"I could drop dead any time."

I hope not now. I've done a Red Cross first aid and CPR course but would the paramedics ever find us? Christos still smiles, ever affable. I can't tell if it is a symptom of resilience or desperation.

"What does your wife do?"

"She is a dentist. The only good decision I ever made. I go back in the winter but what can I do at home?" He is trapped by penury and the collapse of hope, like so many others since the Crisis.

"You have a beautiful place here."

"Property is theft. My life is stolen…"

I try to imagine myself in his shoes, an impoverished recluse, the occasional conjugal visit, watching the pines and reading Herodotus. Would it be so bad?

"…you are free, my friend. You travel. You have people who love you. You are very rich."

We exchange mobile numbers in the knowledge that some time in future we will look at them in Contacts and wonder who that was. He escorts me to the gate in the fence and watches me kick and kick Harley before I remember to turn the ignition key this time. Does he stand at the chainlink fence, his hands on the wire like a prisoner, watching me leave? I don't know. I concentrate on not falling off as I half ride, half walk Harley down the rocky track.

Oreoi

I take a detour on a winding road into the mountains through planes and pines strobing in the sunlight and the breeze. Harley is not impressed so we take it easy in second, giving time for every trunk and branch to take on character. A faded sign marked *katarraktis* points into the woods. 'Cataract' is not a good description for a slender waterfall springing out of an overgrown cliff into a round pool hung with moss and shielded by tall trees. There are more spectacular waterfalls on Evia but none as evocative of ancient tales of nymphs. I don't mean the pre-Raphaelite wet dream of gormless totties with urticaria lips and ginger hair and girlish tits. I mean fierce women living wild, spirits of nature, as like to rip men apart with their teeth as lure them into forests and pools. Among them was Histiaia, who gave her name to the town where we are going. I have her portrait in my modest coin collection, a silver tetrobol from about 300 BC showing her head in profile with grapes and vines threaded through her hair. On the reverse she sits half-naked on the stern of a boat like an ad for a yachting holiday.

After dawdling by the magical waters we take a captivating road through the mountains and down to a fertile plain along the coast. Istiaia is a modern town with a serious parking problem sprawling around a big square and narrow streets choked with cars. Doubtless it has many hidden virtues that I feel no incentive to unearth. It dates from the nineteenth century and used to be called something else until it acquired Homeric respectability by taking the name of ancient Istiaia, which was closer to the coast and sent ships to Troy.

It is nearly nightfall as we sputter into Oreoi. There are no hotels, only blocks of holiday apartments with phone numbers outside. I try one on a street parallel with the sea front. After ten minutes an elderly woman picks her way over the empty floor of the cavernous lobby. She is not the gouty old granny in black I expected but a petite and elegant lady with dyed-blonde hair, an Hermès scarf and a Jaeger-looking suit. She looks as if she has just got up from the bridge table. Her name is Theodora. She speaks no English and only one word of foreign, *enchantée*. From the pigeon-holes behind the desk, each with a roosting key, it seems I am the only guest. Emboldened by this I grumble about the price, grumbling being the closest I ever get to haggling, and quickly cave in. Fair enough, it is a suite with two bedrooms, a big bathroom and a separate kitchen-diner, newly furnished and equipped, which seems a shame to waste on just me.

The evening is still light enough to see the sights: a long waterfront with fishing boats, a wide beach and a panoramic view over the straits to the mountains, where we are going tomorrow. The main attraction is a magnificent marble bull, three metres long, from the 4th century BC, that was found on the beach. He glowers ready to charge out of a glass case. The plaque says it is a funerary monument, and who am I to argue, except to wonder if it could be more significant, since the bull was associated with the moon-goddess Artemis and features on the reverse of Histiaean coins. I take photos featuring the reflection of the flash in the glass that I hope will pass for arty on Instagram.

It's starting to rain. I plod up and down the front getting wet and looking for dinner before picking Spiros's as it is an *estiatorio*, a restaurant as opposed to a taverna, serving cooked meals not grills. I order *lahanadolmades*, cabbage leaves stuffed with minced meat and rice and lathered with *avgolemono*, egg and lemon sauce, the speciality of the house that Spiros recommends, in other words that he didn't shift at lunchtime. I try to get into conversation by mentioning Athos but Olympiakos is playing basketball on the TV and Spiros isn't interested.

This is the gist of Oreoi's chequered history. It was ancient Histiaea until 446 BC when the name was changed to Oreus, meaning fort. The Romans destroyed it in 199 BC. When the town was revived in the nineteenth century the name was pedantically changed to Oreoi, plural, because there were two forts, one guarding the shore and the other the approach from inland. I don't know why I need to know this but it's in Nigel McGilchrist's excellent guide book.

Yes I do know why I need to know this. Any social media addict, news junkie, or pub quiz bore will tell you that data is a distraction and a bromide that prevents me getting morose sitting by myself in a deserted taverna by the sea on a drizzly evening with nothing to do except look at my distorted reflection in a plastic awning rippling in the breeze. Spiros brings food and drink, a more agreeable sedative. His *lahanadolmades* are delicious.

King Otto

I am trying to cut down on wine so I have a beer with my stuffed cabbage, a Fix. It is the actual name of a brewer, not a corruption of Fuchs as is sometimes said, who arrived with teenage King Otto in 1833. Oreoi was replanned on a grid by one of the architects in a Bavarocracy of regents, ministers, bureaucrats, engineers, and shopkeepers, supported by 3500 German mercenaries. They ran the country like a colony, excluding Greeks from senior positions. The state was managed by a ballooning bureaucracy and funded by taxation. German legal codes replaced those of the republic. Primary education was compulsory. A national army fed by mass conscription and bolstered by German troops crushed the warlords and absorbed their militias. Republican ideas such as a national assembly, a constitution and democracy, were suppressed.

Many Greek intellectuals were anti-clerical. They said there was no place for an ignorant and obscurantist clergy in a secular state deriving inspiration and credentials from an ancient heritage. King Otto's regents from Catholic Bavaria disagreed. They understood the utility of a national religion. They declared the Church of Greece independent from Constantinople and subject to a Ministry of Education and Creeds. Catholic King Otto was proclaimed its head. The Patriarchy in Constantinople was incensed. It was twenty years before it recognised the Greek church. Adding injury to insult, six hundred monasteries were closed and their lands nationalised. American Protestant missionaries were allowed to proselytise and found schools and churches.

Otto's German wife Amalia also had a lasting impact. She designed a simple gown inspired by classical and folk styles known as the Amalia Dress that became the national dress of the middle classes. She introduced the Christmas Tree to Greece and its popular ditty *O Elato,* based on *O Tannenbaum.*

The Bavarians set about recreating the Classical Greece of their imagination. The Drachma was revived to replace the Phoenix. Professors carried on the revision of written Greek to make it more classical. After the capital was moved to Athens from Nafplio in 1834, Byzantine, Frankish and Ottoman buildings were demolished. The Acropolis was scoured to the bare rock of two millennia of history, including its landmark Frankish tower. The medieval town below it was cleared to create avenues radiating from the Acropolis and lined with monuments of Germanic Greek Revival architecture. They began with the Royal Palace, now the Parliament, a barracks of a building with porticoes and pediments, columns and capitals stuck on the middle. Between the avenues a grid of cross streets was lined with neo-classical two-storey cubes with shallow pitched roofs and wrought-iron balconies. The grid and the architecture were replicated throughout the Kingdom.

Otto's government was less popular than his beer. Greeks complained that taxes were higher than under the Ottomans, and Germans were getting the best jobs for more pay. The official language was German. Otto kept his Catholic faith and Amalia was Protestant, scandalising pious Greeks. Opposition was crushed, including the arrest and condemning to death of heroes like Kolokotronis - sentences wisely commuted. Government overspending created a financial crisis. European creditors, led by London, refused to refinance, forcing the government to impose austerity and pay tax revenues directly to them - the first Greek bailout.

On 3 September 1843, ten years after Otto arrived, veterans of the Revolution supported by the army massed in front of the Palace and demanded a Constitution with an elected Parliament. Otto gave way, converting overnight from an absolute to a constitutional monarch. *Syntagma* - Constitution - Square in front of the Parliament building commemorates the event.

Otto hung on for 19 troublesome years until he was deposed by another revolution in 1862. He and Amalia lived out the rest of their melancholy lives in Bavaria, dressed in fustanella and the eponymous Amalia dress, speaking Greek before dinner. The Powers swiped left through the royal princes of Europe for a successor until they found another teenager, George, from a Danish family this time. Britain sweetened the deal with a coronation gift of Corfu and the other Ionian islands.

By the time I've finished a second beer it's pouring down. Fortunately the back door of the restaurant is opposite my digs. Squelching across the hall and gently burping cabbage I hear music coming from Theodora's rooms, rebetiko of Sotiria Bellou, a lovely song about living alone without love. I wonder if it happens to be on the radio or on a record that resonates with her own life. For a moment I am tempted to knock on her door to find out, talk about the time I saw Sotiria live on stage, reminisce about the old days when women wore twin sets and pearls and men wore ties. *Enchantée.*

Stupid idea. She's probably nodding in her chair with her hair in a net and teeth in a glass. I go to my room and sit up in bed reading the *Philokalía* until I fall asleep.

I used to live alone without love in the dark, unhappy,
crying away the nights in my dreary room
Let's have a glass of old wine and talk about love's beautiful song
that's like a flower in spring
Now everything around me is smiling and makes me drunk on love
the sweet kiss of your lips is like a rose in April.

Histiaia

8 ACHILLEAS TO LARISSA

Rain has stopped, not a cloud in the sky, a glorious new day, the open road ahead. Awake at 7 feeling tired and achy, I hope I'm not coming down with something. Perhaps I caught a chill in the rain. A hot shower does nothing for the symptoms. I put on an extra T-shirt and a short sleeve shirt under the denim smock and go in search of hot Nescafé. Nothing is open yet so I trudge along the beach in the young sunshine and say good morning and farewell to the handsome bull. Meandering back along the sea front feeling poorly I wonder whether I should go back to bed and stay there until the risk of pneumonia is past until I tell myself sternly that I feel tired and achy most mornings so snap out of it.

At the end of the front is the Café Tostimo, its logo a happy face on a slice of bread. The name is a play on words, *nostimo* meaning tasty and *tost* meaning much more than toast. A tost is a sandwich of two rectangles of sliced industrial bread with matching rectangles of plasticised yellow cheese and pink reconstituted ham, laminated in a sandwich toaster. It belongs to the same lessish food group as rice cakes, cream crackers and cardboard. Wrapped in cellophane and stacked in the fridge for days it is the staple fare of ferries, airports, small town cafés and available day or night.

Fortified by tost, Nes, ibuprofen and paracetamol, I load up Harley. He won't start. Kick and kick, twiddle the throttle, push and pull on the choke, despite knowing it's been stuck for years. No good. Stay calm. Run through the procedure. Check fuel gauge. Half full. Mistrust fuel gauge. Open tank and stick finger in. Half full. Wipe finger on trousers. Check ignition key on. Turn off. Turn on. Kick and kick. Resist temptation to punch saddle and kick front wheel. Harley stays shtum. Time for the last resort, the equivalent of switching a computer off and on, abandon him and take a stroll to the jetty. When I come back he starts first time. Why? Flooded carburettor? Condensation in the spark plug? Mechanical malevolence? Who cares? We're on the road again.

We splutter cheerfully for a few kilometres to the ferry. The port of Oreoi silted up over the past century and shifted down the coast to Agiokampos. At the ticket booth under an olive tree I hand over Charon's obol, the money ancient Greeks put in the mouths of the dead to pay the ferryman over the Acheron to Hades. Or over the Styx if you follow the Latins. I tell myself again that I'm not that poorly.

We have an hour to linger over a Greek coffee. In a posh resort or a city café I go for a double espresso. In less sophisticated places it is indistinguishable from the Greek version and 50c dearer. They use the same fine ground coffee for both. It is becoming more common for Greek coffee to be made in a whizzer rather than a traditional *briki*, a long handled pot tended over the flame. The result is the same - a chewy brew with grounds at the bottom to be avoided. It takes strength of mind not to take a last sip against your better judgement and get a mouthful of sludge.

The ferry arrives. With my helmet on an elbow and a vrroom-vrroom to impress the foot passengers I navigate Harley onto the ramp without stalling and hand the ticket to a deck-hand. He tells me to park next to a Suzuki 600. Harley is outclassed. I give his saddle a consoling pat, toss my helmet into the crate and swagger up to the saloon for another demitasse of sludge.

The mortal cares and responsibilities and preoccupations of yesterday slough off into the sea. Not for nothing is crossing a river the passage from life into shadowy Hades.

Ghosts and Vampires can't cross water, although I don't know why, other than being convenient for stories.

As we draw into Glifa I saunter to the bikes hoping people think I am going for the Suzuki until I take my helmet out of the crate. With it dangling off the handlebar we breeze off the boat with another vrroom-vrroom and a wave to the port policeman. I'm feeling better.

Glifa is the mirror image of Agiokampos with a quay, a cluster of houses, a long beach. I see no reason to linger and take a steep road snaking up into the surrounding hills. We drive over the neck of a mountain peninsula that makes the lower jaw of the pincer-shaped Gulf that has the big port city of Volos at the hinge. The region is called Magnesia, named after the Magnetes tribe, nothing to do with mining or an upset stomach. The rain has cleared up, the sky is blue, the sun is hot, the light is tautologically luminous. It's a pleasant drive through the undulating foothills.

After half an hour we come down to the gulf side of the peninsula and the port of Achillio in a placid gulflet of its own ringed by hills, with a pleasant promenade and a modest marina for yachts and fishing boats. Flairing the pheromones of frying fish I park beside a waterfront restaurant and within minutes sit before a heaped plate of *gávro,* this morning's catch of little anchovies, like big whitebait, along with garlicky dressed boiled greens, crusty bread and a *tetarto,* a quarter litre of palate-tingling white.

Where are we? *Achillio* is a clue. We are in ancient Phthiotis, say that without your teeth in, birthplace of Achilles, the greatest and most flawed of mythological heroes. Homer's *Iliad* is about his anger, pride, and revenge for the death of his lover Patroclus, his killing and barbaric treatment of the Trojan Hector. On this sunny day I'm not in the mood for manly brutality. I prefer the story of how his mother the nymph Thetis didn't want him to go off to Troy because of a prophecy that he would die young. She took him to the island of Skyros and persuaded the king to take him in to live with his daughters disguised as a girl. He was a good-looking lad so with clothes and a hair-do and a few tips on body language - relax your shoulders, take small steps, speak softly - he fitted right in. In more ways than one. With the King's daughter he fathered a son, Neoptolemus, a nasty piece of work who later used Hector's baby son to beat King Priam of Troy to death.

Another prophecy said the Greeks would not defeat the Trojans without Achilles. Odysseus and some companions went to Skyros looking for him. They pretended to be pedlars and among the trinkets included a sword. Achilles could not resist picking it up and gave his game away. Another tale is about his mother dipping him in the Styx to make him immortal but holding him by the heel that stayed vulnerable and gave his name to the tendon.

I'm not qualified to discuss the value system of Homeric Greece, other than it seems to be based on honour, status, strength, courage, a violent yet meaningful death followed by immortality. Today we've moved on from the warrior virtues and broadened the scope of heroism to include altruism, virtue, a moral sense. So why do people still name their children after Achilles? Why are the Greek heroes relevant to us? Perhaps because they act out our desires, sometimes expressed and more often repressed: incest, murder, rape, hatred, fear, ambition, gender uncertainty, the creatures that swim around in the depths of our subconscious. In ways we do not like to admit to ourselves the heroes are like us.

When Achilles changed his women's clothes for armour he took to Troy two and a half thousand men of his tribe called Myrmidons. The name comes from the word for ant. There are several explanations. One is that Zeus created an army out of a swarm of ants. Another is that he changed himself into an ant to rape one of Achilles' ancestors. She gave birth to Myrmidon, a pre-Marvel Ant-Man, who became King of Phthiotis. Zeus has form in shape-changing for seduction, most famously as a bull or a swan or a dove or an eagle or a stallion. But an ant? A human-sized ant from 1950's sci-fi? An ant-size ant creepy-crawling into her underwear? It's puzzling why the myth-makers even tried to make something of it, other than explaining a name which probably derived from a pre-Greek word meaning something completely different.

Field Of Mars

I got to know Achilles on the Field of Mars, the CCF parade ground between the cricket pitch and the refectory. At fourteen the Combined Cadet Force, was compulsory. On Thursdays we wore khaki battledress and trousers, itchy khaki woollen shirts and khaki ties and gaiters and belts we had to paste with blanco, erroneously named as it was khaki-coloured. On our heads we wore black berets rakishly pulled down over the right ear.

At the beginning of term we queued up for our kit in the quartermaster's stores, a single-storey wooden hut smelling outside of creosote and inside of army surplus serge. Army surplus Sergeant Major Spray eyed us up and down and shoved piles of khaki at us. The only thing we tried on was the beret, a moment of shame I had been dreading all morning. Since my first school cap my hats have been made to measure. I have seen the incredulity of Sarnt-Major Spray so many times on sellers of boaters, panamas, cycle helmets, fedoras, fur hats, charity shop trilbies, headphones. He ransacked the darkest and smelliest corners of his stores. After pulling and tugging and stretching, the biggest beret he found perched on top of my head, rising untamed like a chef's hat. It looked so grotesque that I was Excused Beret for as long as it took to requisition one from the War Office.

What to wear in the meantime? Mixing military and civilian uniform was against regulations. I was not to parade bareheaded since military etiquette forbids saluting without a hat. I still tut when I see hatless men saluting. Instead of learning how to Kwiyuk-Match and Haybout-Tun I sulked in the armoury while my comrades-in-arms tramped up and down and stamped their boots and shouted orders in new-broken adolescent voices. Instead of some pettifogging military chore the CO shoved a Penguin book into my hands.

"Here. Learn to be a soldier."

Bless his barminess. Bless his astuteness. It was the *Iliad*. I was captivated from the first words. *"Anger of Achilles is my story, how it brought the Greeks so much suffering and sent the souls of many heroes to Hades…"* I devoured it at home with only breaks for my tea, my mind on the plains of Ilium.

What did I learn about soldiering? Honour and Brutality. Achilles is angry with Agamemnon for confiscating a slave girl and sulks in his armoury, refusing to fight. Only when his comrade-in-arms Patroclus borrows his armour and is killed by Hector does rage and revenge bring him back to the battlefield to kill and dishonour the Trojan hero. There the *Iliad* ends. You have to go to the *Odyssey* to hear about the famous Horse and how the war ended.

I was too young and innocent then to understand the relationship that some scholars see between Achilles and Patroclus, comrades-in-each-others-arms. It was not unusual among soldiers in Ancient Greece. Chalkis had a monument to a warrior famous for his valour and his boyfriend, leading to the Athenian slang *halkidise,* meaning sodomise. In Alexander's day the Sacred Band of Thebes was a crack regiment composed of homosexual couples. This sort of thing was not talked about on the Field of Mars.

The new beret arrived and I joined the ranks. The War Office took no chances. It was enormous, a floppy artist's beret, a French Onion Johnie's, a Phrygian Liberty Cap. I could pull it down over both ears and still have some left over for the back of my neck. In a breeze it inflated like a Sultan's turban. To my nicknames was added Private Tea-Cosy.

I didn't care. In my mind I wore the crested helmet of the Greeks. My friends called me Jonicles.

Jeff

Brooding on Myrmidons and sleepy from wine I rouse Harley and get back on the road. We leave olive groves and vegetable patches for fields of cotton and cereals. The afternoon gets hotter. I'm glad of the helmet as a sun-hat, the scratchy shirt to absorb the sweat, the flip-down sunglasses tomake rainbows of the glaren. The hills recede, the dead straight road gets tedious. It goes through the innocuous town of Almiro. I should mention the archaeological museum, an elegant neo-classical building tricked out in white and salmon pink. I am happy to see it is closed for the day so I don't have to traipse round it. Open opposite is the Gossip-Coffee-And-More Café, its English name promising international sophistication that I hope extends to a decent espresso. I leave Harley to cool off in the company of other bikes huddled like sheep in the shade of a mulberry tree. Tired and sweaty, knees aching, eyes smarting, I go inside for the air conditioning and free wi-fi.

An email from a friend says that Jeff, an old colleague I haven't thought about for decades, dropped dead walking the dog. There is a link to his memorial service. I swallow the clickbait and am hooked into YouTube. Six months younger than me, loyal Christian, pillar of the community, golfer, hunter, old school banker, 50 years married, father, grandfather, all over now. As the *kafetzis* puts my coffee and a complementary biscuit on the table I flash back to the day his eldest son was born.

We were trainees in Pittsburgh, sitting at massive desks in the neoclassical mausoleum of a banking hall. I suffer from a minor complaint. If I put on socks even slightly damp, I have shooting pains in my legs within the hour. Usually I pop the socks in the oven for ten minutes while I get dressed but that morning twelve-month-old Jack thew up over my feet and I risked an unbaked pair off the drying rack. The pains started when I got off the bus. I went straight to the lavatory, took off my shoes and socks and wrapped toilet paper round my feet like *portyanki*, Russian foot wraps. I put back the socks, squeezed my feet into loosely laced shoes, checked for trailing tissue, and went to my desk. Jeff beamed behind an open box of cigars adorned with a blue cigar band. He explained to the ignorant limey the happy event that this announced. I shook his hand and took a cigar but didn't know if I was supposed to light up in celebration or pop it in my top pocket for later. Although it was only just after eight I took the safe option, bit off the end and lit up, toasting and nodding and liberally expressing congratulation and good will.

I suffer from another minor complaint. Cigars make me ill. I felt queasy at the same time as the next bout of shooting pains in my legs. I made it to the lavatory without mishap, sat down, tore off shoes, socks and toilet paper, tossed the cigar on the floor, and head in hands, eyes closed, willed myself into the inner world of consciousness where you battle with the urge to puke. I was jerked out of it by the smell of smoke. There's nothing sharpens the senses like your trousers on fire. I leapt up, trampling with bare feet the smouldering toilet paper that had ignited my turn-ups. With extraordinary presence of mind I lifted the seat and plunged my feet into the toilet bowl one by one while I pressed the flush. The day was saved. With the bonus of evacuating the banking hall due to the fire alarm, the cause of which was never discovered.

My abiding memory of Jeff is his beaming face as he handed out cigars in honour of the son, who now buries him.

His eulogy filters into the Thessalian street. Oh this iced triple espresso tastes good. Scratchy shirt, itchy knee bandages, incipient boil on my bottom, sweat filled boots, glint of sun on Harley's shiny saddle of torture, it all feels so GOOD. Sorry Jeff, rather you than me.

I pay, pee, mount, kickstart and accelerate to my own fate.

Sugar Dogs

I decided from the outset not to drive on the National Road from Athens to Thessaloniki. A 50cc bike is permitted but is not in the spirit of the venture. The real reason is that I am too nervous. But after Almiro the regional road turns into motorway without warning or possibility of escape. We cringe on the hard shoulder while trucks and cars thunder by. There are no bumps or potholes so it is safer than a minor road but much more boring and stressful and only a concrete wall at the side to look at. After an hour I turn off for airy Aerino and take a country road north to Velestino, gently undulating over sun-damaged fields acned with olive trees.

Velestino is barely awake from the siesta, if siesta is anything to do with its somnolence. Doddering along Riga Fereou street the unmistakeable effluvium of sugary doughnuts and savoury cheese pies induces me to park outside a bakery. I pore over the tasties and plump for a chocolate-filled *koulouri*. Imagine a warm ring of pizza crust stuffed with Nutella. With an iced Nes at a table outside, I run the velvet gamut of sensation from heavenly deliciousness to feeling sick, taking me back to school holidays, when I'd scarf half a pound of Woolworths fudge and spend the rest of the afternoon lying on the settee reading the Beano with a prophylactic sick bucket handy.

As I reach the stage of nausea when you can't resist taking another bite, the chocolate penny drops. Rigas Feraios, who drew the wonderful map of his imaginary Hellenic republic, was born here. The inhabitants of Velestinos were Vlachs and spoke Aromanian. It was built on the ruins of ancient Pherai, hence Rigas's adopted name. He never used it himself, writing under the Slavic Velestinlis he was born with, but was rebadged later to enhance his Hellenic credentials. He was sent away to school where he stabbed an Ottoman official and fled to join a band of klephts on Mount Olympus. I wouldn't dare question this revolutionary credential, except that it is hard to imagine him using a knife for anything other than his dinner.

I brush off the crumbs, get back on Harley and cross the border into Thessaly, the original frontier of the new Kingdom of Greece in 1833. A T-junction has two signs to Larissa, emphasis on the first syllable, one pointing right, the other left. I give Harley his head and he chooses left, ending up on a regional road linking Larissa and Volos. We are now on the Great Plain of Thessaly, the most fertile area of Greece, formerly famous for livestock. The earliest coins of Thessalian cities feature a cow or a horse. Now they grow grain and cotton and sugar beet. Surrounding hills are a smudge on the horizon. The road ahead is dead straight, disappearing into the vanishing point.

The flat and featureless landscape is aflame with burning stubble, acrid white fog drifting over the fields and over the road into eyes watering with smoke, nose snivelling with smut, sinuses choking with snot. Six-wheel, eight-wheel, twelve-wheel trucks hurtle down the two-lane road in both directions, pumping diesel filth into the miasma. Dopplerish crescendos and diminuendos coalesce into a pulsating roar. The airy bow waves of oncoming trucks take the breath away and thump my helmet to the back of the head, throttling me with the chin strap. Peering into the smog, buffeted in slipstreams, as far over to the right as I dare into the ragged edge where the asphalt peters out into debris, hardcore and a ditch, I could reach out and touch the sides of the trucks as they whoomph past. An unstowed strap whacks me on the back, a windscreen washer asperges my sooty spam. Smoke and flames and smuts and embers all around, it is so thrilling.

Too thrilling. I decide to test my cross-country map-reading and by-pass Larissa, the capital of Thessaly, Greece's fifth biggest city, of which I have heard nothing that tempts me to visit. *'Larissa is not the kind of place you would choose as your prime holiday destination'* says my Lonely Planet. My copy is a first edition, 1994, with the prices in drachmas. But how much can change in twenty five years? The advice surely does an injustice to the citizens, who are surely as charming and hospitable as any in Greece. The real reason is that I am nervous about driving in cities with the fear of running over jay walkers and being shouted at for holding up the traffic.

I turn off down a road signposted to Achilio, our friend Achilles again. The map says it goes due east over a reservoir and into the hills. I want to go north so turn left on a gravel road. It isn't on the map, but the sun is out so as long as I keep it more or less on the left ... this is not the first time I have navigated across country by dead reckoning and it has always ended in confusion and humiliation but you learn from your mistakes how to make more mistakes so we press on. At least the fields are not on fire. They are green with big cabbagy leaves of sugar beet or white with cotton balls on dark green bushes, thriving on fertile earth, copious water and generous EU subsidy. Greece is Europe's cotton king, producing 85 percent of it, a factoid that might come in useful one day but not as I go further astray along dirt roads and gravel pathways through an unhedged maze of turns, junctions, dead-ends and diversions. I am soon lost.

We come across a road with crumbling tarmac and potholes heading towards the distant cube of a tall building, where I can surely ask directions. Some hope. It is, or was, probably a sugar factory, windows broken, gates hanging off the hinges, conveyors stripped and rusted. There is no time for dismay. The two-wheel enemy rouses the inhabitants, a pack of feral dogs. They yelp out into the yard, led by a yellow brute the size of a small pony with pointy ears and vicious eyes. Behind him is a Cruft's of all sizes, breeds and miscegenations, from unshorn poodles to Rottweilers, yapping and howling and slavering. Thank God there is room to turn and Harley doesn't stall. The leaders snap and snarl inches from the back wheel, egged on by the baying pack. I daren't go at top speed because of the potholes and ruts. I stay in second and go as slow as I can to avoid falling off but fast enough to stay out of reach, an incitement but better than fresh dog meat. Weak from starvation and disease they give up after half a mile and I stop to tremble and breathe deep, not turning the engine off, just in case. I close my eyes and breathe a thank you to Harley.

In the countryside packs of strays are a real threat. There are more since the Crisis as owners can't afford to feed them and vets generally refuse to euthanise a healthy animal. Farmers put down poison, a constant fear of dog walkers and horse riders. City strays are usually harmless, as they can easily find food and water.

I keep the sun over my left shoulder, willing Harley not to have a puncture. The treeless plain is ploughed now, scraped of vegetation, fertilised, pesticided, no sign of wildlife, in a word farmed. I lapse into a cataleptoid reverie, Harley grumbling along in second as the sun gets lower. At last a T emerges from the blue, a lovely telephone pole. In half an hour I am battling the slipstreams again.

Thessaly was Turkish until 1881. Nineteenth century travellers admired Larissa's slender white minarets, the colonies of storks, its convenience as a stop on the way to somewhere else. My idea is to find a hotel outside town where the road I am on meets the National Road as it bypasses the city. It is an obvious place for a truck stop or a motel but not obvious enough for anyone to build one. The four lane highway narrows to a congested city street until I am in the centre, crowded by traffic, moythered by pedestrians, confused by diversions, junctions and traffic lights. I stop at a taxi rank in a noisy square and ask a huddle of taxi drivers where to find a hotel. One of them points over the road to a massive neon sign, *Hotel Dionissos*.

Forty-five euros is way beyond what I usually pay but it's been a long day on the fiery plain. I feel stiff, weary, tarred and feathered in my itchy new shirt. To the elegant receptionist I look a scruff, worse than usual. I hope that a helmet on the elbow is an excuse. I take Harley in a sinister industrial elevator, like the lift down to a morgue, to his lodgings next to the laundry. After a shower and a wi-fi and a lie down I go looking for my dinner but tavernas are as hard to find as hotels. I settle for a tost round the corner.

Waffles
Crepes
Ice Cream
Pies (pastry)
Sandwiches
Beer
Drinks (glasses)

9 LARISSA TO AMBELAKIA

The advantage of paying through a niggardly nose for a three star hotel is that breakfast is included. I go down to the All-You-Can-Eat-And-Surreptitiously-Sneak-Into-Your-Pockets-For-Later Buffet. I pig out on things that don't travel well in the trousers: scrambled eggs, fried eggs, funny-tasting sausages, fat-drooling bacon, crispy hash brown patties, nuggety mushrooms, chocolate croissants, baklava, yoghurt, fruit salad, muesli, honey, Nutella, yellow label Lipton tasting vaguely of tea. Into my shirt and trousers I cram hard boiled eggs, slices of ham and yellow cheese, apples, oranges, dried figs, crusty rolls, cinnamon biscuits. I waddle up to my room to pack my bag and the day's provisions.

Feeling bloated and queasy, I retrieve Harley from the basement and we launch out into Larissa's confusing one way system. My mood is not improved by driving past the Hotel Dionissos for the third time. At last we break out and head east, the plan being to get on the Old National Road. It is bright sunny morning, delightful in most circumstances but not when you're driving straight into the sun. The grandad flip-up sunglasses are useless so I have to shade my eyes like a tar in the crow's nest, increasing the anxiety by having only one hand on the handlebars.

The Old National Road is as nerve-wracking as the New. Two lanes each way, potholes inadequately patched, thundering trucks, teeming cars, howling bikes. On the right is the military airport. Larissa is the headquarters of the Hellenic Air Force. It has about 200 fighters and 200 bombers, compared with 90 and 170 in the RAF. They are away on missions today, or grounded to save fuel, as the skies over Thessaly are quiet, unlike the ear-bashing highway.

This road and the rest of Thessaly, along with a good chunk of Epirus to the west, fell into Greece's hands in 1881 as a reward for staying neutral in a confused war and messy treaties between Turkey and Russia. King George had been twenty years on the throne. He kept it for another thirty, the longest reigning and on the whole the most successful Greek king. He had changed his title from King Of Hellas, as Otto had been, to King Of The Hellenes, in other words of all Greek people inside or outside the frontiers. The overriding policy of his government and the dream of his subjects was the *Megali Idea*, the Great Idea, to expand the borders of the state to include all Greeks within them and, for the most fervent, Constantinople. For a small agricultural country it was ambitious.

Black 97

Greece had more than the Ottomans to deal with. The political landscape changed with Bulgaria, Serbia, and Romania struggling for independence under the patronage of Russia. Bulgaria has been a traditional enemy of Greece for a thousand years. Greeks have a soft spot for the tenth century Byzantine Emperor Basil the Bulgar Slayer. Between them was the rich Ottoman province of Macedonia and its capital Thessaloniki, a bone of contention gnawed by Greece, Bulgaria and Serbia ever since.

I have to be careful here. Passions still run high. Twenty five years ago a Greek American scholar writing about Macedonian Slavs received death threats from Greek nationalists as did her publishers, who cancelled her contract. It was taken over by an American university press.

Who were the Macedonians? A macedoine (I couldn't resist it) of communities with different religions, languages, customs and dress. They could be Greek Orthodox or Bulgarian Orthodox or Jewish or one of the Muslim sects. They might speak Greek, Macedonian, Turkish, Serbian, Bulgarian, Albanian or Aromanian. Greeks and their language were in the minority but dominated trade, towns and ports. Nationalists on all sides used similar tactics to assimilate the inhabitants. They sent agents over their borders to politicise the villages, win their allegiance and set them against rival neighbours. Village by village they competed with propaganda and violence, setting up churches, suborning the leaders. They set up hundreds of free schools competing with each other for children to indoctrinate. They sent terrorists to enforce loyalty, often army officers under aliases, officially disowned and privately financed by wealthy entrepreneurs and emigrants of their diasporas. They fought each other as well as Macedonian nationalists and Ottoman troops trying to keep the peace.

In 1897, buoyed by nationalist fervour and a flood of volunteers, the Greek army under Crown Prince Constantine crossed the border from Thessaly into Macedonia to settle the issue, the first time since the Revolution that it had confronted the Ottomans. The war lasted a month before the Greeks were routed. Turks marched into Thessaly and down the road I am driving on. Their flags again flew over Larissa, Volos and Rigas's Velestinos.

The Great Powers persuaded Turkey to give back Thessaly and Epirus in return for crippling reparations, triggering an economic crisis. Since its creation Greece had depended on international borrowing. Investment in roads, railways, ports and the spectacular but impractical Corinth Canal were financed by unsustainable debt. War reparations were the last straw. In 1897 The International Financial Commission, in other words the City of London, paid off the Turks, took over Greece's finances and imposed austerity. It was the third time default had led to bailout and the humiliation of foreign control of the treasury. But not the last.

The humiliation of 'Black 97', as the defeat was called, dampened the elation of the first modern Olympic games the year before. It deflated but did not puncture the Great Idea.

Scandal

We putter at a gentle 40kph/25mph across a deserted plain under a burning sun along a dead straight road, letting the mind wander from the Euclidian definition of a straight line through the byways of geometry into Pythagoras and his dietary prohibition of beans until, despite an enormous breakfast, the neural pathways become fixated on ice cream. A cornet, a tub, a lolly, it doesn't matter. Using all the tricks of meditation I can muster I try to dispel these images until, like a mirage, an ice cream oasis appears in the heat haze, a petrol station adrift in an endless tawny sea. The attendant, a word derived from the French for 'wait' is justly named. He waits outside his office gazing at the empty road across the plain. Balding, pale and pudgy from his sedentary occupation he has given up reading, listening to the radio, telephoning, things which define his solitude. We stop at a pump and he stares at us through black rimmed spectacles, making sure we are not a figment of his residual expectations before slouching towards us. Three, I say, which he verifies by contemplating the fingers I hold up. In slow motion I raise the saddle onto its flakey metal strut and unscrew the cap, careful not to let bits of rust fall inside. He plucks the nozzle from the pump and places it delicately on the rim of the tank. We watch the counter until with hardly perceptible twitches of his fingers, he coaxes it to the exact number. Heady with volatile organic carcinogens we count the drips as he shakes the nozzle. He replaces it on the pump while I screw on the cap and scrawp the strut down and lower the saddle. I hold out three shiny coins.

Do you have ice cream? I ask. He looks puzzled for a moment. Did I use the right word? Or did I say the word for frost or glacier or peacock? I'm sure I said *pagoto*. He turns and slouches back to his office. I follow and my heart leaps to see a freezer chest against the wall with lovely promises of Scandal, Shock, and Nirvana. He comes out jangling a bunch of keys. The top of the chest is secured with four padlocks the size of my palm at either end of two hefty metal bars fixed to hasps on the sides. I wonder about the incidence of ice cream rustling in Thessaly. There must be twenty keys on his jailer's ring and he doesn't have a system for trying them, opting instead for random selection. Craving for Scandal, Shock or Nirvana rises to a pitch where I am about to brain him with his windscreen squeegee and snatch the keys from his hand. At last he hefts the bars from the chest. It's like Indiana Jones when the Nazis open the Ark Of The Covenant and find only sand. A few lollies lurk at the bottom like mammoth poo in thick frost. Little does our attendant know how close he is to the wrong end of a squeegee handle. He reaches in and scrabbles under the lollies and comes out with a touch of frostbite and a vintage tub of *Sikago*, Chicago.

I suck the lovely stuff off a plastic spoon as we sit at a metal table under the awning. He smokes a roll-up and in reasonable English suddenly launches into his CV, or resume if you are American. He has the Cambridge Lower and thinks he will do the Proficiency. He lives with his parents on a fifty stremmata farm, twelve acres, not big enough to make a good living. For six years he dabbled in informatics and multimedia at a technology college in Crete until the army lost patience and drafted him. He spent ten months on sentry duty in Cyprus. Because of the Crisis he could not afford to get his remaining five degree credits He came home to a job pumping petrol. That was eight years ago and he is now 35. There are no other jobs. Unemployment is 30 percent. What can he do? His laptop was stolen so he can't practice his informatics. He used to have a bike like mine and that was stolen too. He looks enviously at Harley, which must be a first. I thank him for his company and leave him to his life, gazing out over the endless Thessalian plain, dreaming of the might-have-been, filling the ash tray with butts of brown rollups.

Balkan Wars

King George and his army under Prince Constantine recovered their reputations fifteen years after the debacle of Black 97. In 1912 the Christian kingdoms of Montenegro, Serbia, Bulgaria and Greece joined in an unlikely alliance of convenience to throw the Ottoman Empire out of Europe and annex its territories to their own. Why unlikely? They were deeply hostile to each other. Montenegro wanted northern Albania, Serbia wanted Albania and Kosovo, Bulgaria wanted Macedonia and Thrace, including Thessaloniki and Constantinople. Greece also had aspirations but was seen by the others as too weak after Black 97 but they had the best navy and could blockade Turkish reinforcements. In newspapers across Europe it was billed as a Holy War, a Crusade, Cross against Crescent. With God on their side and cholera on the enemy's, Bulgaria drove the Turks south east through Thrace to the last defences of Chatalja, 70 kilometres from Constantinople. Serbia took Kosovo and northern Macedonia. Montenegro got some of Albania. Greece's navy seized strategic islands at the mouth of the Dardanelles, while their modernised and reformed army did much better than expected. It took southern Epirus, its main city Ioannina, and the great prize of Thessaloniki, which they reached a few hours before the furious Bulgarians.

It was the first war of the modern age and anticipated the First World War that eclipsed it. A million and a half men under arms, trenches, mud, Maxim guns, artillery barrages, balloons, spotter planes, Red Cross medics, ambulances, field hospitals, refugees, censors herding war correspondents and photographers, cinema news cameramen. A little boy called Memet, a station master's son in Edirne, was the first ever civilian killed by a bomb dropped from an airplane.

A peace treaty lasted a few weeks. Bulgaria resented having only Thrace and still coveted Thessaloniki so declared war on Greece and Serbia. It was repulsed and invaded by the others while Romania and a revived Turkey joined in the mayhem. When it ended Bulgaria lost most of its gains. Turkey got back eastern Thrace as far as Edirne. Serbia doubled its territory with Albania and Kosovo. Greece did best, doubling its population and its territory with Epirus, Macedonia, western Thrace, the north Aegean coast, a handful of islands and Thessaloniki. Which is more or less what it has now.

It was pouring with rain when the Greeks of Thessaloniki came out to welcome Prince Constantine. They were a minority. In general Greeks dominated trade and shipping, Muslims were bureaucrats and landowners, Jews were manufacturers and merchants. Fears of massacre receded and the transition was relatively peaceful. It was different in the countryside where Muslims fled from the extirpations of Christian neighbours, nationalists and refugees. King George paraded with his son a few days later. A madman assassinated him the following year, which took the gloss off his triumph.

Until the outbreak of the First World War the new King Constantine enjoyed a brief political honeymoon with Prime Minister Eleftherios Venizelos - travellers will recognise the name from Athens airport. Constantine wanted to remain neutral. He was related to the Kaiser and, like his general staff, believed in the superiority of German and Bulgarian arms. He was also concerned for the Anatolian Greeks at the mercy of Turkey, who Germany had offered to protect in return for Greek neutrality. Venizelos plumped for the British and French Entente as he had a secret undertaking from the British Prime Minister David Lloyd George that Greece would be given Smyrna, today's Izmir, an international trading port on the west coast, half of whose population was Greek. Greece stayed out of the war until 1916 when Allied troops were evacuated from the Gallipoli defeat to Thessaloniki with Venizelos's approval and against King Constantine's wishes. The streets milled with troops in fustanellas, kilts, breeches, leggings and trousers of all colours among hawkers, beggars, refugees and Cretan gendarmes keeping the peace.

Spurred by the Allies' declaration of martial law in Thessaloniki and the Bulgarian invasion of western Thrace, Venizelists split from the King and his government in Athens and set up the 'Provisional Government of National Defence.' in Thessaloniki. The Allies backed Venizelos against King Constantine, who surrendered his throne to his second son Alexander and went into exile in Switzerland. Greece declared war on the Central Powers and joined with the Allies against Bulgaria on the Macedonian Front. The so-called National Schism between Venizelist republicans and Royalists divided the country until after the Second World War.

A hundred years later our rebetiko band still sings the rousing anthem 'The Children of the Defence'. I bellow it out loud to the rhythm of Harley's spluttering:

It will be written in history one day.
That he kicked out all the brutes from Athens.
That he kicked out the king, the senators, the crooks and the clowns.
And in the Defence, with all the officers, Venizelos is fighting...

The distant hills on either side get closer. We come to the end of the tedious plain and the beginning of the famous Vale of Tempe, a narrow gorge between two mountain ranges. The excitement is too much for Harley who starts to wheeze and falter at any speed, not only when we touch 40kph/25mph. Perhaps the fuel at the ice cream station was mouldering underground for want of passing trade. We stop at a roadside café outside the village of Tempi for coffee and a rest. I squint at the oil in the spy hole under a chrome bulge beneath the petrol tank but can't see anything through the dirt. I don't know what else to do except hope for the best.

I sit on an outside balcony next to the desultory talk of two portly men my age, whose idea of a day out is to potter down from the next village for coffee. I butt in with tried and tested gambits - the economy, Merkel, the price of petrol, Athos, grandchildren, football, minor surgery, but they seem to lead eventless lives, unless they are keeping thrilling secrets not divulged to strangers. Chewing on the coffee sludge from a sip too many I coax Harley back onto the road. I am glad that the rest has done him good, clearing whatever was troubling him and leaving only his habitual stutter.

Exchange Of Populations

After the defeat of the Central Powers in the First World War the victorious Allies divvied up the Ottoman Empire. Smyrna was given to Greece to administer. In 1919, with the support of David Lloyd George, and the opposition of the rest of the Allies, the Greek army advanced east into the heart of Turkey with the Great Idea of taking back Asia Minor that Byzantium lost to the Ottomans nearly five hundred years before. They hesitated when King Alexander was bitten by a pet monkey and died. His father King

Constantine came back from exile to popular acclaim, appointed new commanders and led them into battle.

The victor of Gallipoli, Mustafa Kemal, later known as Atatürk, Father of Turkey, created a break-away government to resist the Allied Powers' carve-up. He pulled his troops back to Ankara, made a stand, and routed the ill-advised, ill-led, ill-supplied Greeks. Terrible atrocities were inflicted by the retreating Greeks on Turkish civilians and by pursuing Turks on Greek civilians, culminating in the bloodbath and chaotic evacuation of troops and civilians from burning Smyrna. The Asia Minor Campaign became the Asia Minor Catastrophe. King Constantine abdicated for a second time in favour of another son, George II. The Army Commander and five politicians were summarily executed. Constantine's brother Prince Andrew, one of the commanders, escaped a death sentence and was sent into exile with his infant son Philip, the future Duke of Edinburgh. George II did not last long. After a failed Royalist coup he was deposed.

In 1923 the Treaty of Lausanne recognised the Republic of Turkey and Mustafa Kemal as its first president. Both he and Venizelos wished to build modern nation states and create a lasting settlement between them. One of the impediments was the Greek minority in Turkey, almost 25 percent of the population. At the League of Nations Philip Noel-Baker engineered the appointment of its first High Commissioner for Refugees, the famous Norwegian explorer Frederick Nansen. The two of them shuttled between Athens and Ankara to negotiate an exchange of populations: Christians would be relocated to Greece and Muslims to Turkey. In the following year more than a million Christians were expelled from Turkey, adding to the million who had fled Asia Minor as a result of Turkish genocide during the war. Half a million Muslims were expelled from Greece.

Where were the refugees to go? The Greek government settled many in Macedonia and Thrace, bolstering the Greek population against native Slavs. The rest were planted wherever land could be found. They named their new settlements after those they had been uprooted from, hence towns like Nea Artaki and Athenian districts like Nea Smyrna and Nea Ionia. Refugees were not universally welcome in communities struggling with poverty and unemployment. The word refugee itself became denigratory, *prósfigas*. A jealous nickname for sophisticated young Smyrniote women buzzing round the local men was *prósfinkes*. *Sfinkes* means wasps.

Some years ago we lived in Kifissia, a wealthy northern suburb of Athens. The neighbouring municipality was the less fashionable Nea Erythraia, created by refugees from Erythrae, now called Çeşme, opposite the island of Chios. Our house was in pastures and olive groves next to a riding stables. Panayotis the local shepherd brought his magnificent moustaches and his flock into the garden to keep the grass down. After warnings of snakes and wells we let the children roam around our Arcadia. One afternoon we found them on the balcony arranging bones in the shape of a human skeleton, guided by the Usborne Book of The Body. They were arguing about tibias and fibulas, humeruses and radiuses. The bones were smooth and brown and some of the smaller ones, fingers and toes for example, were missing. Only the cranium was left of the skull.

"Darlings..." said Arfa and was lost for more words. They ignored us while we struggled between encouraging their interest in anatomy, tearing them away to scrub their hands, explaining what happens after death and calling the police. We settled for asking them to show us where they found the remains, hoping it was not a cemetery. They led us to a ruined mud brick cottage in an overgrown olive orchard. Inside was a single room with an earth floor, empty but for a femur-long wooden chest, the lid open. Inside were scattered little bones.

"We thought it was treasure," said Jack.

"Is there a ghost?" asked Kate.

"Yeah. And now you've taken its bones it'll come into your bedroom," said Jim and made woooo noises.

Whose were they? The size of the pelvis indicated they were male. Otherwise there was no clue. We consulted Panayotis. He was shocked and made signs of the cross. He tried to pass them off as animal bones but they were unmistakably human. All he could tell us was that as a child he remembered a deaf old woman called Thea living in the hut with warts and cats. With our Greek friends we tried to come up with an innocent explanation but our theories led back to murder or necromancy. When we suggested we take the bones to the police they laughed. It is a rule of life in Greece that you don't go to the police unless absolutely necessary. The most likely explanation was that the hut had been built by a refugee, who had brought the bones of a loved one from Asia Minor.

It is traditional among Greeks, especially in the countryside, to exhume the bones of the dead three years or so after burial and store them in a little box in a bone house. It explains why Greek cemeteries are so small.

Meanwhile the children put the bones in a black plastic garbage bag and kept them next to the Lego in the playroom to amaze their friends and startle their grandparents. My dad gave us a spirited version of *'dem bones dem bones dem dry bones'*, knowing he was dying of lung cancer.

After a time we needed space for more Lego and made discreet soundings about a Christian burial for our anonymous playmate. Without papers, without even knowing if he was a Christian, or whether he had been properly buried before, it was a problem. There is a liturgy for provisional baptism but not for provisional burial. I thought of taking them back to the mud brick house but that solved nothing and I might be seen, which would get me arrested. So at the dead of night, the children holding candles, we buried him ceremoniously in the garden with the goldfish and guinea pigs and thought no more about it until the day my father died and I remembered him singing on the balcony and playing the bones, cheerful and defiant, which I suppose is the best way to deal with the business.

Balkan belligerents:
Turkey, Greece, Bulgaria,
Serbia, Montenegro,

(Courtesy of the Illustrated London News)

10 TEMPE TO LITOCHORO

The Vale of Tempe is a narrow gorge with vertical sides and a river at the bottom. The road runs along one bank and a railway line along the other. From Persians to Germans it has been the main invasion route into southern Greece, and the main retreat route. Roads north used to bottleneck through it, turning into a two lane death trap. Shortly before I got there tunnels 6 km long were opened beside it.

Mythological Tempe was not a great place for a woman. The nymph Daphne was pursued here by lustful Apollo. She appealed to her river-god father who turned her into a laurel bush. Eurydice, wife of the proto-poet and musician Orpheus, running away from her half-brother bent on incest was bitten by a snake and died. Orpheus was so distraught he went down to hell to bring her back, charming Hades with his lyre. Latin poets were effusive but inaccurate about Tempe's charms so that by the Renaissance it became a model of an idyll that in poems and paintings are nothing like the real thing. Google Turner's picture *The Story of Apollo and Daphne*. He painted a U-shaped valley from a geography text book.

Lay-bys serve souvenir stalls and a restaurant reached by a pedestrian suspension bridge that gives excellent views up- and down-stream without the effort of puffing up cliff paths. At a pier below the restaurant a Love Boat is advertised, although in the context a Rape Raft might have been more appropriate. For half an hour I potter about limpid green pools, scattered with golden leaves, and throw twigs in the river and rack my brains for the words of Kathleen Ferrier's *'What is life to me without thee?'* from Gluck's *Orpheus and Eurydice.* We had the 78 ever since I could remember. Although it was my mother's favourite it made her sad to remember dead relatives so I'd put it on the radiogram when I was cross with her, which is how I got to know the words. Children can be bastards. I am sorry now but it means I can sing to Eurydice in the Vale of Tempe. On so many levels it brings tears to my eyes.

What Is life to me without thee?
What Is left If thou art dead?
What Is life; life without thee?
What Is life without my love?
What Is life If thou art dead?
Eurydice! Eurydice!

In an Orphic reverie I make myself comfortable on a mossy stone beside the river and picnic on looted breakfast goods. For all it's cracked up to be over the millennia, the Vale of Tempe is dramatic and beautiful but not uniquely so. It benefits from some good stories over the years but there are many wilder, more striking gorges with less traffic. Its big advantage is location. After the Plain of Thessaly the Vale of Streatham (a suburb of London) would be linctus to the soul.

How did I get onto this? Let's get back on the road.

Metaxas

After the Asia Minor Catastrophe and the Exchange of Populations the new Hellenic Republic had an eventful decade with 23 changes of government and 13 army coups ping-ponging between Venizelist and Royalist officers. A rigged plebiscite brought King George II back from exile in 1935. He appointed General Ioannis Metaxas Prime Minister.

Metaxas declared martial law, dissolved parliament, banned political parties. He persecuted communists with police brutality, imprisonment and exile to island concentration camps. The multicultural, multilingual, multiracial roots of Greece were cleansed by burning books and rewriting text books. Classical theatre was revived in Athens and Epidauros. Minority languages were banned. *Katherevousa*, the 'purified' language of officialdom and education, was revived and revised again to look like ancient Greek. The propaganda ministry controlled press, radio, cinema and censored every other form of media and entertainment, including vulgar, immoral, dissolute Anatolian-imbued rebetiko.

Metaxas's fans point out stability, the establishment of IKA, the social security institute still flourishing today, the 40 hour week, maternity benefit and holiday pay and other corporatist innovations.

With the noble omission of anti-semitism, Metaxas' totalitarian regime echoed the German and Italian Fascism that he admired, even to the proclamation of a 'Third Civilisation', based on ancient Sparta and Orthodox Byzantium. He called himself *Archigos*, the Greek equivalent of *Führer* or *Duce*, that sat uneasily on his appearance. He was a tubby little fellow with a moustache and round glasses, a shopkeeper in his Sunday best. The Hitler salutes that greet him in photos look more like taking the mickey out of his size than *Sieg Heil*.

His last act transformed him from a tinpot dictator into a national hero. In April 1940 Italian troops crossed the Adriatic and annexed Albania. In the middle of the night on 28 October the Italian ambassador woke up Metaxas at his house in Kifissia with an ultimatum. Either he allowed the Italian army into Greece or the two countries would be at war. His exact reply is disputed but legend has it that it was one word, *Oxi!* - No! I cannot imagine a Greek using one word when ten would do but, whatever he actually said, *Oxi!*

became a headline and an inspirational rallying cry. The Greek army drove the Italians back over the mountains into Albania. Metaxas enjoyed the victory until January 1941, when he died.

In April Germany invaded through its ally Bulgaria, swatting away an exhausted army and inadequate British forces. Greece surrendered. King George II and his Metaxist government sat out the war in Cairo.

Platamon

After the excitement of Tempe we chunter into Macedonia along a humdrum highway beside the National Road. Mountains on either side alleviate the tedium of farmland. In the middle of nowhere the modern-looking HELNIC furniture factory and store provides some passing interest and I stop to browse among their speciality, pharmacy furniture, a niche so far unknown to me, until a keen young woman approaches. So I don't have to explain that I've only come in to stretch my knees in the air conditioning I shuffle off quietly before she chases me out. The road descends towards the coastal plain of the Thermaic Gulf, with views of the sea on the right and lush green hills on the left. The Gulf takes its name from Therma, the ancient name of Thessaloniki. Therma meant fever as it was built in mosquito infested swampland.

As we gently climb the ridge of a foothill sloping to the coast I am hooked out of the depths of tedium by the apparition of Platamon, a fine Crusader castle built on a natural motte next to the sea. A coronet of crenellated walls crowns the hilltop and encloses a handsome octagonal tower of white stone. According to a convenient display board in the car park it was probably a Byzantine fort from the tenth century, rebuilt by a Lombard Crusader knight after the heroes of the Fourth Crusade established their Latin Empire.

The Byzantines took it back fifty years later only to lose it to the Ottomans in the fourteenth century.

The last time the castle saw action was in April 1941. Germans invaded Greece, took Thessaloniki and blitzed down the coast road to Athens, led by battalions of *Kradschützen*. *Schützen* means troops. *Krad* stands for *Kraft-rad,* power-wheel and is military speak for motorcycle. Made by BMW and Zündapp, Krads were integrated motorcycle and sidecar combinations, the rear wheel of the cycle and the wheel of the sidecar on the same axle. The passenger in a sidecar sits much lower than the driver so it looks like he's brought along a hobbit. They went over almost any terrain and carried more arms and equipment than two individual soldiers. In the early years of the war, they were a rapid assault and reconnaissance force attached to tank regiments.

The New Zealand 21st Infantry Battalion was ordered to hold Platamon hill to cover the retreat of Anzac and British troops. They fought off Krads and Panzers for thirty-six hours and then fell back to join an Australian battalion for a last-ditch rearguard battle at Tempe lasting another two days. The survivors were taken prisoner or found their way to Crete for more last-ditch action.

I am just in time to get into the castle before it closes. A steep but short pant up the hill leads to a grassy enceinte, shaded by trees. It is remarkable that it was not more damaged by tank and artillery shells. There is a great view of Mount Olympus, the long sandy beach of the Thermaic Gulf curving away to the north-east, and the nearest finger of the Halkidiki peninsula on the other side. I sit under a tree and try to imagine waiting for the enemy and am thankful I have never seen war. Gratitude to the lads who sat up here on an April afternoon eighty years ago, as well as countless other young men and women, is tinged with the suspicion I might have missed out on something but I can live with that.

My father had a motorcycle and sidecar until he met my mother. She refused to get in it. This was partly because it was unfashionable and messed up her hair but mostly because of experience. When she was about seven years old and her sister was four their father came home with a cycle and sidecar chassis for the family to enjoy. He made a plywood box for the girls to sit in. Even after getting one-legged Father Mallarkey to bless it, Grandma would not trust her daughters to an open sidecar, so insisted that Grandad put a lid on it. They had to crawl inside the coffin and lie on a cushion in the dark and noise, hugging each other, shaken and bounced, an eye glued to an air hole. Every so often Grandad would thump on the roof and yell "y'all roit in dere?" The girls had to thump back in reply. They were left with claustrophobia and a life-long aversion to sidecars.

The museum café is still open for a quick iced Nes and a jumbled meditation on my mother, the invasion of Greece, the Fourth Crusade, the strange taste of the sweaty dried fig from my back pocket, the probability of life after death, whether Harley would like to be called a Krad, and many other unacknowledged notions and emotions swimming around in the soup of the semiconscious.

Leake

Mount Olympus, home of the Gods, 3000m high, brow wreathed in cloud, rises out of the plain on the left. I follow a quiet road parallel with the new motorway and try to decide if I'm going to chance a spectacular sunset view of the Home of the Gods from the village of Litochoro, gateway to to the mountain, or turn down to the coast and find a swim and an ouzo. No contest. At the junction, a complicated interchange with confusing signage, I find the road towards the beach.

Beside the old railway line is Litochoro Station, abandoned now. There's a hotel nearby belonging to the time when the railway brought visitors to Olympus. It has a wide verandah looking over the sea and a glass door with gold lettering. I don't bother to go in and ask the price, it's not for the likes of me, guv'nor. Harley and I potter along the gravel road parallel with the railway line for half a mile but there's nothing else so I go back to the hotel. Inside it's not so posh. A middle aged man is doing a crossword at a table in the dining room. He looks me up and down and I struggle not to see myself through his eyes, dishevelled, sweaty, travel and breakfast stained. I tell him I am going to the Holy Mountain on a *papaki*. He asks where I'm from and I play the Irish card. He shrugs and spreads his arms in apology that money must come into our conversation and names his price. €25! Including breakfast! Does he feel sorry for an impostrous pilgrim? Who cares? His name is Dimitris-call-me-Jimmy.

It's a pleasant room overlooking an untended garden and the beach. Over the bed is a colourful portrait of a bosomy Romani and a photograph of the Eiffel Tower, both of whose relevances to Olympus are hard to fathom. Before the luxury of a nap is the chore of laundering my wardrobe in the basin using the give-away shampoo. A useful tip from my Russian experiences: if the plug is missing or doesn't work, a plastic bag does the job. And always carry a long piece of string and clothes pegs for drying.

I change my mind about the nap and go for a swim. The beach is perfect - pale fine sand, gently shelving into the deep - and sublimely uninteresting, like tropical beaches in holiday advertisements. But the sea is choppy and invigorating, with the added frisson of not knowing if the squidgy thing you brush against is seaweed, jellyfish, or a used diaper. Invigorated and refreshed I dry out with a jog along the watermark until I remember how much I loathe running and change down to a stroll. I collect a retinue of strays, sustained by the leftovers of nearby restaurants, peaceable companions unlike the sugar dogs of yesterday.

Over an ouzo and a plate of sausage and cucumber I am joined on the hotel verandah by Lieutenant-Colonel William Martin Leake, courtesy of Kindle. He came to Greece in 1802 as a twenty-five year old British artillery officer on the staff of Lord Elgin. On his way back to England from surveying Egypt he was on board a ship carrying some of Elgin's loot that was wrecked off the island of Kythera. It took two years to get the marbles back up. In 1805 he was sent back to Greece by the Foreign Secretary to survey the interior and persuade the Turks to stiffen the coastal defences against Napoleon and the Russians. He spent two years riding around Greece, taking advantage of his mission to map and explore and re-discover classical sites identified only in texts. His guides were the first century geographer Strabo and the second century Pausanias and the only maps were ones he drew himself. A classicist by education and a surveyor by training, his scholarship was as remarkable as his military expertise, both of them fuelled by extraordinary powers of observation. Sites with ruined walls and broken columns and plans on display boards that we traipse round today before looking for the café were then no more than a bump in a field or an inscription on a stone or a handful of coins dug up by the plough. Tomorrow I will visit one of his discoveries, Dion, at the foot of Olympus.

Leake's best-known and most useful books are the three volumes of *Travels in the Morea* and the five volumes of *Travels in Northern Greece*. The Morea is the old name for the Peloponnese. In 1976 we were given a leather-bound early edition of the Morea by a neighbour, Bertie, when we set off for Greece in our VW camper. He bought them when he was posted to Greece as an army officer thirty years before, helping the National Army hunt down andartes. Like Leake he patrolled the mountains with a pistol and a military escort.

For the next five years Leake, Pausanias and the Blue Guide lived in a cupboard over the engine compartment with towels and beach mats, getting stained and tatty but well-thumbed. The Leakes are still on our bookshelves. They shed grains of sand when you get them down.

Chicago

Leake and I go inside for dinner. An elderly lady sits at a table by the serving counter doing something technical with vegetables. She is dressed in black but wears gold earrings and a necklace, indicating there has not been a death in the family for a few years now. For her generation, traditional gradations of mourning are rigorous. You start off in total black without jewellery or makeup. Over time pearl buttons are permitted, then a black patterned dress, while jewellery is introduced bit by bit. Timing depends on the degree of relationship, husband being the most demanding followed by parents, children and so on, moving out through the degrees of consanguinity. There are often overlaps as relatives get older so you can be stuck indefinitely in total black. In our part of Evia there is an exemption for the traditional island scarf, mustard yellow with black patterns. There is no lack of precedent or advice for the first-time bereaved but in doubt you can go to the Widow Shop, like a Bridal Shop but for later, where they will put you right. And the men? They wear a black armband for six weeks. For younger women these customs have gone the way of traditional scarves, something granny did.

"Kalispera," I say.

"Hi Howarya," she says. I am torn between conflicting desires for conversation and for my dinner. "Siddown." Resigned to a garrulous half hour I sit next to her and prepare for the customary interrogation along the lines of a mortgage application - name, age, address, marital status, children, profession, income, outgoings, children's' marital status, grandchildren - but she is remarkably uncurious.

"Where you from?"

"Ireland."

"I know Irish good people was born in Chicago married a man older than my dad came back built this."

"Nice place."

"Chicago."

"I mean here."

"Eh we live. You know Chicago?"

"I've been a couple of times. It's too cold for me. When it's not too hot."

"You get used it's a good place."

"Did your parents emigrate?"

"Sure before the war lucky for them."

Between 1890 and 1935 one in every four of the male population of Greece between the ages of fifteen and forty-five went to America, over half a million men. They went to the cities of the East coast, New York and Chicago of course but also Detroit, Boston, St Louis. The first Greek Orthodox church in America was built in New Orleans in 1866. They went to the New England mill towns to work in the textile and shoe factories. By 1920 Lowell, Massachusetts, had the third largest Greek population in America, behind New York and Chicago. They went to Colorado and Utah and California to work in the mines and on the railroads. By 1925 Salt Lake City had the biggest Greektown in America. A few used their native skills raising sheep in the mountains of Utah, recreating the mountain villages of home. Sponge divers from the Dodecanese colonised Tarpon Springs Florida. Many emigrants left with two things apart from a change of clothes, an icon to keep them safe and a bag of earth from home to be sprinkled on their coffin if they died.

"Where were your folks from?"

"My Dad from Smyrna lucky to get out my Mom from Katerini down the road we had a good life."

Greeks in America were looked down on, exploited and victimised. Greeks and Italians were not considered white. The Ku Klux Klan saw them as the next worst thing to Afro-Americans and Chinese. In 1922 Greeks founded the American Hellenic Educational Progressive Association, acronymed AHEPA as a defence against the Klan, to help with citizenship, to set up schools for children and adults. Today it is an educational foundation and one of the biggest lobbying organisations in Washington DC.

One of AHEPA's roles was to find women for all those single men. They organised charters on ships that toured the Aegean recruiting brides. When the boat came in the girls lined up in the main square for speed dating. Not all were happy to go. A song of 1937 says "*I don't want the AHEPA with a fez, however rich he is, I love a lad with a thin waist...*' For some reason well-nourished suitors thought that wearing a fez with a tassel and the AHEPA logo would distract from their paunches. Other men proposed to photos of 'Picture Brides' through marriage brokers or friends who had sisters. The FBI suspected white slavery until they discovered that while money changed hands it was not the man who paid but the woman with a traditional dowry.

There's another sad song from the time:

Yiorgo, my love, I'm leaving you,
And I'm going far away.
They're marrying me off into exile
They take me like a lamb to be slaughtered,
And there, in my grief, they will bury me.

"Why did you come back to Greece?"

"Mom's cousin came back from the war couldn't settle down came back the year we married said it was cheaper than Chicago sure was nothing to spend your money on here dirt poor."

Not all emigrants stayed. About half of them came back when they had made some money. *Amerikanákis,* little American, was 1930's slang for a sucker, a pigeon to be plucked - not all Americans but returning Greeks, flashing the cash, 'showing them up' as my Grandfather said when he went back to Ireland on holidays in a new hat. A 1935 song *The American* tells of five lads from Piraeus ripping one off.

"My wife's grandmother was born in Wisconsin," I said, "They came back to Ireland. The boat must have been empty, everyone going the other way. Cheap tickets though."

She sighs and stands up and takes her vegetables behind the counter to the kitchen. I think of our daughter Kate, emigrated to California, husband and two boys now, we see them once or twice a year. The pain of being left behind. At least these days there's Skype and FaceTime.

I get up and go to a table a safe distance from the counter. The other diners are a young French couple with eyes only for each other. Jimmy comes over to take my order.

"Did mama talk about Chicago? She's never left."

The faded decor and crepuscular lighting of the dining room matches the *ancienne cuisine,* an excellent feed of juicy fried aubergine with pungent garlic purée, a massive serving of grilled pork belly with succulent fat, thick chips oozing lubricity, salad swimming in smokey olive oil, a brimming jug of extra-virginal sea-dark wine. Delicious. Hello dreams, hello night sweats, you're worth it.

Occupation

The pork belly does its work on mine. Karagiozis characters in coal scuttle helmets on Krads pursue me through the night until Harley whisks me away to oblivion.

After *Oxi!* and the Italian defeat there were no more heroic victories. The full repertoire of Nazi occupation was visited on Greece. Reprisals, hangings, shootings, mass executions, torture, burning villages, starvation. Germans occupied Athens, Western Macedonia, Crete and some islands. Italy was trusted with the largest but strategically less important territory until it capitulated in 1943 and Germans took over. Bulgaria annexed Eastern Macedonia and Thrace to the satisfaction of the Slavic-speakers. The Bulgarian policy towards Greeks was expulsion and extermination. Italians killed about 11,000 people, Germans 20,000 and Bulgarians 40,000. As despicable as the others, Italians get off lightest in the roster of baddies, possibly because they did not deport Jews. And possibly because the *makaronádes* were feared and mocked in equal measure.

More lethal than 'pacification' was plundering Greece for food, fuel and raw materials, coupled with an Allied blockade. 300,000 people, about 5 percent of the population, died of starvation. The Oxford Committee for Famine Relief, today's Oxfam, was founded to lobby a reluctant British government to let food supplies through. Public opinion in America and Britain finally persuaded them. To this day food is a frequent topic of conversation. Perhaps the preoccupation with food is long embedded in Greek culture, perhaps it is a collective memory of devastating starvation.

Resistance to the Nazi occupation was driven by EAM, the communist National Liberation Front, and its guerrilla wing ELAS. It included other left-wing groups and unaligned patriots. They prepared to take over when the war was over. Building a Soviet-style government they called 'Free Greece', and eliminating rivals was more important to them than helping the Allied war effort, to the frustration of saboteurs of the British Special Operations Executive, the SOE. With violence and terror, expulsions and evacuations, EAM/ELAS eventually controlled 80 percent of the mainland outside the main towns and roads.

While Britain supplied ELAS with arms in return for cooperation, its policy was to prevent them taking over at the end of the war. Churchill supported the King, his Metaxist ministers and right wing army officers exiled in Cairo. Inside Greece Britain armed EDES, the royalist National Democratic Greek League that did battle with ELAS as well as the Germans. It recruited from royalists, republicans and people victimised by ELAS. Pitched against both in a three way civil war were the collaborationist Security Battalions of the Greek puppet government, kitted out in fustanellas and pompom shoes, working closely with the Wehrmacht. They numbered over 20,000 anti-communists, Nazi sympathisers, and men anxious to feed their families.

Most of the officers of the British SOE, who were parachuted into Greece to organise and arm resistance did not speak Greek. Some respected and admired the resilience and courage of the Greeks while many followed the Churchillian line. In 1944 Major D. J. Wallace, advisor to the British Mission and a Greek speaker, was attached to the right wing EDES. A few weeks before he was killed observing an attack on a German position, this was his assessment:

In spite of much kindness and hospitality I can see no reason to modify my view of Greeks as formed in the Middle East. I am convinced that they are a fundamentally hopeless and useless people with no future or prospect of settling down to any form of sensible life within any measurable time. Our effort in Greece, in men and money, has not only been out of all proportion to the results we have achieved against the Germans but also to the value to the Greek people, who are not capable of being saved from themselves nor for themselves worth it. This is also the unanimous opinion of all British liaison officers who have long been in the country.

Distinguished officers more sympathetic to the Greeks like Eddie Myers and Monty Woodhouse were thought by the foreign office to be too close to ELAS, the left wing resistance, and were shunted off to other theatres.

Our band plays a song called Haidari, written by Markos in 1943. Haidari, near Daphne monastery, was the site of a notorious concentration camp. Over 20,000 people, including Jews, Italian POWs and Greeks passed through on the way to Auschwitz, forced labour in Germany, or execution.

Run, mother, fast as you can.
Run to save me from Haidari.
I am condemned to death,
17-years-old child in chains.
From Sekeri Street they are taking me to Haidari.
Any time now Charon will take me.

Gestapo HQ, since demolished, was between Merlin Street and Sekeri Street, where the Italian Embassy now is.

In a walled enclosure by the road a couple of kilometres away from our house in Horio is a monument to a local resistance hero who died on 3 September 1944. Germans were withdrawing from Greece. A convoy of trucks led by a jeep was ambushed by ELAS. A young fighter was killed. In bas relief on the monument he wears the beret and bandolier of the andarte. I happened to pass by during a remembrance service. Half a dozen elderly men in raincoats, berets and red scarves stood in a group on the left. One of them was making a speech. On the right stood another half dozen elderly men in overcoats and trilbies and blue scarves listening to one of them making a speech at the same time. When they finished shouting each other down the men in berets sang the International. The men in trilbies produced a battery operated turntable and put on the National Anthem, joining in. Finished and hoarse, they saluted in their various fashions and left, each group ignoring the existence of the other. One man was left, in beret and red scarf, standing in front of the carving of the hero, tears streaming down his face. Through his sobs he told me the lad was his big brother.

One of our neighbours told us what happened. He had been at school with the boy, fourteen years old. A gang of half-starved schoolboys heard the gunfire and went to watch. When it was over and the Germans lay apparently dead the boys ran to rifle their pockets for food. Our lad started to pull the jackboots off the officer, who came to and shot him dead with his pistol.

'Oxi Day' on October 28 is a national holiday with parades and speeches, second only to Independence Day on 25 March. *Oxi!* resonates not only with the Italian campaign and the Nazi occupation but deep inside the Greek character as deep-seated resistance to domestic despotism and foreign domination. After 'liberation' in 1944 they had both, which is perhaps why Greece is the only country that celebrates the beginning of the war and not the end.

11 LITOCHORO TO OLYMPIAKI

Sunlight floods the bedroom. It's already nearly nine o'clock and I shower and dress in a hurry in case I'm late for breakfast and the best things are gone. Phew. There's no-one else in the dining room. Chicago Gran potters around the kitchen in a long black dressing gown but no-one else is here. The remains of my dinner are still on the table where I left them. I'm surprised everyone is up so late until I see the clock behind the bar. Half past six. I must have read my watch upside down. From vital and alert after a good night's sleep I instantly switch to dozy and stupefied from not enough. A congealed chip from yesterday's plate is meagre consolation.

Too cross with myself to go back to bed I decide to start early for Olympus. It's chilly outside so I go back to my room and put on a second shirt and a fleece. When I come down again Gran beckons me over and hands me a stale chocolate croissant and a mug of tepid Nescafé. She stands at the door to wave me off, which I find touching and inauspicious.

Sunrise is worth getting up for, not a phrase I often use. The reborn sun limelights Olympus ahead of me, no longer tonsured with a fringe of white cloud but double peaked in snow white. The road goes dead straight to the village of Litochoro past a sprawling military base.

Litochoro is situated at the head of the slope, immediately at the foot of the great woody steeps of Olympus, on the right bank of a torrent which has its origin in the highest part of the mountain, and here issues between perpendicular rocks five or six hundred feet in height. The opening presents a magnificent view of the summit of Olympus, the snowy tops and bare precipices of which form a beautiful contrast with the rich woody heights on either side of the great chasm above Litochoro. The rising sun now lights up the snowy summit, as well as all the rocks, woods, torrents and precipices below it; distinguishes them from one another by the strongest shading and seems to bring them all within half their distance… I couldn't put it better myself so I won't but crib this paragraph from Colonel Leake.

There are two things I want to see, the police station and the Maritime Museum. What is a maritime museum doing half way up a mountain? As it doesn't open until 9 I must leave you as much in the dark as me. The police station marks the spot where the Greek Civil War started on 31 March 1946. In retaliation for brutality against communist sympathisers thirty three guerrillas of ELAS, the left-wing resistance against fascist occupation, attacked the police station killing a dozen policemen. I find it easily enough, although it seems too modern to be the original and probably not in the same location. It's not a significant landmark anyway. The origins of the Civil War predate 1946 by generations and its repercussions ripple on today.

Civil War

The wounds of the Civil War of 1946-1949 run deep and silent. In the centre of Athens a moving sculpture bears mute witness in a square appropriately called *Klathmonas*, Weeping, originally nicknamed for civil servants fired when the opposition got in. Otherwise the memory is too raw. It is not taught in schools. To my knowledge no museum deals with it. In Athens the National History Museum and the War Museum end with the German invasion of 1940. Two private museums about concentration camps on the islands of Agios Efstratios and Makronisos are moving but not informative about the context.

In 1944 Germany withdrew from Greece and was replaced by 6,000 British troops and a government of national unity that notionally included EAM, the political wing of ELAS, the communist resistance. Churchill was determined to crush the communists, bring back King George II and install a right-wing government. In December 1944 shooting broke out at an EAM/ELAS demonstration in Syntagma leaving thirty dead. EAM/ELAS occupied the city. The government re-enlisted collaborationist Security Battalions and Gendarmes to fight alongside British troops with tanks, artillery and warplanes. The so-called *Dekembriana* of street fighting in Athens lasted a month until EAM/ELAS was driven out of the city and laid down their arms. Athens, unscathed during the Occupation, was left with the ruins of a battle ground.

Dissuaded from imposing the unpopular King, Churchill installed Archbishop Damaskinos as Regent. He presided over a succession of five prime ministers and the 'White Terror', the persecution of leftists, real or suspected. Nazi collaborators went back to their old jobs of torturing and jailing people who had resisted the occupation. Thousands of presumed leftists were executed in public or sent to island prison camps. Severed heads were displayed in village squares. In 1946 a rigged plebiscite voted for the return of King George II. He died a few months later and was succeeded by his brother Paul.

EAM/ELAS picked up its arms and took to the mountains again, setting up a Provisional Government. Near-bankrupt Britain handed over the task of saving Greece for capitalism to President Truman and his eponymous doctrine of arming vulnerable countries against Soviet expansion. In March 1946 the attack on the Litochoro police station was the starting pistol of the first proxy war of the Cold War. ELAS was rebranded as the Democratic Army of Greece, a conventional regular army funded and supplied by Yugoslavia, Albania and Bulgaria. Facing it was the National Army sustained by the USA and $2 billion of aid. Alongside both were guerrilla bands and militias winning the acquiescence, if not the hearts and minds of the population, with atrocious cruelty.

The Civil War was more destructive and lethal than the Occupation. More lives were lost than in any conflict since the Revolution of 1822. 10 percent of the population was killed or exiled. Villages have memorials to those killed by both sides. Swathes of agricultural land were left uncultivated, villages and infrastructure destroyed. For decades afterwards a succession of right wing governments presided over death squads, purges and show trials, leaving a residue of dislocation, bitterness and irreconcilable tension between Left and Right that still reverberates. Legislation officially ending the Civil War was passed by Parliament in 1989.

A few years ago on Evia I drove into the mountains between Kimi and Mount Dirfis to Makrichori. The name means distant village. I wanted to see the frescoes in a Byzantine church dating from 1303. Their state of preservation is described with enthusiasm in a guide to Evian frescoes published in 1932. I arrived on a sleepy late summer afternoon. Half a dozen elderly men were sitting outside the café. I asked where the old church was. Their spokesman, whose bald pate had so many liver spots it looked like a leopardskin skull cap, said it was in the cemetery too far away to walk but in any case not worth visiting. Besides, it was locked and the man who had the keys had gone to Halkida for the day. Too bad. On the way back to the car I noticed a faded blue signpost to 'The Old Church' so I went to have a look anyway. It was no more than twenty yards to the cemetery, there was no lock on the gates and a rusty chain wrapped a couple of times round the door handles of the church had not seen a padlock in years.

It was a little cross-domed church, exquisite if you ignored the breeze block extension, which accommodated the faithful until a new church was built on the main road. The frescoes were a disappointment. My 1932 guide evidently had low standards of excellence. In several places the plaster had crumbled away and the rest was soot blackened and streaked with water. Saints and prophets who survived to the height a man can reach had their eyes gouged out. They looked more alive than the fierce looking sighted ones above them.

I was peering at the founder's inscription when the place was suddenly flooded with light. For a moment I thought I was blessed with a visitation, which indeed I was. One of the men from the café had followed me and switched on the lights from a codged-up fuse board in the porch. He was in his eighties but with a gentle unlined face that I was tempted to compare with John the Beloved above my head until I decided I was getting carried away by my surroundings.

"Very beautiful," I said.

"Eh, you should have seen it in the old days."

"Of course," I said, trying to conjure out of the patchy and peeling shadows the brilliant colours and tumultuous animation of the life of Christ that the anonymous medieval painter had brought to this isolated mountain village.

"When I was a boy it was wonderful. Now look at it."

He came over to me and gently poked two fingers at the pale eye sockets gouged into the face of Saint Michael.

"Andartes," he said.

"Andartes?"

"Andartes camped in here. They gouged the eyes that accused them."

This explains why the 1932 guide was enthusiastic about the frescoes. They had survived from Byzantine times until the Civil War. Ten years later I took Arfa to Makrichori. The old roof had been repaired with new tiles, fresh cement laid round the outside to stop the walls falling out, and the peeling plaster inside rendered over. The eyeless saints survived. A new crop of old men mouldered in front of the café. The owner wanted to practise his German and told us he had just turned sixty and was the youngest man in the village. We told him we had just visited the old church. He said it used to be beautiful but the Turks desecrated it. 'Wasn't it the andartes?' I asked. He jerked his head up and tutted, the Greek gesture for 'no'. Andartes were Christians. The village was still divided.

Olympus

The road continues out of sleeping Litochoro to Prionia, trailhead for the hike to the summit. I could take a hiking trail 18km from Litochoro to Prionia but gone are the days when I could do a 36km walk. (There were about three of them). The brand-new National Park Information Centre, containing a wealth of information about the history, archaeology, fauna, flora, monasteries and mythology of the mountain is the first stop and a short one as it's closed until 10 o'clock. A couple of kilometres further on the New Monastery of Saint Dionysios is open for business. It replaces the original sixteenth century foundation a few kilometers up the mountain that was shelled to destruction in 1943 by German troops, who suspected it harboured andartes.

The monastery precinct is beautifully kept and swept, grey stone flags, mellow stone walls, cream and red stucco, lustrous wood, red tiles, manicured trees and plants in pots. If a monastery garden is inspired by heaven, we'll have to be very tidy in the after-life. Monks in the church are chanting. I sit in the narthex, as I don't know their rules for non-Orthodox going into the nave. Monasteries are more fussy about heterodox and heretics than secular churches. I try to give way to the music, strange and thrilling with its scooping quarter tones and twelve-tone melodies, but I'm restless and eager to be up the mountain. I make my apologies to Saint Dionysios and rejoin Harley in the car park.

I have second thoughts about taking Harley a thousand metres up the mountain to Prionia. If he conks out 18km is a long way to freewheel down to a Litochoro garage, assuming there is one. First thoughts win out. I pat his saddle and off we go. The first few kilometres are relatively gentle, a couple of hairpins and crystalline views. The forest begins, thick and variegated in every colour and variety of bushy tops and Christmas trees. At a trailhead called Gortsia I leave Harley to snooze in the car park while I venture a safe distance along a narrow path through…

…I'm not going to describe the scenery because when I try it's a disappointment. I fail to do justice to the breathtaking beauty of the place. I struggle to find the vocabulary. I don't mean for listing trees and rocks and streams and views, shapes and colours, this only needs a thesaurus. Bringing to life the sensation of being apart and yet part of the landscape, to embrace and exude the air and the silence and the light and the space, to revel in being intimidated yet inspired, is a rare talent and I don't have it. Sorry about that.

After 5km the road ends in a car park already patronised by early risers. A rustic log-clad restaurant is open for hot Nes and sinful sugary doughnuts to compensate for the tingly effects of altitude and other self-justifications. Weighed down with guilt and pastry I cross a wooden bridge that takes a trail upwards into the forest, following the sign to a waterfall created by the Enipeas river, named after a god. For Ancient Greeks all rivers were gods. Most of them had similar stories of miscegenation with mortals, who came to bad ends. His waterfall is two parallel streams frothing together erotically into a pool of clear green water surrounded by gossiping trees. Half way up Olympus, bemused by the scene, altitude and lack of sleep, the stories don't seem so daft. I mooch around the enchanting pool until the first tourists arrive and then go back to the restaurant. Actually they are the second tourists because I have no illusions about my own status.

According to the map on a display board it is 4km to Saint Dionysios's hermit cave along the trail back down to Litochoro through the Enipeas gorge. The restaurant owner kindly agrees to look after my stuff. I pack a bottle of water and another sinful doughnut and set off. It takes me well over an hour as there are more ascents and descents than are obvious from the map and I left my knee bandages with Harley but mainly because it is too beautiful to rush. In front of the cave is a wide clearing under a massive overhang where the Saint's followers built a tiny whitewashed chapel extruded from a cleft in the rock. I join a queue to go inside. There is barely room to stand up. The murky air is thick with damp and old candle smoke and stale incense. It feels that what was once important here has departed.

I scramble down from the path to find a solitary stone for an eremitic lunch of squashed doughnut and the last of the figs that have been making my right buttock sticky since Larissa. You can see why Saint Dionysios chose the spot, apart from the convenience of a cave. The numinous of the place is almost palpable. Yet it is not concerned with me, no more than I am concerned with the ant crawling up my trouser leg to a fugitive fig pip. The landscape exists on its own terms whether I exist or not. I am absorbed in it but separated from it by the impenetrable barrier of consciousness. The only way I can be at one with it is by moulding it to my own perceptions. How then is it holy? Is holiness intrinsic to the place? Or am I kidding myself, indulging in the self-delusion of the spiritual? What is the spiritual anyway? I understood what I was talking about when I jotted all this down on my phone.

I follow a stepped trail uphill to the original monastery Dionysios founded, twenty minutes on the map plus another twenty for knees and puff. His mosaic portrait above the gateway shows him fierce in the prime of manhood with a lush brown beard. The church has been restored while the rest remains in ruins from the German bombardment. Full of resolutions to come back to the mountain one day with hiking poles, knee bandages, ibuprofen gel and other geriatric accessories, I rejoin Harley and coast down to Litochoro and then to the beach for a swim.

Dion

The next morning I wake up at eleven by my watch but am not going to be caught out like yesterday. It's only half past six. I pull the sheet over my face against the light and try to go back to sleep, tossing and turning for over an hour before the lavatory summons me to get up. I look at my watch and see that I've done the opposite of yesterday, I read it correctly. I slept until eleven and now it's nearly one. The sense of achievement from sleeping twelve hours and only having to get up twice in the night is undermined by missing breakfast.

After brunching on a wholesome Greek salad and assuring Jimmy and Granny Chicago that I would come back with cohorts of family and friends in the spring, they wave us off from the steps and we set a course for Dion archaeological park. The sanctuary of Olympian Zeus was the religious centre of ancient Macedonia. It is a delightful change from the bomb-sites that most excavations look like. Sure, it has the usual rubble strewn amphitheatres, vestigial temples, traces of shops and houses, mosaic floors, slab roads, phallic columns with curly tops, baths with hypocausts laid bare, a communal latrine with holes in the benches for twenty bums, and other amenities. What makes them attractive is that they lurk in nymph-flitting, muse-chattering, god-whispering meadows and glades, trickling streams and sunlit pools, tree-shaded paths meandering past grass-grown ruins. I spend a happy afternoon mooching round, avoiding tour groups and the display boards they huddle over.

My favourite corner is the captivating sanctuary of Isis with her statue in a reed-lined pool. She is an interloper in a sanctuary to the Olympian gods, an Egyptian, divine mother of Horus incarnated as the Pharaoh, compassionate to us mortals in life and at the hour of our death. From the fourth century BC her worship spread throughout the Greek and Roman worlds. There is a contentious theory that Isis evolved into the Christian Mary Mother of God. They have several similarities. But also many differences. Isis and Mary are not alternative names for the same goddess but fill a god-space in our hearts for an archetypal mother, who will intercede with Daddy so he doesn't smack us for being naughty and when we are dying will cuddle us and tell us to go to sleep and everything will be all right.

The museum is close by in a light and airy neo-classical building. It displays a lively mosaic of unmotherly Medusa and the typical collection of pots, busts, statues and marble steles - gravestones with bas-relief effigies of the Dear Departed sitting down to say goodbye to relatives. The living are often smaller, giving the impression that they are further away, that you the observer are already in Hades about to welcome the Dear Arriving.

I want to see the *hydraulis*, an ancient organ in which the flow of air to the pipes is regulated by water pressure and not to be confused with a hydraulic organ powered by water. It dates from the 1st century BC and is the oldest surviving keyboard instrument in the world. Air is pumped through a water reservoir into twenty four metal pipes, the longest being just over a metre long, so sounding more like a flute band than a church organ. I linger over the display of silver coins and spot one which we gave to Harry for his fortieth birthday, the head of Alexander the Great peeping out of a lion's head. We give the children something ancient for their fortieths to put their advancing age into the context of millennia. Happy Birthday kid, your life's a spark in the abyss of eternity.

On a bench in a garden next to the museum I finish the bread and feta pocketed from brunch washed down with water from the museum toilets. I share a crust with a well-mannered stray, his portly figure showing he is in no need of well-wishers, an Epicurean dog and certainly no pleasure-shunning Cynic. Cynic means 'dog-like'. The 'joke' might have gone down alright on a University High Table in the last century. Haw haw Professor. Get on your bike you pretentious git. So I do.

The Junta

After the Civil War Greece became an anti-communist client state of the USA. Nazi occupation, civil war, famine, displacement, ethnic cleansing, poverty, emigration, political turmoil, few natural resources, no industry to speak of, rudimentary infrastructure, backward agriculture, chronic underinvestment, swollen and inefficient bureaucracy, Greece did not have a lot going for it. Its survival was remarkable, let alone an economic transformation thanks to the Marshall Plan and sound economic management.

Alekos was the last person born in our house in 1960. Six people lived in two rooms. They slept on the floor, collected water from a spring, baked bread in a collective stone oven, cooked on charcoal. Mule was the only transport. There was no sanitation, no lavatories inside or out. I have never had the nerve to ask where they went. Mitsos, a son of a neighbour, said in the fields, whatever the weather. Then electricity came along the main road in the valley and everyone moved down to new concrete houses with piped water and septic tanks.

Buses took men to the lignite mines in Aliveri to bring in cash. A rich neighbour, Costas, my age, ran away to Athens aged 13. He was taken in by a distant relative and earned a living selling electric fans door to door in blocks of flats just electrified. He graduated to refrigerators out of his shop and then his own factory. In a decade lives were transformed.

Meanwhile the political establishment went back to its old ways, the leftists under George Papandreou, the rightists under Constantine Karamanlis. In 1964 the left won an election for the first time. Shortly afterwards King Paul died and was succeeded by his 24 year old son Constantine II. He dismissed Papandreou for threatening to reform the army and made several attempts to form a new government. The interference of King Constantine and the military sparked conspiracy and mayhem. Those of us old enough to have seen the film Z, the Greek pronunciation of which means 'he lives', based on the real-life assassination of a leftist politician, have a flavour of the anger and paranoia of the time.

On 21 April 1967 a group of right wing army officers proclaimed martial law, shut down Parliament, arrested politicians. The dreaded Greek Military Police, ESA, arrested and tortured suspected leftist sympathisers before sending them to island concentration camps. The Colonels grew up under the dictator Metaxas before the Second World War and fought in the Civil War that followed it. The leader George Papadopoulos had been in a collaborationist Security Battalion during the Nazi Occupation. Their ideology looked back to an imaginary Greece of 'Christian Hellenes' with patriarchal families, traditional communities, everyone going to church, dancing in circles, no communists. Demotic Greek favoured by the left was branded a degenerate dialect and suppressed in favour of Katherevousa. Cultural events were censored, left-leaning books and music banned, especially rebetiko and anything by the communist Mikis Theodorakis.

They revived the Great Idea, sending men and material to support Greek insurgency in Cyprus for union with Greece.

King Constantine turned down the job of figurehead and attempted a counter-coup but the army liked the new regime and he fled the country. Royal watchers in Greece had to be on their toes. Of its seven kings, four were deposed, one of them twice, one was assassinated and one died of a monkey bite. Two died naturally on the throne. As Constantine's uncle King George II is supposed to have said, the most important equipment for a Greek king is a suitcase.

Many Greeks and liberals blame the coup on the USA. 'CIA-backed' is a conventional modifier to the words Coup or Junta or Military Dictatorship. Maybe. Many Greeks prefer to blame foreigners for their misfortunes. The USA probably did not engineer the coup but certainly gave the resulting regime its enthusiastic support.

The church played its part. The much loved papas of a village near us was the grandfather of a friend. Snow white hair, bushy beard, shiny red nose and a booming laugh suited his name, Nicholas. A fine chanting voice had no need for the microphone which was just as well, as his frequent slapping of it to make sure it worked made sure that most of the time it didn't. His cheerfulness and his nose were fuelled in equal measure by the Holy Spirit and ouzo. He drove an old Toyota whose speedy days were over, which saved his life on several occasions when he ran into a tree or a ditch and had to be taken home by the police, protected by his calling from further repercussions. He had been a mechanic by trade until he answered the call to the priesthood in his forties. Service as a sergeant in the National Army in the Civil War made up for lack of education. A few weeks at a seminary to pick up the basics and he was ordained like hundreds of right-thinking others, recruited for their faith in Christian Hellenism and deployed in country villages.

For the first few years of the Junta the economy grew by 7 percent a year and standards of living rose. The government invested in infrastructure, especially electricity, television and tourism. If conversations today in the café are to be taken seriously, some Greeks left behind by the economic boom of later years or swallowed up in the Crisis that followed look back to the Junta with nostalgia. It remains an inspiration to extreme right-wing parties.

When the global recession of 1973 began to bite there was growing agitation for change. Resistance was led by students. On November 17 it culminated in a tank assault on the Athens Polytechnic university leaving at least 25 dead and more in the days that followed. Thousands were arrested and beaten up. A coup within a coup dismissed the original leaders for going soft and replaced them with harder liners. They supported the overthrow of the government of Archbishop Makarios of Cyprus that led to a civil war between Greek and Turkish Cypriots and the Turkish invasion. Abandoned by domestic, international and American support the regime collapsed. The joint chiefs of staff invited the former rightist Prime Minister Constantine Karamanlis back from Paris to form a government.

The anniversary of November 17 is commemorated with demonstrations, wreaths, streets closed off and extra police in the streets of central Athens.

Tobacco Road

The road from Dion to Katerini is dead straight across a flat plain crossed by wide rivers and their tributaries, a dreamscape for blank-eyed revenants, gaping mouths on stilts, ragged men with deadly clobbering sticks and other figments and mirages to while away the ennui of motorcycling. More prosaically it is fertile and fertilised land for the principal crop, tobacco. When Greece, Bulgaria and the recently renamed Republic of North Macedonia were part of the Ottoman Empire, Katerini gave its name to a type of what used to be called Turkish tobacco and is now less contentiously called Oriental. It has smaller leaves than Virginia and is more aromatic. This year's crop has been harvested and is drying in the sun. The land has been ploughed and raked level, waiting for future plantings, insecticides and fertilisers, while it digests and drains the chemicals of the past year through streams and rivers and estuaries into the murky soup of the Thermaic Gulf. Most of the crop is exported, the rest used by domestic manufacturers like Papastratos, whose Assos and Marlboro alleviated the tedium of many hours of my brief banking career. Greek Marlboro, with more oriental in the blend, should not be confused by the taste buds with the American version, although it retains the services of the Marlboro Man cowboy and not a hunky Greek shepherd. Greece accounts for about a third of total EU raw tobacco production, just behind Italy. Greeks and Bulgarians are the heaviest smokers.

Right now on the bike I'd love to light up a Balkan Sobranie or an oval Sullivan Powell Special Turkish Number One, Prustian throwbacks to undergraduate life. For poncing around at parties we flashed around Black Russians with gold tips or the variegated pastel colours of Sobranie Cocktail for effete effect. They were camp alternatives to existentialist untipped Gauloises Caporal with an Asterix helmet on the packet or Gitanes rolled in yellow paper made of corn husks that smouldered forever from a packet graced by a Romani dancer wreathed in smoke. The vending machine in the Junior Common Room had untipped Player's Navy Cut, a decent hit after breakfast. The packet featured Jack (High) Tar, a beardy hipster in a sailor suit with Hero on his cap and sailing ships in the background. Inside the flap was the motto, *it's the tobacco that counts,* punchline of lame jokes. In the women's colleges they smoked Benson and Hedges Gold or Embassy with soapy tasting filters and coupons to collect. They were all a step up from the working man's luscious Woodbines of schooldays in packets of five with an orange and green vegetal motif of the woodland creeper. Further back in time were chocolate cigarettes in the Christmas stocking, not very nice chocolate but a promise of more grown-up treats to come. It's been over thirty years since I last lit up but I could go back to the gaspers tomorrow, except at my age I should probably ease back into it gently. I considered nicotine patches as a transition but these days vaping is probably a better way back to the lovely weed.

We puff across the toxic plains of nostalgia to Katerini. Macedonia's second city seems to have done well out of the tobacco business, modern and prosperous. Colonel Leake found little to say about it either. I take a road to the sea, signposted Olympiaki, and after a couple of kilometres stop for a pee round the back of a deserted house on the edge of a field and take a photo of myself in the wardrobe mirror of a bedroom suite in the front garden. It captures a moment when an old geezer in baggy clothes and a helmet steps out of the wardrobe into the Narnia of a Macedonian littoral, wondering what the hell he's doing there.

Olympiaki

We gasp into the beach resort of Olympiaki, a serried phalanx of holiday flats and hotels, many of them owned and inhabited in summer by South Slavs, a collective name for the citizens of Bulgaria and the countries that used to be in Yugoslavia. Yugo means south in their languages. I find a simple and adequately appointed room for €15. A record! The chambermaid, Dejina, is a shy philosophy student from Leskovac in Serbia, whose claim on our attention is an internationally famous week-long barbecue festival featuring the world's biggest burger. She is disappointed that its fame has slipped me by. She pays for her studies in Belgrade by working here for the summer. Not being in the mood to discuss philosophy, I reminisce about the extraordinary snowfall that brought Belgrade to a halt a few years ago and delighted the white tigers in the zoo and their cubs, who had snow fights. Grandfatherly small talk yields the bonus of an unsolicited toilet roll with the extra pillow I ask for.

I pad barefoot over a patch of weeds to the beach. To be accurate, the resort does not have a beach, the beach has resorts. Along the so-called Olympic Riviera seventy kilometres of sand selvedge the coast from Stomio to Methoni. The sea is choppy and I can't help thinking of the run-off from inland agri-business, although I'm sure the clammy murkiness of the water is to do with the sand being churned up and seaweed carried in by the breeze. Can water be clammy? The *mot* feels *juste* if not technically accurate, and I stick to the breast stroke to keep my mouth out of it. But the dip does its job and I paddle back for a deep untroubled sleep.

By the time I wake up the sun is setting over Mount Olympus. I was looking forward to a wonderful sunset created by the pollution of great lignite-burning power plants in the foothills round the back of the mountain in Ptolomeida. Alas the wind is blowing in the wrong direction so it is only hazy. We have plenty of lovely sunsets to look forward to as the EU has given the Public Power Corporation a grant of €1.75 billion to build two more plants there, using the filthiest coal in Europe. To pay lip service to the battle against global warming they gave Greece free carbon allowances meant to reduce greenhouse gas emissions, if you follow me. Good news for the economy though. Thousands of new jobs will bring prosperity to Western Macedonia, while booming cancer rates and declining life expectancy mean less to pay out in pensions.

The evening promenade is in full dawdle. My fellow flâneurs are mostly South Slavs. Unlike the jolly Greeks gesticulating among them, they take holiday making seriously, quiet and solemn. Restaurants cater for their varied clientèle with a choice of Slavic or Greek names for the same dishes. Nestling among the kebab-kebapi-kebap-chevap joints is a fish taverna. Fresh *gavro,* a tempura-light *fritto misto* of aubergine, courgette and peppers and a tangy chilled white are well worth stepping out of the wardrobe for. My phone is dead so the only entertainment while I wait for the food is watching the girls go by, the world would say like a dirty old man. It's not out of lust, there's not much of that left, but nostalgia. I'm happy for their youth and I'm happy for mine.

The person who looks lustfully at a woman has already committed adultery in his heart (Matthew 5:28) and even if he has not sullied his body is regarded as already guilty.
Saint Symeon Metaphrastis 10th Century The Philokalia

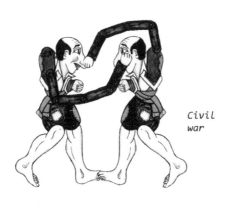

Civil
war

12 OLYMPIAKI TO AGIA TRIADA

There's a blank page in my journal. Only the day and the date. Nothing in the phone. Nothing in the photographs. Nothing in the memory. I was in Olympiaki but that is all I know. I probably stayed there another night because it was cheap. There could not have been any event, experience or thought worth remembering, recording, embellishing or inventing. Breakfast-walk-coffee-sit-down-lunch-lie-down-cup-of-tea-sit-down-dinner-bed. Was there nothing else to this day? Was I really here? Blank. Gone. One day I will stand before The Son of Man on his Throne of Glory, tongue tied, a gormless grin, mind a blank, like meeting the Queen.

"Have you come far?" He will say and turn to the Archangel Gabriel.

"How has he spent the life I gave him? What has this man done for me?"

"Not a lot acksherly." Gabriel will answer.

The Son of Man will raise the finger of judgement saying:

"Heaven does not want you and nor does Hell. You will hang around the gates doing bugger all for eternity with the other *anime triste di coloro che visser sanza 'nfamia e sanza lodo,* as your man Dante puts it, the wretched souls of those who lived without disgrace yet without praise. The Numpties, Fence-Sitters, Time-Wasters, Empty Suits, Don't-Knows, Agnostics, Couldn't-Be-Arsed. The ones with all those blank pages in their journals."

How many days have I got left? Averaging five online life expectancy calculators I should make it to 85. That is about 4,000 days or one day if I don't concentrate on the road. A dozen Christmases. Every wasted day counts, or rather doesn't count.

A worry shared is a worry halved.

"Harley, is there life after death?"

"Vrroom"

"You're right. Nobody knows."

"Vrroom vrroom"

"Thing is, Harley, the 'I' that sees and hears and touches and tastes and is conscious and having this conversation will be extinct along with the pound of jelly inside the skull where it lives. If I have an immortal soul the 'I' won't know anything about it. Goodbye Mole Soul. Have a nice eternal life."

"Vrroom"

"You live in the present. No past. No memories. No guilt. No future either. No anxiety. No hope. You could give classes in mindfulness."

"Vrroom vrroom."

"You're right. There's no point fretting. If it's true it's true and if it's not it's not. I'll find out soon enough."

"Vrroom vrroom"

I know what I do the day after. We take the beach road to Katerini. The town buzzes with the political excitement of a local election. As far as I can tell the central plank of all the candidates' platforms is the site of a new landfill. Competing loudspeakers mounted on pickups tour the streets spouting garbage. They bring back memories of the election we lived through in November 1977, when we lived in Athens.

We enjoyed the razzmatazz of the second election after the collapse of the Junta three years earlier. Demonstrations, marches, loudspeakers blaring over empty streets. Elections are on Sunday. Many Athenians were registered to vote in their family towns and villages. The parties gave away free tickets home to their voters, including flights for the furthest away, and the day off on Monday. A holiday atmosphere livened up the villages but in a deserted Athens the residual fear of a coup was tangible. Shops were boarded up, bars and tavernas closed. Soldiers in jeeps patrolled our posh suburb, tanks and armoured cars were stationed at the main crossroads downtown. It was forbidden to cross Athens. We picked a friend up from the airport and had to get a permit from the police to show at roadblocks.

The rest of the century was dominated by two charismatic politicians from opposite sides of the aisle, Constantine Karamanlis on the right and Andreas Papandreou on the left. Andreas was known by his first name, a sign of his populism and his popularity. They founded their own parties, Karamanlis the centre right New Democracy and Andreas PASOK, the Panhellenic Socialist Movement. They presided over the boom years that brought Greece into the European mainstream and sowed the seeds of its downfall in 2009.

New Democracy won the first post-Junta election in 1974 by a landslide. Karamanlis skilfully neutralised the bitter opposition of left and right. He took the military out of NATO. The Communist Party was legalised. Demotic Greek replaced Katherevousa as the official language. The Colonels and hundreds of officials were put on trial resulting in long jail terms for a handful of ringleaders. A new republican constitution followed a referendum that voted 70 percent to abolish the monarchy. Application to join the European Economic Community was restarted and Greece became a full member in 1981.

Andreas was a rabble-rouser. He promised to join the non-aligned nations, expel American troops, cancel the application to join the European Community, bring socialism to the people. His slogan was 'Change' which he symbolised by wearing a turtleneck to a scandalised Parliament instead of a white shirt and tie. I experienced the Andreas effect at a foreign bankers' meeting, hardly the most sympathetic audience. The word charisma is overused but not in his case. In his trademark turtleneck he charmed the suits.

In the election that we witnessed in 1977 PASOK became the main party of opposition. It spread through the grassroots of the country with shopfront party offices adorned with a green and yellow rising sun. The payoff was victory in the 1981 election. Communist resistance to the occupation was acknowledged and political refugees allowed to return from the Soviet bloc. Veterans of the left became eligible for pensions that had previously been awarded only to collaborators and royalists. Adultery was decriminalised and civil marriage legalised over the expostulations of the church. A national health service was launched.

A new internationalism filtered down to our village. Squeezy pots of mustard and ketchup appeared on taverna tables. In the 1970s, we ate pork at Christmas and Saint Basil brought presents on January 1. In the 1980's Santa Claus muscled in with reindeer, turkey, plastic nativities and snowmen for the mantlepiece. Greece became a destination of migrants as well as a source. Filipinos were among the first. Immigration from Albania was matched by Russia and Ukraine and the Indian subcontinent. Bangladeshi seasonal workers displaced Roma. Families who once had country girls and then Albanians as maids had Russians then Filipinas.

Reneging on Grexit, Andreas milked Brussels for cash to feed his gargantuan social projects. New Democracy had already given wings to patronage, rewarding votes with favouritism. PASOK took it to new heights by ballooning the public sector with make-work jobs and soft pensions. Lax tax collection curried favour with the rest of the electorate. Corruption scandals tripped up ministers and even Andreas stumbled. Politics invaded the streets, schools, universities and workplaces with favouritism, demonstrations, and strikes.

Bill, an American friend newly in Athens, haggled with the owner of a flat he wanted to rent. There were two contracts, one covering half the rent paid in drachmas and the other paid in dollars to an offshore account. This was illegal but standard practice to avoid tax and hedge against the ever depreciating drachma. To collude was against his employer's code of conduct. Bill persevered, groping for arguments why he couldn't do this. Finally he said

"Look, it's illegal for you too, what happens if the tax inspector finds out?"

The landlord twirled his worry beads and slapped them on his leg.

"I am the tax inspector."

In 1996 Andreas died and was succeeded by Costas Simitis, as diffident as Andreas had been brash, a moderniser who preferred technocrats to politicians. His achievements were to take Greece into the eurozone and bring the Olympic Games to Athens. Massive infrastructure investment in transport and public works financed by borrowing at German rates of interest gave a boost to the faltering economy and to immigration of foreign builders. 2004 was the high point of the new millennium. In July Greece won soccer's European Cup in Portugal, a taster of Olympic euphoria. In August the Games opened. They were acclaimed a success, ten billion euros well spent. They were a fillip to national pride and a sign that in little more than twenty years Greece had metamorphosed from a Balkan dictatorship into a respected member of the West's democracies. Normally sceptical and critical, our Greek friends were misty eyed with patriotism and goodwill, proud of themselves and their country and their place in the community of nations. It was a good time to be Greek.

Nea Agathoupoli

On the way out of Katerini I stop for petrol from a grumpy man in his fifties, probably the owner, with groomed grey hair, white summery pullover and a gold chain. Why so glum? I speculate a) hangover b) argument with wife c) argument with girlfriend d) employee not turned up e) anxiety about cancer/HIV/syphilis/blood test f) congenital disposition g) none of the above and you and I will never know the reason as he flits in and out of our lives to be instantly forgotten while he lives out his own life with all its joys and tragedies oblivious of us except that on a bright late summer morning he puts €3 of petrol in Harley's tank in return for the exact change an encounter which he completely forgets within ten minutes unless he is afflicted with total recall so he can relive his life in unreconstructed detail as if he were drowning in a living hell of meaningless experience.

I find by trial and errantry a secondary road to Thessaloniki. After the peripheral traffic peters away on important business among the superstores and furniture outlets, the road is delightful, gently winding and undulating, lit by the morning sun strobing through trees trying on their first autumn colour. Behind them are fields of olives, fruits, crops I can never remember what they are, glinting metal sheds, brown jobs flaffering in the hedges and a hawk soaring in the sky. Further away on the right is the deep blue sea, to the left the mottled foothills of Olympus. A straggle-bearded man in a field leans on a herdsman's stick. We wave and smile to each other, relics from a slower time.

It is 10 o'clock and I've had no breakfast. At the village of Paleo Eleftherochori, adrift in the sea-rolling plain, I pull up at a café on the corner of a crossroads and order a hot Nes. I have to go to the mini-market over the road for something to eat. I point to a *koulouri* rather than ask, just to be on the safe side, and come back with a soft pretzel not a rag rug and distract two young men from their mobile phones with an exchange of views on the Champion's League.

A couple of kilometres further on is the turnoff to the Axio-Loudias-Aliakmonas National Park, not the snappiest of monickers. They are the names of rivers whose conjoined deltas create an extensive wetland, popular with many kinds of bird, home to locals and a lay-over for migrants. Inside the entrance to the park at Nea Agathoupoli is an observation tower with telescopes, binoculars and an enthusiastic warden, a youngish woman keeping middle age at bay with hennaed hair and careful make-up. Through the binos she shows me an egret preening, a cormorant perched on a branch to dry, a marsh harrier, a selection of ducks and out in the bay a flock of brown flamingos. Human fishers in a boat pull up mussels for which the bay is famous. Her mind is not on the job.

"Do you live in London?"

"Sometimes."

"My son is in London for three months. I took him to the airport this morning." Her lip trembles and she looks into a telescope as if she can see him in the distance.

"What is he doing?"

"Erasmus programme. He studies physics." She sniffs and blinks.

"He'll be back before Christmas."

"I don't know where he will live. Is it easy to find a house?"

"In London? Very easy. Lots of nice places." What's the point of telling her the truth?

"I said to take a taxi. He has two cases."

Enormous ones I bet. Packed by a Greek mother. Olive oil in sellotaped plastic bottles, freezer boxes of her stew, moussaka, stifado, feta, cheese pie, spinach pie, baked butter beans, stuffed tomatoes, tzatziki, olives, all leaking into ninety pairs of clean pants, forty five T's, forty five pairs of socks, a score of lovingly laundered shirts. When he opens his cases they will look like a taverna laundry bin at the end of a busy night.

"He will be fine in London. England loves foreigners."

She wipes away a tear and gives my forearm an appreciative squeeze. I escape before I blurt out an empty promise to give him a call and make sure he's all right.

The rivers and marshland have long been an obstacle to roads. The new National Road ploughs on over bridges but my nerves are too delicate to take it. My ornithological adviser mentions a bridge in the marsh that cuts out the hairpin detour I would have to make inland on the old National Road. Harley and I set off down a narrow track to find it. In the next hour or so I become more familiar with the topography of a wetland than I ever hoped to be. Dirt roads, rutted and waterlogged, between beds of reeds and sinister grasses, weave an intricate maze ending up at the same mocking river. Birds wheel unhelpfully above and chirp and flitter unseen in the reeds. Harley coughs in the mud. Wrapped up against a swarm of insects, the more I sweat in swaddling the more attractive I become. Swatting away images of bog bodies and marsh mummies and cerebral malaria I struggle to navigate by shadows cast by the bulrushes. There is no need to panic, only a growing compulsion. After nearly an hour I catch a glimpse of the observation tower. Phew. On dry ground at last I strip off my Invisible Man togs, scrape the mud off my trousers with a stick and with a jaunty wave up to the disconsolate mother resume my journey inland on asphalt.

After a couple of kilometres, where the old National Road crosses the main railway line, is the Café Aeroplano, a concrete two story block with a full-size Douglas DC3 pancaked on the roof. It was bought at auction and lovingly re-assembled there by Mr Ioannides, a motor mechanic, at the beginning of the 1980's. His idea was to bring the glamour of air travel to Macedonians. Kids could play in the cockpit while their parents sat at tables and gazed out of the windows at passing traffic. Disappointingly it is closed, an entertaining folly and a monument to barminess.

The nearest river crossing I can find takes me further north than I would have liked, to Niselli, where a bakery provides a slice of pizza for lunch. I share a table with the baker, about my age, under an outside awning. I force down his indifferent creation out of a paper bag while he munches slices of unappetising nectarine, crunchy as an apple. I open with a *kalimera,* the conventional Queen's Gambit of sociability, which he declines with a grunt. I try the conversational equivalents of the King's Indian, the Ruy Lopez, the Vienna Game, the Caro-Kann, the Grivas - a local boy - finally in desperation the Fried Liver Attack, but he's dour, deaf or depressed. Or fed up with passing writers fishing for material. Later I reflect he may have been up since three and dying to go to bed. His pizza serves its purpose, not so much satisfying the appetite as discouraging it.

After a confusion of junctions we burp along a freshly asphalted and deserted country road signposted to Thessaloniki. Beside us is a rippling tributary of the Aliakmonas River skimmed by insectivorous brown jobs with flashing white tails. It is one of the countless man-made channels that drain the delta to make a fertile plain known for fruit, especially peaches. Regiments of trees are rigorously marshalled so it feels like taking the salute as we pass. We putter as quietly as we can through sleeping villages, a transferred epithet because it is the villagers who are sleeping. Or not: when we lived in Athens the government decreed that all businesses should keep western European hours, 9-5 with an hour for lunch, instead of traditional hours 8-3 followed by lunch and a sleep before getting up again at 6 for coffee. There were massive demonstrations, the main objection, understood but unspoken, being that 3-5 was for sex.

Josif

There are no signposts in the villages but the main road is easy to pick out until we come to a T-junction in the open plain. My paper map was jolted out of the veggie crate by a pothole somewhere. The phone is dead. A Harley Davidson probably has a power adapter and a humidor and a fridge and a Nespresso, a La-z-Boy on wheels after all, but my travelling companion has barely enough leccy for the indicators. So what to do? Ask someone. Not Siri or Alexa but a real person, who feels good about helping a stranger or proud of their special knowledge or entertained by your accent or all the other possible rewards of a simple human interaction, something that Siri and her kind will never know.

Fifty yards up the road is a house with a flat roof and a man in the garden trimming the front hedge and not sleeping or anything more saucy. He is burly and bald, wearing a black pork pie hat several sizes too small, like Mr Potato Head. He welcomes me literally with open arms, glad of the company. My simple greeting unstoppers a deluge of inquiries, reminiscences, comments on the weather and the political situation to which I can only nod and smile as I understand no more than half a dozen words of his Greek. I think his name is Josif and says he comes from Skopje.

If I heard right I am surprised. Skopje is the popular name in Greek for the Republic of North Macedonia. In 1913 at the end of the Balkan Wars it was carved out of historic greater Macedonia and given to Serbia. The rest was given to Greece. During the first half of the twentieth century refugees ebbed and flowed in tides of blood and misery. A population exchange between Greece and Bulgaria launched vigorous Hellenisation. The population exchange of 1923 with Turkey bolstered the Greek population with refugees from Anatolia. In the Metaxas dictatorship of 1936-41 Slavs and their language were oppressed. Linguistic and ethnic

to fate and carry on north in the hope of a sign. We cross the lazy Loudias river by a Bailey bridge with green steel trusses and rattling wooden floorboards. Two men in Public Power Corporation overalls stand on the bank with lift nets a metre square on the end of stout wooden poles, scooping up the catch from the bottom. Their PPC van is parked nearby. They say they are fishing for *kefálopel,* whatever they are. I doubt they put them on their time sheets

One reason I like to travel is to create the illusion of purpose. Bored by this pointless landscape, searching for a narrative where there is none in random events, illusion turns to disillusion. Skating on ice over hidden depths of significance, I suspect it is three inches deep with only concrete underneath like Streatham ice rink. I try to think of evocative descriptions but it's no good. There's nothing I can pin a telling phrase on but flatness and sky and empty musical staves drooping between the bar lines of electricity pylons. Unlike in a book, this one for example, you can't skip over the boring bits in life. Nothing to do but press on.

In a dreamish yellow plain under a monotone sky the melancholy road comes to an end near the intersection of the 1 going north to the border and the 2, running east to Thessaloniki. Under a humming motorway junction on stilts a truck stop, *Open 24 Hours,* is shut and shuttered. It looks Wild Western, all made of grey weathered wood, a porch running the length of it, only the hitching rail is missing. Next to it is a field with over a hundred trucks, equally forlorn, caked mud up to the hubcaps and covered in dust, no other human being in sight. I sit down on the porch and watch the tops of vehicles whizzing past on the flyover above me. An odd way to spend the time but calming.

A stunted one-eyed man in a blue boiler suit creeps out from nearby bushes carrying a child's cot. What is he doing here? Among the questions I should like to ask I settle for the road to Thessaloniki. His directions are easy to remember, a drill sergeant sequence of left-right-left-right-left-right along minor roads that will bring me to the Via Egnatia, the highway from the Adriatic to Istanbul, built two thousand years ago when Gnaeus Egnatius, Roman Governor of Macedonia, immortalised himself.

For the sake of riding the ancient highway I chance my luck on it. Foolish boy. As we get closer to Thessaloniki it becomes more lumpy and potholed, the surroundings more industrial, the traffic denser. Four roaring torrents of filthy metal flutter the hairs on my arms with their slipstream, driving me over the white line at the edge of the road into the rubble of the shoulder. Concentrating on keeping the shiny side up chases any other thoughts from my mind. I opt not to take the inner ring around the city but go straight through it on the Egnatia in the hope that the urban traffic will be slower and the road smoother. Some hope. The buildings close in on either side, radiating heat and reflecting noise. I am hooted at for being too far over left or too far over right. I chicken out of a narrow, twisting overpass and end up on a concrete lane the wrong side of a railway track in a maze of degentrification, hanging doors, broken windows, fly-tipped asbestos, oily smells, women in white chadors and shock-headed dark-skinned men. A kind melon merchant under a flyover puts me right - who buys melons in a wasted land? Then through the centre of the city on the Egnatia with darting pedestrians, slaloming delivery bikers, humphing buses, kamikaze skip lorries, diversions, roadworks, red light starting grids, and onto a drumming three lane rat race before I can turn off into a suburban street and stop and feel dizzy safely and have a drink of warm toilet water. It was all nightmare and terror. But very exciting.

Thessaloniki

We stop at the Queen Street café, spilling out onto the pavement through open glass doors where two streets cross. On the corner made by two kerbs is an immaculate Harley Davidson with silver studded black leather panniers, lustrous yellow paintwork, glittering chrome, an outsize scooped saddle for a big American arse and behind it a pillion perched high up to catapult the passenger over the head of the driver in a head-on. Heritage Softail is written on the front mudguard. It's a bike for tooling up and down the main drag on a Saturday night, cruising up to glitzy cafés, feather dusting at a Harley fan club. We park next to it.

"Don't be cowed, Harley, pity him, tell him how you braved thundering juggernauts and cavernous potholes, consorted with saints, crusaders and janissaries, breasted the heights and breached the forests of Evia, ploughed the waters of Artemision, traversed the blazing plains of Thessaly, ran the velvet gauntlet of the Muses of Tempe, scaled divine Olympus as far as wheels can go, and tomorrow will gaze on the Holy Mountain of the All Blessed. He is a toyboy, Harley, you are a hero."

Over a restorative cheese pie and a refreshing iced Nes I consider Thessaloniki, Greece's second city. I could stay a night or two in a scruffy hotel I know in the centre on the Egnatia; stroll down the wide, majestic Aristotelous Square to the sea front; wander the picturesque streets of old Jewish Ladadika and browse all manner of delicatessen in its redolent shops; gorge on pork and aubergines at the excellent Negroponte Restaurant, started by two lads from Halkida. Thessaloniki is second only to Athens as a hotbed of music and a first stop after dinner would be a cool music bar I know near the Forum. Last time I was here the Ukulele Society of Thessaloniki was jamming George Formby hits, a surprise but no more than dropping into a London pub and finding bouzoukis and baglamas twanging rebetiko.

With my little ukulele in my hand,
Of course the people do not understand
Some say why don't you be a scout, why don't you read a book?
But I get lots more pleasure when I'm playing with my uke.

I should like to know if Thessalonian ukulelists get the double-entendre.

Then tomorrow morning one of the finest archaeological museums I know in Greece, not because of the artefacts but because it is the best explanation and evocation of ancient Greek life and art and politics I know.

The museum also displays the first book in Europe, the Derveni papyrus, dating from the end of the fifth century BC and discovered in 1962 when they were building the National Road. It had been put on a funeral pyre, part of it consumed by the flames and the rest carbonised. Black ink on black paper needed fancy photography to decipher. Scholars are still working on piecing together the fragments and arguing about what order they come in, the date of the text, its significance, its likely author, and above all, what it means. It seems to be a treatise on a poem about Orphic initiation rites. It allegorises creation myths and the nature of the Olympian Gods and explains them in terms of the philosophy and science of the day. Abstruse for most of us, but there are some interesting snippets. For example the author says there is only one all-powerful God, who is Mind, the creator of all things and living within them.

I wonder what the author of the papyrus would think of the annual miracle of Thessaloniki's most revered son, Saint Demetrios the Myrrh Gusher. Non-Orthodox can be forgiven for confusing him with Saint George as both of them are depicted as soldiers on horses spearing the enemy on the ground. George's horse is white and he is killing a dragon. Demetrios's is red and he is killing a man, usually in armour and uncertainly identified. Both saints lived and were martyred during the great persecution of the Emperor Diocletian. The lives of both are confused and probably fictional, not that you would gather from the biographies on ecclesiastical web pages. There's no point in debunking them, so firmly have they taken root in the human need to believe, and none more rooted than the miracle of the myrrh that gushes from Demetrios's relics every year on his feast day, 26 October.

The event takes place in the magnificent early Byzantine basilica that has survived more or less in its present form since the end of the seventh century. Demetrios's bones have never been discovered and his silver casket might contain his scarf and his ring, what you now know are relics second class, but no less potent for that. The casket is carried out from its shrine into the middle of the packed church. At the culmination of the liturgy the Archbishop fumbles with a set of silver keys to unlock a hatch in the top to release the powerful scent of coffee-coloured myrrh that unguents the inside. Priests mop it up with cotton wool balls and hand it out to the faithful crowding around them, a manifestation of the divine and a powerful cure-all. So explain that, you sceptics.

I decide to put the museum, the basilica, the Forum, the Arch of Galerius, the house where Kemal Ataturk, founder of modern Turkey, was born, the tavernas and bouzoukis and ukuleles and all the other attractions of Thessaloniki on The List. The city is hot, polluted, and noisy, too much concrete and not enough green. I sign into the café wifi and find a room in a beach resort along the bay south of here.

Agia Triada

Agia Triada is ten kilometres as the seagull flies across the bay from Thessaloniki. This side of the bay is a long beach carved up between a succession of resorts, a wonderful amenity for the Thessalonians. The sand has a greyish alluvial look to it but is pleasant enough. Unlike most tideless Greek beaches that shelve quickly down a few metres from the water's edge, the sea here is shallow for a hundred yards, a plod to get deep enough but without the nagging anxiety of getting a cramp out of your depth. I bob about, letting the dust and stress of the day wash away and consider giving up the whole Athos idea and staying for a week or so. I dry off on a lounger and watch the city across the water sprawling white like fungus up the hills behind and along the shore.

Poor Thessaloniki, whited sepulchre washed in a blood dark sea. In 1941 the spreading stain on the conscience of Europe arrived at its gates. In 1943 55,000 Jews were made to buy one-way rail tickets to Auschwitz and Treblinka. The Sephardic city of Europe was annihilated.

In the rest of Greece another 30,000 Jews were deported to death camps by Germans, Bulgarians and Greek collaborators. Some were saved by courageous mayors, police, clergy, friends and neighbours. In Zakynthos the Archbishop and the Mayor were told by the German commander to bring back a list of Jews on the island. They came back with two names, their own. In Athens the Archbishop publicly defied the German commander and the police chief issued 1500 false identity cards. The father of our friend, an engineer, had official business in the Peloponnese. Each time he went he smuggled Jews in his car from Athens into the Italian zone. Others fled into the mountains and joined the resistance.

After the war most survivors emigrated to Israel and the USA. Many who came back found their homes expropriated by refugees, their property confiscated. A thousand or so still live in Thessaloniki, more in Athens, a few in the cities like Halkida and Ioannina. The island communities like Corfu and Rhodes are gone. Europe is demeaned and depleted.

Thanassis is my hotelier. His bulk fills a padded throne behind his desk like mousse in a mould. He spends the day watching foot/hand/basketball on TV and keeping a beady eye open for the heinous smuggling of room towels to the beach. He struggles to reconcile my old biker's bandy-legged shuffle, matching geriatric bike, Irish passport, Evian address and Athonite aspirations, gives up and takes a €5 deposit for a beach towel. If not world-weary, Thanassis is hotel-weary, doing the minimum to keep the enterprise going. It's fine for me. A lawn in front and a glassed-in terrace are an improvement over what I am used to. A few drooping brochures in English and a dog-eared poster or two advertise excursions to places like Meteora. I have a fancy black tile bathroom to wash my vest, pants, elastic stockings, knee bandages, ankle bandage, arch supports, wrist bandage, and a drying rack on the balcony to hang them out on. Wrapped in a sheet and contemplating a picture on the wall of a Norwegian fjord I sink gratefully into sleep.

Thanassis only provides breakfast so at nightfall I go foraging along the front. I opt for what claims to be a family-run taverna with traditional recipes handed down through generations of grandmothers. I have my usual - aubergine salad, boiled and oiled weeds, *gavro*. Tucking in I feel a wave of sympathy for generations of grandchildren and suspect they took every opportunity to eat at other people's houses. It is the worst aubergine salad I've had since I first tried making it myself forty years ago, the greens are boiled to a consistency of tinned spinach and the anchovies that came suspiciously fast to the table, taste pre-fried from frozen in a batch that morning and finished off just now in end-of-the-day oil. The bread is OK and they can't do much with a bottle of Mythos beer except serve it warm. My mistake was choosing a seafront joint squeezed in between glitzy cafés with sofas and skimpily dressed waitresses. A seasoned tourist knows to look in the side streets for a dowdy joint with uncomfortable chairs and no view, where the locals go.

Grumbling to myself I get back to the hotel and decide to stay a second night, if only to make sure my washing gets properly dry.

No pleasure is a bad thing in itself, but the things which produce certain pleasures entail annoyances many times greater than the pleasures themselves. - Epicurus

13 AGIA TRIADA TO OURANOUPOLI

I wake up early and read the *Philokalia* before breakfast, a mistake as it takes the zip out of the morning. I'm on holiday for a day. No rush, breakfast at 9, omelette, *tost*, yoghurt and honey, cake and honey, tea and honey. I smuggle a plate of tomato and cucumber salad and half the *tost* upstairs for lunch. The rest of the day is idled away between sleeping, swimming, sunbathing, lounging, strolling along the front past the Holy Trinity church, after whom the place is named, to ragged cliffs at the end of the beach where sociable stray dogs make camp. I try to read improving books on Kindle about the monastic life I am about to sample again but after a few pages doze off in the sunshine.

I have a listless swim in the shallow sea and lie on a sunbed watching sporty types play paddleball. It cannot be classified as a sport or a game because there are no rules and no scoring. The principle is to bat a tennis ball to each other as many times as possible with wooden paddles. The idea is to keep it going. When you smash the ball or make a zinging return of the other player's smash it is not to beat them but to demonstrate your prowess. If you force them into an error both of you suffer. To win is to lose. Cooperation combined with demonstrating superiority is at the heart of Greek life. You collaborate and compete at the same time.

I have an ouzo in the lobby to prepare for dinner, chatting to Thanassis behind his desk over the noise of basketball on the TV. We have to shout so it seems as if we are arguing but most Greek conversations sound like this. We discuss the perfect *bougatsa* and the relative merits of the Ioannina and Thessaloniki varieties. Greeks talk about food like the British talk about the weather.

We move on to the Euro Crisis, Bailouts, Austerity, that Thanassis blames for the downturn in his business. British, Germans, Americans, Turks, Albanians, Catholics, Muslims, were all blamed at one time or another for Greece's disasters. This time men in the Horio café shouted at the TV that Italy wanted the olives, France wanted Aegean gas, Germany wanted the sunshine. Thanassis says something I have not heard from a Greek in forty years.

"It is our fault."

In 2001 Greece joined the eurozone under false pretences, concealing the true size of the budget deficit, trade deficit and debt. It mined the bonanza of subsidies and credit at German interest rates. International banks queued up to lend, domestic banks expanded, businesses took on easy loans. Motorways, railways, trams, metro lines and a brand new airport fuelled a country-wide building boom. The populace was showered with credit cards and mortgages. Until then Greeks were inveterate savers. If you built a house you borrowed from family or saved up for the ground floor then waited until you had the money for the second floor. Seduced by easy money they now clocked up unsustainable debt.

In 2005 the government confessed to fudging the numbers. The European Commission placed the country under 'fiscal monitoring.' The global financial system began to unravel in 2007 as a result of various banking crises. In 2009 Greece could no longer borrow on international financial markets to roll over existing debt and to finance a ballooning budget deficit. In return for bailouts by the Troika - the International Monetary Fund, the European Central Bank and the European Union - the government inflicted fourteen austerity packages between 2010 and 2017. They included public pay cuts, layoffs, tax rises, pension cuts, retirement age increases, cuts in health and defence spending, privatisations, bank mergers, deregulation of monopoly professions like pharmacies and taxis, and more besides. It created a downward spiral of recession as employment and tax revenues collapsed, leading to pressure for still more cuts. The economy shrank by 25 percent, a collapse paralleled only in wartime. Businesses failed and unemployment soared to 27 percent, 40 percent for young people. Anger ignited street riots, strikes, fire bombings, violence and suicides.

Bailouts came to an end in 2018. The Troika left Athens but tough budget rules remain for the next decade or more. The situation has stabilised because it can hardly get much worse. The poor have become poorer while the middle class struggles under a growing burden of taxes, static wages, lower property values. Children of our friends in the village have emigrated, among the 700,000, over 6 percent of the population, who went abroad since 2010. In the past emigrants were agricultural and manual workers feeding the appetites of the New World. These days 90 percent have degrees. 18,000 are doctors. In Horio we are not kept awake throughout Saturday nights by wedding music booming over the countryside as those who stay can't afford to marry. There are fewer baptisms but the burial business stays buoyant. Deaths nationwide outnumber births.

The pain is not only economic. It is an assault on personal and national *philotimo*, self-respect and the respect of others. Greeks are proud of being European and Europe has turned against them. Demeaned by the Troika, insulted by ministers of German and other European governments, pilloried by the foreign press, it was a humiliation.

Dinner this time is in an ouzeri on a side street with fishing nets on the walls, a table for one shoved up against a pillar, a plump lady wiping her hands on a fishy apron. She brings water, bread and half a litre of white and slips a till receipt under the ashtray, €7 fodder for the tax inspector. The rest I will pay for in cash. Automated systems have not suppressed tax evasion, just make it more complicated. A popular explanation is historical conditioning - Greeks hated to give money to Turks, Bavarians, Nazis, foreign banks, Merkel. They mainly hate giving money to other Greeks, especially the ethically challenged who govern them.

Sitting on the terrace of our house in Horio after breakfast some years ago we watched Mikos leading his horse up the hill with jerrycans of water for his sheep. I invited him for a slug of duty-free McSporran and a couple of Marlboro that would keep us in tomatoes for a few days. He brimmed with good spirits, not out of the glass but because his son just got into the police academy. Nikos was a charming lad, who we watched grow up from stoning frogs to galloping bareback in search of lost sheep. Mikos told us a complicated story about the *meson* and the *fakelakia* he deployed.

Meson, contacts, is the glue that binds communities. People rely on who they know and who owes them a favour for advancement and advantage. Reciprocated favours, sweeteners, family ties, old schoolmates, friends of friends, things also known in the sanctimonious north, are expected in the Mediterranean. Want your son to have a cushy office job in Athens for his military service instead of staring at the Turkish coast from a cliff on Samos? *Meson* at the Ministry of National Defence. A paid internship for your daughter? *Meson* at Head Office. Need a building permit for a house you built last year? *Meson* at the town hall. *Fakelaki* means little envelope and contains cash, a top-up for the underpaid functionary or a tax-free incentive for the professional. Friends from Horio who were sent to London for hospital care did not believe that they did not have to slip the consultant a *fakelaki* and suspected they were not getting the best service. Foreigners in Greece usually don't know the etiquette or the going rate or are too embarrassed, so best to find a local go-between. The *fakelaki* is grease, paying people to do what they are supposed to do. Bribery is for what they are not supposed to do. Every so often a corruption scandal hits headlines, dirt is thrown, libel writs issued, investigations begun, arrests made - often of the investigative journalists and whistleblowers. With a handful of exceptions when eye-watering commissions and kick-backs cannot be ignored, complicit politicians and compliant judges ensure that stories fizzle out for want of hard evidence or because the five year statute of limitations is up. The effect is to distort and depress the economy.

Whatever their responsibility for the Crisis our friends pay an exorbitant price for it. Irresponsible borrowing, fraud, tax evasion, outlandish pensions, and the rest of the victim blaming hardly justify the misery inflicted on them. They are also paying for their government's mismanagement, politicians' corruption, exploitation by foreign banks, bribery by foreign multinationals and arms suppliers, and the fundamental flaws and inequities of the Euro.

Lightly grilled octopus, aubergines fried to perfection and a dish of perfumed courgettes make up for the previous evening's coarse dining experience. When I get back to the hotel I settle up with Thanassis as I'm going to leave early in the morning. He gives me a euro and asks me to light a candle for him and wishes me a good pilgrimage. I am touched. He doesn't give me a discount though.

Migrants

With a light heart and laundered orthopaedics I am on the road at 7.30 the next morning, heading along the bay towards Thessaloniki against a bitter north wind and the sun in my eyes. Just past the airport, chilled, dazzled and disoriented, I get lost in a curlicue of junctions and end up in the suburban satellite of Thermi. Stopping at a café for a hot Nes, a *koulouri* and directions from the obliging cafetier, I take my bag into the lavatory and come out wearing two T-shirts, two long sleeved shirts and a fleece.

The directions prove inadequate so I succumb to the digital temptation of Google Maps and its bossy Miss Directions. I am grudgingly converted as she guides me through the asphalt doodle of Thermi until we hit a noisy main road and I can't hear her voice from inside my top pocket. When I stop to consult her she sulks in silence and I can't see the screen for the sun. I also can't cope with the way the map swivels so the direction arrow always points up. It reminds me of persons I am close to, who have to turn a map round so it points in the direction they are going. Anyway, I turn it off because it drains the battery. I ask directions from drivers at red traffic lights, which is more satisfactory.

In any case I'm put off by the robominatrix in the phone. When I hear Miss Directions and her digital sisters I imagine what she would be like in real life, perhaps a granny womanning a sex line in a bulging pink nightie and curlers on the sofa scarfing diet coke and donuts watching the shopping channel on silent while she turns on a programmer on the other end. Her male colleague Mister Turning is no better. His confident bonhomie sound like he's about to sell me a pyramid scheme.

At last we tootle along the straight road into the peninsula of Halkidiki. The name comes from the ancient city of Halkida in Evia, which colonised the peninsula in Homeric times. It is like a hand with three fingers and we are heading for the top one. The other two are known for more secular pleasures, the four s's, sun, sea, sand and the one I'd better not mention on a pilgrimage. On this last day of the journey I am more nervous than ever with so-near-yet-so-far syndrome.

My *diamonitirion,* my visa for Athos, begins tomorrow so there is no leeway for delay.

On the two lane road I build up a procession of vehicles behind me between places where I can pull over to let them pass. At one of the pit stops I park beside a chainlink fence and peer through rusty rhomboids at empty chicken sheds that once housed over a thousand Syrian and Iraqi refugees. It opened in 2016 for migrants bussed down from an encampment at an EKO gas station near the northern frontier when North Macedonia cut off the route to the north. It was run by the military in conditions no soldier would tolerate. People lived in tents inside the massive sheds. In high summer there was no running water, rudimentary sanitation, no kitchens, occasional electricity, the stink of chicken shit no hose or bleach could dispel. With volunteers and donations they themselves recreated the EKO Project with school, library, language lessons, playgrounds in nearby land lent by the local papas. It was closed at the end of 2017, the inhabitants shipped to another battery.

The EU has paid Greece some €1.5 billion to help with refugees. Where did it go? Surely not to ministers and officials and their friendly contractors. Accused of siphoning it off the Defence Minister filed a libel suit in late 2018 against a newspaper alleging mishandling of EU funds meant for refugee camps, so he was obviously innocent, unlike the three journalists he had arrested in handcuffs. Four days later, the Greek Supreme Court ordered an inquiry into the handling of European funds paid to assist the country with the refugee crisis. Fat chance that will get anywhere. But we must not be quick to assume corruption. Incompetence and mismanagement may also be to blame.

However honestly they spent money the government would have been overwhelmed. In 2015 and 2016 a million migrants came into Greece before the northern borders were closed. The flow was also reduced in March 2016 by the EU agreement with Turkey to send back 'irregular migrants' in exchange for 'vulnerable' asylum seekers in return for €6 billion, visa-free travel for Turks and resumption of the EU accession process. Both sides have been dragging their feet and accusing each other. Only half the cash inducement has been paid. The numbers are on the rise again. 32,000 came into Greece in 2018 and 50,000 in 2019. Greece is a holding pen for some 70,000 registered refugees and migrants. Over 1,000 unaccompanied minors are held in appropriate facilities, another 4,000 in detention centres or living on the street, prey to pimps and paedophiles. Who knows how many unregistered people are scratching a living and finding smugglers to get away? Almost all want to leave for northern Europe where they have family or the chance of work. Some are stuck in Greece for ever. Arfa does work for a charity called Last Rights that tries to identify the drowned, register the deaths, inform bereaved families, give them burial. In 2019 there were about 1,000, many of them children.

In contrast with the authorities Greek individuals do their best to help. By spring of 2015 5,000 refugees a month were landing on Lesbos alone. Local volunteers were on hand at all hours with meals, clothing and shelter, medicines, toiletries. One family dried shoes soaked in the sea, another collected dirty clothes and took them back laundered next day. Hoteliers donated rooms and bedding, drivers gave them lifts in their cars until they were arrested for trafficking. One evening a week a taverna gave them an evening out with a meal and music. Parishes ran soup kitchens and clothing stores. Young Greek lawyers, activists, teachers, nurses, interpreters, work tirelessly to help, although they are paid a fraction of international agency workers parachuted in. There are now over 70 ethnicities on the island, mainly Syrian, Afghan and Iraqi but also from all over Africa and even Central America.

The refugee crisis came on the heels of the economic crisis. Some residents complain that the influx is bad for tourism and fascists stir up trouble on the street. An argument against making conditions more tolerable, in Greece and elsewhere, is that it encourages people to come. The fallacy is that however bad you make it, it's hard to make it worse than where they are coming from. I suppose if you inflicted famine and drought on the camps, denied them medical supplies, raped a few women and dropped a barrel bomb every now and then, it would persuade people not to pay predatory bandits to cross war zones at night, deserts on foot, seas in rubber boats to come and live in tents, containers and chicken sheds.

In 2019 the New Democracy government came up with more practical solutions. It opened new tented camps in military bases, for example in Corinth, too far away from the city to offend the citizens or for children to get to school. Legislation giving access to national health care for foreigners from non-EU countries has been cancelled. This leaves them prey to illness and epidemics and prevents children going to school, for which they need a health care number. In Athens police put on a big show for the media with helicopters and armed police evicting migrant squats in downtown Athens. A police spokesman said the operation was like a "silent vacuum cleaner" that "will gradually suck up all the garbage". After protests from local residents the remarks were retracted.

El Dorado

Sharing angry thoughts with Harley, as much about Britain and the rest of Europe as Greece, tinged with guilt that I don't put my energies where my mouth is, I come to a fork in the road just before Agios Prodromos. We take the left prong, heart leaping to see the first sign for The Holy Mountain. The road goes uphill and is even narrower now but I am second in the procession behind a long truck loaded a dozen racks high with live poultry and enveloping us in a miasma of diesel and chicken shit. It stops in a village, and I carry on uphill, no longer mouth breathing. Like a worried parent with a sickly child I take Harley's every gasp and grunt and whimper to heart as he labours in second. At last we reach a parking lot with a view that marks the summit and he can get his breath back while I strip off layers of clothing and wave my arms about under the delusion that this modest exercise does me good. This is not the first laborious hill we have to climb, not the first stuttering descent. With each one, Athos seems to get further away not nearer.

We are now in Greece's El Dorado, where people have been grubbing for gold and silver since classical times. The silver for our Alexander's coin probably came from here. The Ottomans called it the *Mademochoria*, the mining villages. The mint at *Siderokafsia*, 'blast furnace', was one of the three most important along with Cairo and Istanbul. At the beginning of the sixteenth century Suleiman the Magnificent brought in six thousand mine workers, numbering Turks, Jews, Serbs and Gypsies. They made Suleiman's gold *sultani*. Being Islamic they have no pictures but are covered both sides in bewitching Ottoman script and decorations, including a gorgeous *tughra*, the ornamental monogram of the reigning sultan.

I say El Dorado knowingly because it is the name of the Canadian mining company that bought the three surviving mines of Halkidiki in 2012 for two billion dollars. Eldorado is the biggest foreign investor in Greece and has ambitious plans for expanding its operations. They have already spent a billion on construction and remediation of the facilities and employ two thousand people. The curse of gold has sown dissension among miners, hoteliers, farmers, populist politicians, and ordinary people who value clean water and fresh air. There have been violent demonstrations on both sides of the jobs-versus-environment dilemma, here and in Athens. Torn between its two constituencies, the Greek government has been dragging its heels to sign the necessary approvals. Eldorado has resorted to the usual blah-blah about environmental sensitivity along with lawsuits, and at the end of 2017, threats to mothball operations.

In 2020 the newly elected New Democracy government broke the stalemate and approved test drilling and investment. For the time being we can putter along between the trees, the air free from arsenic dust, the water clear of mercury, the road empty of ore trucks, the livid scars of the mines hidden in the mountains, if not from Google Satellite. The thousands of jobs at stake, the foreign investment crisis, the ten percent arsenic content of the ore, the hazardous waste dam on top of a seismic fault, the untried flash smelting technology... it's not my problem. I'm a tourist. I pay to escape from that kind of thing at home and live for a time in a happy world of entertainment and pleasure, free from earworms of worry.

I put such thoughts out of mind by focussing on the benefits of biking, the world you miss in a car or bus, the richness of experience it brings. I feel I know every blade of grass, every stone, every tree I've passed. Some experiences are richer than others, for example the bouquet of roadkill dog on a hot day. I am now a connoisseur - first day tart and zesty, second day flamboyant and on-the-nose, third day the peak of pungency with chewy tannins and an earthy mouthfeel. Tyro tasters should take short sniffs to avoid the gagging reflex.

I stop for coffee in the main square of the most important of the Ottoman mining villages, Arnaia. The houses are traditionally Macedonian, built of stone, some of them three or four stories, with wooden overhanging balconies. One of them announces that it was a working smithy until 1992, another that it housed a family making kilims on an old-fashioned wooden loom until a few years ago. That life is all gone now, ossified in the folklore museum, houses for mining executives and second homes for Thessalonians.

We follow the road past the underground silver mines of Stratoni. Before reaching the port where metal was shipped to Istanbul and now there is a processing plant, we turn right and over a ridge into the next valley through pines and glimpses of the sea, sniffing resin and salt through petrol and dust.

The port of Ierissos serves the north coast of Athos but is not much used. The exposed shore means boats can be cancelled because of rough seas. We press on to the neck of the Athos peninsula at Nea Roda. Here the Persian King of Kings Xerxes had a canal dug to Tripiti on the other side in 483 BC. He was preparing an invasion of Greece and wanted a short cut for his fleet so it would not have to sail round the rocks, currents and winds at the end of the peninsula, where ships of his father Darius perished ten years before. It took three years to excavate, was two kilometres long and wide enough for two triremes. Darius's invasion ended badly for him at the battle of Marathon. Xerxes' came to grief at the battles of Salamis and Plateia.

I stop on the verge by a sign advertising the canal and look for it, proving to myself that its outline can only be seen from the air. It was a grandiose white elephant. Herodotus thought Xerxes could more easily have dragged his ships across the isthmus but wanted to show off with a memorial to himself. Perhaps he wanted to teach Athos a lesson, just as he had ordered the sea to be whipped when a storm blew away his bridge across the Hellespont. Once the fleet was through, the canal was never used again. Athos enjoyed its new status as an island for a decade or so before it silted up.

At Tripiti the road turns left along the shore, between the sea and gentle hills planted with hotels and holiday homes, to

Ouranoupoli. City of The Heavens, gateway to the other world of monastic Athos, is the end of one journey and the beginning of another. Having travelled through time and space on Harley, it is time to leave him behind and take a dip in another dimension.

Orthodoxy

A word for those hazy about Orthodoxy. The Orthodox Church, also known as the Eastern Orthodox church should not be confused with the Oriental Orthodox Church, a separate entity comprising mainly Copts, Armenians, Syriacs and Ethiopians. There are about 260 million Eastern Orthodox Christians worldwide of whom Russia has 100 million. Ukraine 30 million, Romania 16 million and Greece 10 million. The remaining 100 million or so are distributed among the former Soviet Union, the Balkans and the diaspora. About 10 percent of the EU population is Orthodox. Serbia and Greece have the largest proportion of Orthodox in their populations, over 95 percent. These are census figures so do not necessarily reflect belief or church attendance.

The Orthodox Church is not a centralised institution. It is a federation of independent entities - in the jargon a Communion of Autocephalous churches - that share the same faith. It has no Pope, no Head, no central authority. Matters of faith and practice were agreed in seven Ecumenical Councils, the last in 787AD. Any change in doctrine can only be made by all the churches agreeing. Ecumenical is another jargon word. It does not mean different denominations getting together to find some sort of unity, as in the ecumenical movement, but universal, speaking to the whole world. Autocephalous churches can choose their own language of worship. Some have opted for ancient versions, like New Testament Greek in Greece and Church Slavonic in Slavic speaking countries. Others have opted for the modern vernacular, like Romania, Georgia and America.

In 1054 Cardinal Humbert went from Rome to Constantinople on an undiplomatic mission that ended with him slapping down on the altar of Hagia Sofia a Papal Bull, technical term for an edict, excommunicating the Patriarch. This was immediately reciprocated. The rock on which Christ built his church was split down the middle. The Great Schism partly resulted from disputed doctrine like the *filioque* that Catholics added to the Creed. They maintain that the Holy Spirit comes from God and Christ together, *'proceeds from the Father and the Son'* while Orthodox maintain he comes from God only. Disputes like this seasoned the competition between the Eastern and Western Roman empires for political and religious jurisdiction in the Mediterranean, Mesopotamia and North Africa. There have been several attempts at reconciliation since 1960, resisted by those on both sides, who consider themselves guardians of the one true faith. Dialogue with the Anglican church was more lively until the ordination of women killed it off.

In the Ottoman Empire religion was the most important element of individual identity. During the Greek Revolution religion defined which side you were on. Those caught up in the struggle saw themselves as Christians or Muslims fighting for their faith, whatever their language or ethnicity. In the exchange of populations between Greece and Turkey in 1923, being Orthodox or Muslim decided who was Greek and who was Turk, rather than language or geography or self-identification. Christians who spoke Turkish were exchanged for Muslims who spoke only Greek. Protestant Greeks in Turkey were excluded from the exchange, although most went voluntarily.

For historical reasons most of Greece comes under the jurisdiction of the Archbishop of Athens, head of the independent Greek church, while Athos, Crete and the twenty six Dodecanese islands clustered around Rhodes come under the Patriarch of Constantinople. In the Greek Constitution Orthodoxy is termed the 'prevailing' religion and strives to prevail in political and social matters as well as religious. While the church is governed by the Holy Synod, of which the president is the Archbishop of Athens, it is answerable to the Ministry of Education, Research and Religious Affairs. The salaries and pensions of the approximately 10,000 clergy are paid by the state. There is no passing round the plate as the congregation has already paid through their taxes.

Go into an Orthodox church during the liturgy. The main difference with western churches is the icon screen between the nave and the sanctuary. The key part of the liturgy takes place behind it, hidden from the congregation, enhancing its mystery. Other differences include what to a western-trained ear is discordant chanting by a cantor or two. They and the priest chant most of the service. The majority of the congregation stands, the elderly and infirm propped up in stalls round the edge. They do not join in hymns or responses except for the frequent *amin* and *kyrie eleison*. The conventional western way to pray is kneeling down, scrunched up, head bowed and eyes closed, communing with an internal presence. Orthodox stand to pray with their eyes open, lighting candles, kissing icons, making the sign of the cross. Communion is taken in both kinds from a little spoon dipped in the chalice. At the end of the liturgy chunks of bread, *antídoron,* are handed out to everyone as they leave, Christian or not. It is blessed but not consecrated.

Western Christianity is a religion of the mind, Orthodoxy a religion of the heart, says the old cliché. Orthodoxy is mystical, symbolic, intuitive. Worship is tactile, oriented around ritual activities. God intervenes in everyday life with miracles. The Mother of God and to a lesser extent saints intercede with Him for favours. Faced with life-changing events - illness, accident, marriage, childbirth, examinations, promotion - you can go to a shop selling religious articles and buy a *tama*, an ex-voto, a tin or silver plaque with an image representing what you are asking for to hang on an icon.

Religion has been an anchor for people adrift, isolated, living precarious lives in Greece's history of turmoil and upheaval. For individuals, families and interest groups constantly competing with each other it is constant that binds them together.

Religiosity imbues daily life. Shops, cafés, tavernas, buses, and cars are protected by blessings and icons. People of all ages cross themselves when they pass churches, although why they favour some and not others is a mystery to the outsider. Priests grace civic and social events. In the countryside little churches proliferate. Most host a liturgy at least once a year. In the evening the cemetery in our village twinkles prettily with oil lamps lit on every grave. Bereaved people offer *koliva* to passers-by in memory of a relative, ancient food for the dead and Dionysos, lord of the underworld, now a symbol of the Resurrection: boiled wheat, pomegranate seeds, sesame seeds, ground almonds, cinnamon, sugar, raisins.

The traditions and values of Orthodox practice permeate secular behaviours. Intercession and favour, pleading and indulgence, reciprocal favours, hospitality and community, belief in self worth, resilience in misfortune and hope for the future, the long wake of history, the sense of being chosen as guardians of the one true faith, the mingling of natural and divine, all these spill out into the secular world.

The ceremony of the 2004 Olympic Games ended in a massive double helix. One strand in the DNA of Greek identity is culture from the age of myth to the present. The other is religion, not only its institutions, which are part of history, but shared beliefs. It is an essential element of Greek identity and I hope I can get closer to it on Athos, its spiritual home.

Ouranoupoli

We stutter along the main street down a gentle hill to the sea front past hotels, restaurants, cafés, mini-markets, souvenir shops and windows glittering with icons and gold. Advertisements are written in Cyrillic and Greek and Roman script. The town is multilingual in the languages of Orthodoxy: Greek, Russian, Serbian, Bulgarian, Romanian. Flocks of pilgrims, sometimes shepherded by a cleric, wander the streets, huddle in cafés, sit soberly at taverna tables.

We park in a spacious square where buses turn beside the fourteenth century Byzantine Tower, landmark and logo of the town. It is known as the Loch Tower, after its last residents Joice and Sidney Loch. They were a formidable Australian couple, who spent a lifetime working with refugees from two world wars. In 1922 they moved into the tower and were joined the following year by refugees of the Exchange of Populations. After Sidney died in 1955 Joice set up a rug weaving business to bring income to the women of the village. Her autobiography, *A Fringe of Blue*, and Sidney's *Athos: The Holy Mountain* are evocative glimpses of Athos and post-War Greece Until she died in 1984 the tower was open house to many on their way to the mountain.

Until 1923 monks lived in the tower. Athos extended to the neck of the peninsula, where Xerxes dug his canal. The government appropriated the land up to the present border for refugees. In 1946 the name of their village was changed from Pyrgos, Tower, to Ouranoupoli, an ancient city on the other side of the peninsula. In 1959 the villagers took up shovels and made their own road to Ierissos. Until then most travellers came overnight to Athos by sea from Thessaloniki.

A simple room at the Hotel Zeus is a haven of luxury compared with the monastic accommodations ahead. I drop my bags and meander down to the town beach to join a shoal of other well-larded pilgrims swimming on the spot against a choppy onshore sea. This is the last swim we shall have before taking the ferry. Famous travellers like Robert Byron took dips on Athos, but since then swimming is prohibited, to avoid the carnal temptations of naked skin. I let myself be washed up on the sand to dry off and give my sinful flesh a last taste of the sun. On the way back I stock up with peanuts and chocolate in a crowded mini-market. Packets branded in various scripts jostle with icons, religious gew-gaws, souvenirs, sun cream and beach toys.

Before dinner there is time for a mile hike along the shore to the perimeter wall of the Autonomous State of the Holy Mountain. For much of its thousand year history, power and influence was contested by Greek, Serbian, Russian and other Slavic monarchs. Beginning with the liberation of Northern Greece from the Ottomans in the Balkan Wars of 1912/13, Athos gradually came under Greek sovereignty that was finally given international recognition in 1923. Public order is the responsibility of the Republic of Greece, which provides a police force and a fire service integrated with those of the rest of the country. The Greek Foreign Ministry appoints a resident civil governor. Whatever their original nationality, monks admitted to one of the twenty monasteries automatically become citizens of Greece.

In most other respects Athos is independent. The monasteries own the territory and appoint the Holy Council with an executive committee of four abbots. Much of their work is reconciling the ways of the outside world with a traditional way of life. For example, Athos sticks to the calendar and time-keeping of Byzantium. The monks live by the Julian Calendar that was replaced for the rest of us by the Gregorian in 1582. They are thirteen days behind. If you think you are going for the Easter festivities you may find yourself fasting for Lent. The day begins at sunset so times of liturgies and meals change according to the season. To avoid confusion in practical matters, like what date your visa is for or what time the ferry leaves, a concession is made to standard timekeeping. Many monasteries have two clocks showing secular and monastic time.

Although legally part of the European Union, Athos is exempt from freedom of movement and anti-discrimination legislation, so it can issue visas and remove temptation from monks by banning female animals and women. In Greek law a woman trespassing on Athos is liable to an automatic prison sentence of two to twelve months. An exception is made for cats to keep the mice down and hens for eggs to eat and to make tempera for icon painting.

Arfa and I walked to the frontier a couple of years ago. The road ends at a stone wall with a green wrought iron gate out of a garden centre catalogue. I took photos of her rattling the bars. Many women, especially my feisty daughter, bridle that half the human race is banned from seeing the wonderful sights and treasures that I have now learned not to bang on about in their presence. I have also learned not to mansplain the ban. Some of the ripostes I have tried include

- In a monastery there is an 'enclosure' where women may not go, and in a convent where men may not go. It's called an *avaton* in Greek. Think of Athos as a big *avaton*.

- You wouldn't like the toilets.

These and other justifications release only vituperation. I preempted Arfa's complaints.

"Tell me, fruitful vine and helpmeet, you are a woman, wife, mother and grandmother to girls, distinguished in the defence of the marginalised and the victimised and the pursuit of equality for all before the law. Tell me what you feel about the prohibition of women as a European human rights practitioner. Is it inhuman and unrighteous?"

Short Silence

"Who cares?"

"What?"

"If it's private land they can probably do what they like. There are a lot more important things to get het up about."

I miss her now as I peer over the garden gate at a collection of old trucks and the Arsanas of Chromnitsa. Arsanas means arsenal in its original sense of dockside warehouse. A couple of buildings bravely fly the blue and white striped flag of Greece and the black double-headed eagle on a yellow field of the Greek Orthodox.

The arsanas serves the Chromnitsa winery, three kilometres up the hill on the other side of the wall. A hundred years ago it was a hospital for Russian monks. After the Russian revolution it became derelict. The legend is that Evangelos Tsantalis, head of a famous wine and spirits company, sheltered there when caught in a storm while out hunting. He planted a vineyard and built a winery. Its Metoxi Kormilitsa Red is at the top of the Kremlin's wine list. You can get a bottle of red or white in the UK for under a tenner.

A short distance uphill on this side of the garden gate are the ruins of Zygou Monastery, or the *Frangokastro*, the Frankish Fort. St Athanasios, the founder of Athos's first monastery, the Great Lavra, began his ascetic life here in 958. Close to the sea and convenient for pirates, by 1200 it was deserted. In 1204 the knights of the Fourth Crusade gave up on the Holy Land and sacked Constantinople instead, setting up a Latin empire. In 1206 one of them, who may have been a bishop and whose name has been spared infamy, settled in the ruins of Zygou with fellow ruffians, rebuilt the fortifications and set about looting the monasteries. The monks appealed to Pope Innocent III, who had the Franks forcibly ejected in 1211. It has been known as the Frankish Fort ever since. Fortunately the site is closed for the day so I am spared having to make sense of the ruins when what I really want is an Avaton Tsipouro - ouzo without the aniseed - distilled in the winery on the other side of the wall.

At nightfall I have a last meal to prepare spiritually and physically for the ascetic days ahead. I consider monastic little fish and boiled greens but plump instead for a little bottle of Avaton tsipouro, a jug of sea-dark red and a steak with chips and fried vegetables. The toast is Harley for bringing me safe here.

Gluttony and intoxication. I love the feeling of walking round in a different skin, a different mind, out of my usual too solid self. I know I will pay for this as I struggle through headache and nausea to get up in time to catch the boat tomorrow but for the moment this is a glimpse of what I might have been, what I could be, what I want to be, a liberated spirit. What makes it doubly joyful is the knowledge that it will end. Without beginning and end everything is nothing, it is and is not. In the street I gaze up at the starry firmament, or where the starry firmament would be without the bright shop windows and street lamps. Insects zip in the neon like shooting stars and I'm grateful for this fleeting taste of gladness. With the insouciant bravado of a stray dog owning the road I saunter back to the hotel.

The vine produces wine, the wine drunkenness and drunkenness an evil form of ecstasy.

Second Century Text. The Philokalia

MAP OF ATHOS

Visitors to Mount Athos are asked not take photographs of monks without their permission or the blessing of their abbot and I think the same goes for writing about them. The conversations with monks are as verbatim as I can recall. But I have changed their identities out of respect for their privacy.

14 ZOGRAPHOU TO KONSTAMONITOU

The swifts of Loch Tower wheel and dart over the busy port. Fishing boats arrive with the day's catch. Monks and pilgrims queue to take the ferries to Athos. Tourists board boats for the daily tour to see the seaside monasteries of the Holy Mountain from the water. Open caiques with white canopies ferry holidaymakers to the island beaches opposite.

I say goodbye to Harley, who has brought me safely here, through the trials of nature and civilisation, struggling with his own infirmities and mine. He is my spiritual model: patient, obedient, hard-working, struggling, frugal, modest, gentle, uncomplaining, unpretentious, derided, idiosyncratic, world-worn, servant, companion and friend. I park him in an alley beside the hotel and leave the key in the ignition in case he is in the way. I do not need to take much, the clothes I stand up in, a change of underwear, a hat, travelling pharmacy, toothbrush, phones, Makarios's books. I dump the rest of my disposable life in bag-lady's bundles in the hotel basement. With them I leave doubt and scepticism and reason and logic so I can open my mind to ideas and sentiments refined in medieval Byzantium.

My plan is to get off at the main port of Dafni and take a bus to the capital Karyes. From there I can walk to Makarios's monastery. I will give him his books and carry on the conversation we started last year. The next day I will walk, knees permitting, to the monasteries of Simonopetra and Dionysiou at the end of the peninsula. From there I can take a crack at climbing the Holy Mountain.

It will take two hours to get to Dafni, half way along the south coast of the peninsula. We will stop at half a dozen monasteries on the way to set down passengers and pick up others. I have stayed at some of them in previous years so we will sail into the past as well as through the present.

First task is to collect my *diamonitirion*, my visa, from the Pilgrim's Office. It costs €30 and is valid for three nights. They let in a hundred men a day of whom ten can be non-Orthodox.

Then down to the port to get a ticket for the ferry, jostling in the queue to hand over Charon's obol. I have plenty of time to go back for the Zeus's excellent breakfast: boiled eggs, yoghurt, honey, bread, cheese, butter, cake, jam. As a first step to monastic self-denial I squirrel nothing into my pockets but munch it in the early sunshine on the terrace next to a table of three jolly priests in holiday mood. They leave in stately procession and I order a leisurely espresso, too leisurely, so have to scamper down the road to the ferry, scrambling onto the ramp as it starts to grumble up.

The vehicle deck is packed with vans and trucks with food and materials. Above it is a half deck with a saloon fuggy with men who have seen the coast before and have no interest in seeing it again. A wizened monk sits in a corner making *komboskini*, prayer rope bracelets, out of knotted wool with a bead to mark the beginning and end of a round, the equivalent of rosary. Thirty three knots mark the years of Christ's life, each made of seven crosses of thread to keep demons at bay. He charges a euro each or six for five euros. He sells more on the way back from Dafni to men clinging to the experience or remembering who they forgot to buy souvenirs for.

Above the saloon is an open deck canopied against the sun, the port rail crowded with photographers and gawpers bagging their first monasteries, the benches packed with huddles of pilgrims and a few singletons like me. I sit next to a thin, old, sweet-faced, odiferous monk cradling a cardboard box tied up with string, fishy eyes peeping through gaps in the lid.

"*Yortazete?* Are you celebrating?" I ask. Fish is only for Sundays or Feast Days.

"Thank God" he says, which leaves me none the wiser. He closes his eyes to avoid further conversation.

The ferry chugs down the coast. A continuous line of hills drops steeply down to a narrow shingle shore. The peninsula is about 50 km long and 10 km wide. Water courses, ravines and valleys run down on either side of a central ridge rising to the Mountain. Low-lying land and plateaus are cultivable for market garden crops, orchards, bee-keeping, vineyards and olive groves. The rest is thick forest, a source of timber and wild food to forage, home to boar, foxes, jackals, wolves, reptiles and birds.

Those of us with maps try to spot the frontier. On the secular side the hills are stripped to grey rock and scrub by grazing. On the theocratic side, where flocks are forbidden, the green hills flourish. A scattering of buildings dot the hills, some ruined, others whitewashed and inhabited, a few with solar panels on the roof. Photographers take action snaps of seagulls plucking tost crusts from the fingers of pilgrims excited with the novelty of it all, kids on school journey. An all-boys school, obviously, although I instinctively recoil at the door of the toilets before the symbol of a woman in a skirt from the ferry's previous life. I come back and stand at the rail next to three men in their twenties, speaking Greek.

"Have you been before?" I ask the one next to me. He has designer glasses, crimson Polo T-shirt, white chinos, loafers, a lemon yellow sweater tied round his neck, dressed for

Monastiraki not a monastery. The Athos dress code is long-sleeve shirt, comfy trousers and trainers or hiking boots.

"It's the first time. I'm getting married next month. I came to prepare myself."

Men come to Athos for many reasons but a stag do is not that common. He won't wake up handcuffed to a lamp post at five in the morning wearing frilly pink knickers, that's for sure. Before I can ask where the hen party is the loudspeaker announces the first port of call, the arsanas of Zographou monastery. The stags bustle off to their luggage. I move to the front rail of the deck to watch us come in.

A Byzantine tower guards a couple of warehouses and a jetty. A handful of men with luggage wait to embark. Twice as many crowd in the bows to get off. A truck is waiting to cart them to the monastery, hidden in the hills a mile away. A priest, my age, joins me at the rail. He wears a cassock and a cylindrical hat but his white beard looks too trimmed for a monk. He is a big man in every direction with a round, jolly face. He'd be in demand for children's Christmas parties. We, nod and smile at each other, uncertain which language to greet each other in. He chooses *bonjour* and I follow suit. I point to the wedding party heading for the truck.

"See those three? The one in the middle is getting married. He's come to Athos, *pour son enterrement de vie de garçon*, his Bachelor Burial."

"He needs all the help he can get. In another life I was married. It was a taste of hell."

He laughs like Gerard Depardieu. Guffaw.

"Are you married?" he says.

"A trial marriage. Fifty years."

"Bravo. What is your secret?"

"My wife says to have low expectations."

"Marriage is more penitential than monasticism." Guffaw.

"Are you a monk?"

"Me? No. I married again. See my white hair? I'm only thirty five."

"Where is your parish?"

"Avignon."

"Do you have many Orthodox?"

"From all over the world. We say the Our Father in eight languages including Arabic. We have Russians, Greeks, Africans, migrants, refugees, workers from Eastern Europe. Many Syrians. Are you Orthodox?"

"Not yet."

"Good reply."

"It's less confrontational than saying no."

"What if I ask when you're going to be baptised?"

"I say when God wills."

"Be careful. God might catch you one day."

"I'll take the risk."

Zographou

The ferry is cast off and its screws churn us backwards. Papas Depardieu points to the tower.

"You know why it's called Zographou? It means self-painted. Three rich men from Ohrid built it in nine hundred and something. They couldn't agree whether to dedicate it to the Virgin, St Nicholas or St George. They locked a wooden panel in the church and prayed outside all night. In the morning they found the panel painted with the icon of St George. A hundred years ago a visiting bishop didn't believe the story. He poked George's left cheek and his finger stuck. They had to cut off the end with a knife. You can still see it."

I look for a hint of irony, the fun in bullshitting a stranger, but he seems serious. Until he bursts into a guffaw.

"I love those legends. They keep the truth alive. Who would remember three men from Ohrid?"

"So this isn't your first time."

"No. I come here for the exercise." Guffaw. "And for the faith."

"You have certainty. You're lucky. "

"Certainty is good. Uncertainty is better. It keeps us on our toes."

"I have plenty of uncertainty."

"Shall we get in the shade?"

I look up at his hat.

"That must be hot in the sun."

"Not at all. The disk on top shades the rest of it. And there's air space inside that gives it insulation. If it's really hot I put an ice pack inside." Guffaw.

I know the story about the icon of Saint George. I have stayed at Zographou. I took photos of the wide cobbled courtyard made by the church and four-storey buildings. Features included a massive cypress, a chapel, an outdoor font in a pavilion and a cenotaph topped by a crucifix. I tried to make out the dedication on the memorial. An elderly monk, skeletal and stooped, came up to me. In the gift shop he had sold me a mug printed with a picture of the arsanas so he knew I spoke English. His own was fluent, delivered in bursts and deficient in the definite article.

"See. See. What he done?"

"Who?"

"Pope. Burned them. In tower here." He thrust out a hand to conjure the tower. "Twenty two monks. Four workers. "

He beckoned me to follow him to a mural just inside the gates. It featured the blazing tower topped with twenty six haloes jostling over a selection of bearded monks. Soldiers stoked the flames egged on by a man in a scarlet cloak.

"See. Cardinal. See. Pope." He pointed up to a triple crowned figure looking as if he was blessing the scene. "Are you Catholic?"

I accepted my share of guilt.

"Catholics burn in hell. Orthodox only way."

In 1261 the Emperor Michael took back Constantinople from the Crusaders who had captured it in 1204. When the Latins massed for a counter attack in 1274 the Pope gave him grudging support in return for re-unification with Rome. This went down badly in Constantinople and the rest of Orthodoxy, especially Athos. Michael imposed his will by sending in the troops. Setting Greek soldiers on Greek monks would heap fuel on righteous fire so he sent Latin mercenaries to hang a few abbots and monks as encouragement to toe the line. The twenty six of Zographou defied the heretics from the tower with an icon of the Virgin of the Warning for protection. It didn't work but survives with a few scorch marks in the little church in the courtyard. The monks bring it out to fight forest fires.

Latins were not always unwelcome. The fifth monastery to be founded on Athos at the end of the tenth century was Benedictine, a house of Italian monks. For three hundred years, despite the Great Schism, the Latin rite echoed over the mountain. It was dissolved a few years after Michael sent in his troops. The ruined tower still survives as a monument to what might have been.

While firm in their conviction of the primacy of Orthodoxy, other monks I met in Zographou were open and generous to those who do not share their faith, from the kind and otherworldly abbot to an elderly helper in the kitchen.

Monasteries

The word monk comes from the Greek *monachos*, meaning solitary. The basic unit is a hermit in a cave without human contact. When a hermit finds a lonely place to spend his life he grows what he can, starting with onions and then a vine. He takes stale bread from his monastery and forages in the forest for weeds, nuts, berries and mushrooms. He may be joined by others, to a maximum of six, perhaps building a shack with a room for a chapel. This is called a cell, not to be confused with a monk's private room in a monastery. Usually a cell is a self-governing independent unit. The monks earn money for essentials with handicrafts, such as wood carving or making prayer ropes. On Sundays and feast days they go to the liturgy and a meal in their parent monastery.

A *skete*, deriving from the Greek for 'ascetic', is a group of cells clustered around a central church, creating a self governing collective with a leader elected every year or so. The cells organise their own lives but come together for liturgies. There are twelve sketes on Athos, some of which are as big as a monastery.

Monasteries have a basic layout. A ring of walls is the first line of defence against pirates, Latins and Turks. Inside is a stone tower with the treasury and the library, the last refuge against enemies and fire. The focal point is the *katholikon*, the church, repository of icons and relics. Close by are the refectory and kitchen. In a courtyard a fountain spouts mountain water. The gatehouse has a shop for souvenirs and religious articles. The guest house has a room for receiving pilgrims with the registration book and a kitchen for making coffee and washing up. The living quarters are in three or four storey buildings with single cells for monks and dormitories for pilgrims. Other rooms house chapels, meeting rooms, laundry, and whatever is needed for the monastery's craft production. In basements are storage, workshops and wine cellar. The dead are lodged in temporary graves for about three years, usually outside the walls, a mound of earth, a black wooden cross at one end. Permanent quarters are in the bone house where the exhumed bones are heaped and the skulls ranged on shelves.

Outside the walls are vineyards, fields of kitchen garden stuff, orchards of domesticated trees. Cypress trees stand sentry. Cliff-top monasteries have flamenco skirts of cultivated terraces. There may be a few flowers around the courtyard but the primary purpose of horticulture is growing things to eat. The boundary between garden and forest is blurred. One monk has grafted domestic cherry branches onto wild trees hidden in the woods. Another knows a ruined well where he gathers oregano and thyme.

A monastery is an independent foundation with its own constitution, rule, and property inside and outside Athos. They each have their own history and character reflecting the traditions of the great nations of Orthodoxy. Russian, Serbian, Bulgarian houses celebrate the offices in Church Slavonic, the rest in Ecclesiastical Greek. They vary externally in size and wealth, internally in the nature of the community, the rigour of their observance, their willingness to embrace modernity.

There are about 1800 monks on Athos. About half live in monasteries and the rest in hermitages, cells, sketes and farms. They come from all over the world, primarily Greece, Cyprus, Romania, Russia, Serbia, and Bulgaria. The last three have their own monasteries but you find men from these countries and many others in all the houses.

A monk is not empowered to administer sacraments, perform the services, present the relics and other priestly duties. For this he is ordained as a priest-monk, a *hieromonk*. The faithful greet a hieromonk by kissing his hand. All monks are addressed as 'Father.'

The abbot is elected for life from among the hieromonks. His badges of office are a staff and a pectoral cross. In a big monastery he may be given the title of archimandrite. From archimandrites bishops are chosen for the church outside. He has total spiritual and organisational authority over his house and its dependencies. The abbots of the monasteries form the Holy Council of Athos, based in the capital Karyes, and elect their president, the *Protos*.

Elders help the abbot run the monastery. They are not to be confused with a different kind of Elder, who is outside the hierarchy. He acquires his title by general acclaim for his holiness, wisdom and spiritual gifts. He may have powers of healing, seeing the future, mind reading, being in two places at once. Some are canonised a few years after their death.

Monks are not the only ones who live on Athos. Lay workers wear monkish clothes, for example a black tunic and trousers, but take no vows. They work in the kitchen, the guest house, the fields or the building sites. Some are older men fallen on hard times, homeless, widowers, lonely. A few are fugitives from justice or vendetta. Some monks bring in their fathers to end their days. Paid agricultural and building workers live in bothies outside the monastery gates where their diet and routine do not clash with those inside. Finally there are pilgrims, approximately thirty thousand a year to be housed and fed for free, three nights each, close on a hundred thousand nights of hospitality.

Konstamonitou

Papas Depardieu sits on a bench and closes his eyes, his hands joined over his stomach, dozing or avoiding further conversation. The ferry has barely got out into deep water from self-painted Zographou when it turns towards another arsanas a few hundred yards further on. A jetty and a simple two storey warehouse/boathouse with a red tile roof belong to Konstamonitou, hidden in the hills a mile away. The two ports are separate because they serve two different valleys.

The boathouse doors conceal a powerful RIB, a rigid inflatable boat, for emergency medical evacuation to Ouranoupoli. The monk who looks after it gets down to the arsanas on an all-terrain Segway scooter that he keeps on the balcony of his third floor cell and lowers with an electric winch, both machines charged by a solar panel. His robes cover the handlebars so susceptible pilgrims have taken the sight of a monk whizzing effortlessly through the trees as a levitating mystic or a demon.

Technological wizardry is not typical of Konstamonitou, financially one of the poorest monasteries. The buildings have been patched up over the years with DIY cementing and carpentry. The refectory is a simple hall with rough wood beams and no frescoes. They cook with a wood-fired oven and heat the rooms, when absolutely necessary, with wood stoves. An ancient generator meets the most essential needs: workshop machinery, kitchen refrigerators, office computer, phone chargers. Living quarters have no electricity.

The monastery may be cash poor but is asset rich with priceless treasures. The right hand of St Stephen the first martyr is preserved in a handsome silver case. His miraculous icon was thrown into the fire by iconoclasts in Syria. It jumped into the sea with nothing but a mild scorching and fetched up on an Athos beach. Another icon, Our Lady Who-Answers-Everything, the *Panaghia Antiphonitria*, filled up the jars when a monk told her there was no oil for her lamps.

The accommodation would not get stars on TripAdvisor. A monastery is not a hotel. The room I stayed in when I was there last year had eight metal beds each with a thin flock mattress, pancaked pillow, army blanket, two threadbare sheets, a pillow case and bedside chair. I begged the assistant guest-master for a towel the size of a teacloth. Bare boards, hospital green walls and high windows parsimonious with light through the grime completed the decor. The lavatories were down an arched corridor, three cubicles overlooking the hillside. One had a pedestal without a seat, the other two were holes in the ground with garden hoses that doubled as icy showers. The corridors were lit with oil lamps. Going to the lavatory in the middle of the night was never more romantic, with the added bonus of burning oil to mask the smell.

The routine in all monasteries is more or less the same every day of the week. The night is for praying, the day is for working. It starts in the late afternoon with vespers, around 5pm, moving seamlessly into dinner at 6.30pm followed by compline and veneration of the relics. There's an hour or so to relax before evening prayer and bed before 9pm. At 3am a monk wakes everybody up by whacking a wooden plank called a *talanton*, or a metal one called a *semantron*. Monks in their cells pray and meditate until 4am, when they go into church for matins followed by the liturgy, which non-Orthodox call mass. At about 9.30 they go into the refectory for breakfast. The rest of the day is for work and an hour or so of sleep before vespers. The routine is changed by all-night vigils for the great feast days.

In some monasteries non-Orthodox are welcome at services and to eat with everyone else. In Konstamonitou we heterodox may not join the others in church or the refectory. The people most shocked by this are not us, who shrug and tut, but Orthodox outsiders. A Greek pilgrim once tried to drag me into church by the arm saying Christ is for everyone but I shook him off to avoid scandal. I like the Russian proverb *'you don't bring your own rule into someone else's monastery.'*

For something to do during vespers last year I earned my keep by tidying up the flower beds and planters in the courtyard and around the church. With my Opinel knife I deadheaded roses, rooted out bindweed, pruned shrubs. I gave it all a good watering from the fountain. It was pleasant work in the late afternoon sunshine, listening to the chanting from an open church window. A bird in the eves, a swallow maybe with a blue back, pale yellow front and a splash of red on the head joined in with an exquisite, blackbirdish song, all full of life and praise to touch the heart of an old sceptic.

I grew up knowing Franciscans who wore sandals on bare feet throughout the year. So I thought I was suitably monastic doing the same. As I dealt with roses outside the church a late-coming monk, a burly bouncer in a bushy beard, bustled up, adjusting his veil. Expecting his thanks I put on humility but it was not needed. He pointed to my toes and told me I couldn't go into church without socks, a technicality since I wasn't allowed into the church anyway. But it might also apply to the refectory so I didn't take the risk of being barred from my dinner. I went back to my room for a pair of purple Primarks. For once I had license to wear socks and sandals without contumely. As soon as the Orthodox went back into church for compline and veneration of the relics I went inside to eat. The cook was deeply apologetic for the discrimination and made amends with double helpings and custard creams. Dinner was an excellent bean soup, a fresh onion for dessert and a lively new wine.

After the services were over, I loitered on an ancient wooden plank against the church wall. Monks bustled around on mysterious errands, eyes to the ground. It was hard to tell if they were depressed, anti-social or praying. For all the fasting and simple diet and hard work some of them looked well-nourished by the régime. A white-haired monk hobbled over and sat down next to me.

"Howarya" he said in Australian. "Where yez from?"

After chit-chat about cricket and Saint Symeon, whose feast it was that day, I asked why they didn't get EU money for restoration like other monasteries.

"Nah, the abbot won't take it. He says they're all schismatics and atheists in Brussels. They're power grabbers. One day they'll want payback. Better be independent."

"There are many in England, who agree with him."

He stood up and wished me goodnight. I sauntered to the gates for a stroll outside before they shut for the night. Another elderly monk finished replenishing the lamp over the entrance and hauling it up into the arch. He was tall with a bony face and bright blue eyes. We exchanged the conventional greeting.

"Bless, Father."

"The Lord. Where are you from?"

"London."

"Are you Orthodox?"

"Not yet."

"When?"

"When God wills."

"Of course God wills. He brought you here. As soon as you get back to London you must go to the bishop and be baptised. Before Christmas. Take the name Stephen. He is our patron."

"I've been baptised."

"It doesn't count. Orthodox baptism is the true baptism. Do you have a wife?"

"Yes."

"You will tell her to be baptised. Do you have children?"

"Four."

"Do you have grandchildren?"

"Seven."

"You will tell them to be baptised too. Then you will all go to Paradise."

I pictured how to break the news to the family. By now we were sitting on the plank bench.

"How old are you?" he asked.

"Seventy four."

"I am seventy nine. We shall soon be dead. If you are baptised we can sit together in Paradise and talk."

He could have thought of a more attractive incentive. For the next half hour he gave me a quick tour d'horizon of church history and its various schisms. At eight he stood up.

"I must rest. I have to get up at three. Good night."

"Good night Father. See you in Paradise. God willing."

He made a grimace that I think was a smile.

Orthodox believe that baptism has to be by full immersion in water, otherwise it doesn't count. It's not the only difference between churches. Others include the Orthodox rejection of the Immaculate Conception, Purgatory, Original Sin, unleavened bread for the Eucharist. The sign of the cross is a giveaway — thumb and first two fingers as opposed to four fingers flat together. Doing it the wrong way could get you killed in the Balkan wars of the late nineties.

I went outside to the smokers' haunt, an alcove between the outside buttresses of the ancient wall furnished with a bench and a bucket of sand. I gave up thirty years ago but enjoy second hand smoke and the company of smokers. The custard cream cook plumped his rheumatic bulk down next to me and lit up a Marlboro. The health warnings on the pack seemed superfluous in a place dedicated to the afterlife. Bring it on, they should say.

"Deutschland?" he asked.

"England."

"I know England. I was a seaman."

In his broken English and my broken Greek we reminisced, in my case imaginatively, about the docklands of Cardiff, Liverpool and London in the sixties. He offered me a cigarette and I put my palm on my chest. He took a deep drag into his gurgling lungs and pointed through an aromatic haze to sprigs of mountain oregano growing on the rock wall above a fountain on the other side of the courtyard.

"See? Rigani. Everything you want here."

"Have you always been a chef ?"

"I learned when they put me in the kitchen. If you love to eat you love to cook.

"Don't you miss meat?"

"If I feel the need I have a chop with the workers."

"You like it here then."

"What would I do outside? My wife is dead. My daughters have their lives. If they had children, eh, who knows?"

A kitchen helper in civilian clothes and monkish cap sat down with us. He was cross-eyed. When he discussed his chores for the morning with the cook one eye looked at me so I butted in until I twigged. He was gaunt and raddled not from the monastic life, I thought, but a rough life in the world outside. He kept his roll-up in a cupped hand, sat hunched and tense, the wariness of jail. He leaned his head back against the wall and closed his eyes. The gesture said it all. Here is peace. They got up and wished me goodnight.

The fountain opposite was built into the side of a cliff and shaded by a massive plane tree. An old man in monkish dress sat on the rim of the basin and gently dabbled his fingers under the running tap. His habit and cap were patched and green with age, his socks and Crocs faded grey, his hands brown with liver spots, his cheeks sunk and yellow, his beard and bun a grubby white. I went over and filled the tin mug chained to the tap. He stopped dabbling and fixed his eyes on me, so black the irises merged with the pupils, two dark holes.

"Are there Christians in England?" he said. Christian in Greek means Orthodox.

"Yes."

"Drink the water. It is good for the organism."

"Have you been at the monastery long, Father?"

"Not Father. I am not a monk. My mother brought me."

"Why?"

"It was a long time ago."

"Do you go outside?"

Exo, outside, means out of Athos.

"I go to Karyes to help carry things. I've been to Zographou for Saint George."

"What do you do here?"

"I look after the mules."

The monastery had no mules. I let it pass.

"Good work," I said.

"Do you know how to tell a demon from an angel?"

"No."

"Demons are clever. They have conquered outside."

"Of course. So how do you tell angels from demons?"

"I told you. It's difficult. Be careful."

He dug in his pocket for a shiny black banana.

"Here."

Was this kindness? A test? A parable? Should I eat it now?

"Thank you very much I'll have it later. Here."

All I had on me to reciprocate was a packet of Lockets honey and lemon throat sweets that I keep on me in case the incense makes me cough if ever I am allowed in church. He took one, sniffed it, put it in his pocket and gave me the packet back. A bell clanged. The gate was closing against the night. We led each other into safety, halting briefly to make signs of the cross under the lighted lamp.

With misgivings I peeled the demonic black banana before brushing my teeth. It was white, firm and tasty, an angelic banana after all. I wondered if my friend was unwrapping the Locket in his room. They are not to everybody's taste.

15 XENOPHONTOS TO PANTELEIMON

I tell Papas Depardieu about the angelic banana.

"Do you preach to your flock about demons?"

"Sometimes it is helpful to personify our weaknesses."

"And Satan?"

"Pope Francis tells us Satan is a real person. Who are we to contradict him?"

One of the monasteries we sail past served excellent red wine when I stayed there before. It was not on the table in jugs but doled into our tin cups from a plastic flagon by a big blonde lad out of Breughel with a ruddy face and blue eyes and a cap that he wore on the side of his head. Later we chanced to file out of compline side by side into the courtyard.

"Where do you live?" he said in a thick Scottish accent.

"London."

"Have ye been to Inverness?"

"Can't say I have. Aberdeen though."

"Close enough."

"Are you from Inverness?"

"Latvia. What do you do?"

"I write books."

"What about?"

"Greece mainly."

"Och that's dangerous work. Were ye ever on the Acropolis? Behind every statue there's a demon waiting to jump out at ye. Didye know that?"

"I'll be careful."

"You do that. Take precautions."

"I will."

"It's a treat to speak English. D'ye fancy a wee digestif?"

He led the way to a side door in the refectory and pulled out a bunch of keys to open it. We were in the kitchen. He unlocked another door into a pantry, aseptically clean. He opened a tall refrigerator stacked with plastic flagons of wine. He took a couple out, not for our delectation but to retrieve a two litre Kilner jar hidden behind them. It was full of what appeared to be tomato juice with unsavoury green and yellow bits floating in it. He flicked open the top and handed me the jar.

"Will ye get a taste of that."

I was minded to decline but his wide, simple face looked so benevolent, so expectant, I hadn't the heart to refuse. I took a sip. Then a swig. It was the best Bloody Mary I've ever tasted.

"You like it, eh? Totally organic. Totally scratch. My friend brews the vodka from his own potatoes. Everything in the mixer I make from the garden."

"There's a still in the monastery?"

"He lives in a wee cell near here. They make everything. Ouzo. Tsipouro. Raki from the plums."

"What about the tabasco?"

"Och, easy. Hot peppers and salt and vinegar."

We sat at a table in the dark refectory, the frescoes illuminated by the light from the kitchen, transported into a biblically themed bar, passing the jar between us like a loving cup. Rather than reproduce all our conversation I'll summarise his back story.

He was in his early forties. He left Latvia in his teens with his mother and two sisters to work in a fish factory in Inverness. He found more entertaining employment as a barback and then barman in a nightclub. The women stayed gutting fish until they acquired a highland croft where they became Jehovah's Witnesses and now scratch a living from the soil and part-time cleaning. He had no religion until he went on a mixologists' away-day sponsored by Stolichnaya and fell in love with a Russian woman, who would only sleep with him if he was baptised. The woman left him when, in his words, 'ma heid went funny'. Six years ago he was in hospital and had a dream of being on top of a mountain where he was safe from the demons that haunted him. A short time afterwards he saw an American documentary on TV about Athos.

"That was was the place for me."

"Tell me about demons," I say.

"Och, in the night they come and suffocate ye. In the daytime they tempt ye to do bad things. Have ye ever seen a porno demon?"

"On late night TV."

"Ye'd know if you met her. She's hideous. She's got a nice body but the face of a monster. These long black nails, and a black tongue. Her back's covered in pig hair that can cut through yer flesh."

"I can't say I've met her."

"She smells disgusting."

I have to say that the succubi who haunt my own dreams are more attractive. Each to his own. I decided not to delve more deeply for fear of what loose talk and the Bloody Mary might trigger.

"Do you ever want to go back outside?"

"If ye talk about seeing demons they put ye in a mental health hospital. Och, five years I've been here and they still don't make me a monk. I dinna know why."

Monks

The ferry docks at Dochiariou monastery. It is on the shore and well fortified against pirates, infidels, heretics and other sea-going marauders. Over it broods a Byzantine crenellated keep and a rust-red tower crane. Massive curtain walls are overhung by two storey slate-roofed houses painted red, green and blue, jutting out on rows of wooden struts. Tight-packed inside the walls other buildings sprout chimneys around the triple cupolas of the *katholikon*, the main church. The monastery is dedicated to the archangels Michael and Gabriel. One of them on a tall Doric column guards the jumbled arsanas on the quay.

I visited Dochiariou three years ago. First thing you do is announce yourself at the guest house. The guest master's assistant put a tray in front of me. He was young with a straggly beard and unruly hair tucked underneath a soft cap. Like most monks he looked tired.

"My name is John, Father. May I ask yours?"

"It's not important."

"Where are you from, Father?"

"From here."

"Where is your family?"

"My mother lives here. The monastery belongs to her. Jesus is our brother."

He said this in a very unaffected, matter-of-fact way. I suspected he was a novice at the last stage of induction before he was given a new name with the first tonsure. Novices learn to abandon the world outside, their identity, their parents and family and friends. For a surname they take the name of the monastery. Monks almost never go outside for family events, visit a dying parent or go to a funeral. They take literally Christ's stark warning *'If any man come to me, and hate not his father, and mother, and wife, and children, and brothers, and sisters, yea, and his own life also, he cannot be my disciple.'* It is said to take about three years to become a stranger to one's family. It must be very hard on everyone, especially parents whose only sons join up.

Why become a monk? It's a hard life, not a soft option, not an easy escape from the world outside. Bed and board are provided but the work and sacrifice are small compensation. Why do they do it? For as many reasons as there are monks. A vocation to prayer and penitence in a single minded quest to get closer to God is the primary motivation and vital in keeping going through dark days and doubts.

Many young men who come to test their vocation do the rounds of several monasteries in search of one that suits them and will take them. In the current revival some monasteries have no more room for recruits. It is not easy to be accepted as a novice and the drop-out rate is high. He spends a minimum of a year and usually three, wearing a simple black cassock and a soft cap, before being tonsured and given a new name, a wide sleeved robe called a *rason*, a brimless cylindrical hat and a veil. The veil is worn in church draped over the hat and down the back to the waist. Only in death does it cover the face. Some monks stay at this rank for the rest of their lives. There are no formal vows, only a commitment to remain a monk. After a few years the next stage is to take vows of poverty, chastity and obedience and take on the Great Schema, otherwise known as the Angelic Schema, with a knee-length tabard heavily embroidered front and back in red and white with the Cross, a lance and a sponge and below them a death's head.

Monks have one foot in the material world and the other in a parallel universe of the spirit that are both equally real to them. They strive to bridge the gulf by fasting, hardship and prayer. On the wall of many guest houses is a print of the *Ladder to Paradise,* a lively icon based on a 7th century career guide for ascetics. A ladder crowded with monks has thirty rungs from bottom left to top right, where Christ is waiting.

It is a never-ending struggle to climb to the top, egged on by angels above and monks below. Demons hover in the air, picking off the unworthy who tumble down into the gaping maw of the Beast.

At the bottom of the ladder is renunciation of the world and obedience to a spiritual father. A novice spends up to three years in boot camp. He is given arduous menial tasks and has to show absolute obedience, tested by unreasonable demands. His only possession is a notebook in which to write down his sins from ever since he can remember to the peccadillos of the present. He confesses them every other day to his spiritual father. Penitence is in isolation or in public. The equivalent of punitive press-ups is full prostrations. This is coupled with lessons in chanting, praying, ritual and fasting.

The following rungs up the ladder are the ascetic's struggle against the unruliness of the body. The word *asceticism* means training, shorthand for a regime of prayer, sleeplessness, discomfort, exertion, flagellation, fasting and self-denial designed to eliminate emotions, personal relationships, sexual urges and other desires of mind and body. Visions and hallucinations brought on by hunger and sleeplessness or demons are fought off with prayer and the crucifix. Other dangers include clinical depression, lethargy and pride.

Finally the ascetic achieves '*apatheia*', lack of feeling, the severance of all connection with the physical world in return for Enlightenment, meaning a state of mind not knowledge. On the top rung of the ladder is *theosis*, mystical union with God.

Icons

"I stayed here last year," says Papas Depardieu, joining me at the rail as we come into Dochiariou. "They have a miraculous icon of the Virgin. It made a monk blind because he insulted her. The food is very good."

"Which is more unbelievable?"

Guffaw.

"I already said. There is truth inside the legends."

"I like the ones about icons thrown in the sea and washed up on the beach. And the ones which fill up the oil jars when they've run out."

"Ah yes. God will provide."

"Talking of which, would you like a coffee? Sweet, medium or no sugar?"

The first icon was the Mandylion. King Abgar the Black of Edessa, a city now called Urfa in south-east Turkey, heard of Jesus's healing gifts and dropped him a line asking him to come and cure his leprosy. Jesus wrote back saying he couldn't come right now but was sending one of the disciples he had appointed to spread the Good News. He enclosed a picture of his face imprinted on a face towel. The equivalent in the Catholic church is Veronica's Veil. The Mandylion was looted from Constantinople by the Fourth Crusaders and ended up in the Sainte-Chapelle in Paris where it disappeared during the French Revolution. In many Orthodox churches a painting of the Mandylion is on the architrave above the sanctuary. Arfa was thrilled when I phoned her with the news that her birthday was the feast day of Saint Abgar the Black.

Every monastery has at least one miraculous icon. Most of them are of the Virgin with St George running a distant second. The legends that have grown up around them originate in the histories of the monasteries and then take on a life of their own.

The archetypal icon is painted by itself or Saint Luke. It is thrown in the sea to escape iconoclasts or Turks. It is found on the beach on Athos by monks, who take it away on a donkey. The donkey dies on the journey. The monks install the icon in the church but during the night it moves somewhere else, perhaps where the donkey dropped dead. The monks put it back but the same thing happens the next night. And the next so the monks give in and build it a church where it wants to be. Over the years the icon protects the monks by putting out fires or saving them from pirates. When the oil runs out after a bad harvest it fills the empty jars to overflowing. It scolds them when they do wrong and punishes them if they persist. If it is harmed by Turk or heretic it takes revenge. During Turkish times the icon is hidden in a well. Decades later it is miraculously rediscovered.

An icon does more than mythologise the monastery's history. It encapsulates the relationship between man and God, a portal into the divine world, a channel of prayer for mercy and favour, healing and fertility, salvation and eternal life. It witnesses the willingness of God to show favour to the devoted. An image as an aid to intercession takes on a spiritual significance in itself and eventually its own miraculous properties. It becomes a wonderworking object in its own right.

I once visited an icon painter. His studio stuck out from the monastery battlements, bathed in light from picture windows looking over the sea. It felt like the bridge of a ship steering north to the distant smudge of Thassos on the horizon. The painter had the face and figure of an El Greco, with piercing blue eyes and iron grey hair turning white in the beard. His cassock was out at the elbows, showing a grey vest, and his Crocs were mended with wire. So it was a pleasant surprise when he offered me a cup of Earl Grey. He was from Leeds and still had the accent.

He was wary at first then warmed when, for some reason I have now forgotten, I mentioned motorcycles. Like me he had a Lambretta scooter when he was at art school and we chatted amiably about spark plugs and petrol consumption. After college he led a chaotic life in communes and squats, the Lambretta the only fixed point. Obsessed with the transitoriness of life and art he threw away his paintings as soon as he finished them. On his thirtieth birthday he went into a church to get out of the rain. Never religious before, he was moved to talk to God. God answered, telling him to go travelling. On the Lambretta until it was stolen and then hitch-hiking, getting jobs along the way, living rough, he arrived on Athos twenty years ago. After working in the monastery kitchens for a few months he asked the abbot if he could stay. Learning that he was a painter the abbot appointed him assistant to the resident iconographer, an old man who soon died.

"It was all meant to be."

"What if it hadn't rained that day?"

"God sent the rain."

"Of course."

"You should read Philip Sherrard. *The Sacred in Art and Life*. One permeates the other."

An icon on an easel was half finished.

"How do you start?" I asked

I expected the conventional procedure by which the artist fasts and prays for days, painting being an extension of prayer. He opened a laptop and put on a slide show.

"Say I'm asked to do George. I go through the laptop and pick out the colours I like. I make the paints the traditional way, grind the pigments, mix them in egg and wine, your classic tempera. Sketch one of the standard outlines onto a board and away you go."

"It's a straight copy then."

"Not at all. I can vary the colours as long as I don't stray too far. Put a bit more or less detail on the clothing, that sort of thing. Every one is an original."

"What about the faces? To be honest, they all look the same to me. Don't you ever feel like doing something different?"

"Different? It's all been done. Byzantium was the greatest empire that has ever been. The greatest civilisation. The greatest religion. The greatest art. It's our job to keep it all alive."

It seems to me like painting by numbers. Simple colours in two dimensions with no attempt at depth or perspective. But I'm missing the point. They don't depict reality. Iconography is theology not art. An icon is not the expression of individual creativity, not a vehicle for sensual pleasure, not a simulacrum of the outside world or the inner world of the mind, not an evocation of the particular in space or time, not the creation of a new reality. An icon is a prayer, a path into another plane of existence. This is not what George or Mary or Jesus looked like. They are a door into a world of absolute truth. She is not a mother, this is motherhood. He is not merciful, this is mercy. They do not protect, this is protection. He does not judge, this is judgement. He does not suffer, this is suffering. Icons are depictions not of Saints but what they represent, a perfect idea to which we aspire.

They say icons are a window into the divine world if you look long enough. It doesn't work for me. There are one or two icons I find moving. But only because they have a human expression created by accident - flaking paint, soot, a warp in the board. My favourite image of Christ is a photo I took of a neglected fresco in a church on Evia. Something happened to the paint round his mouth so he looks as if he's smiling. Christ never smiles in pictures. There is no laughter in heaven, not the way it's painted anyway.

"More tea?"

"Yes please."

"The Antichrist hates art. It's in scripture. Art is sacred. Where is the art of today? I did five years in art schools. Was there any guidance about what it is all for? All I learned was technique. The Antichrist is out to destroy Christianity. We must fight back with our art."

Xenophontos

When Arfa came with me to Ouranoupoli we took a tourist boat along the coast to the end of the peninsula. It was packed with men and women of all ages on a parish pilgrimage. Seagulls in the slipstream herded us forward, dolphins arcing in the water led us on. It is impressive to see it all from the sea, especially the breathtaking 'monasteries of the rocks' perched on vertiginous cliffs.

Opposite Xenophontos monastery we thought we had broken down. The boat dropped anchor with ominous mechanical growlings. But rescue was at hand. A speedboat of the kind that pulls water skiers zipped on a cloud of spray from the shore, manned by four monks, two of them standing in the cockpit, robes streaming behind them. The two sitting in the back were older and more solemn than the lads having fun in front. Our boat lowered a platform at the stern and they climbed aboard. They had indeed brought salvation, a spiritual kind, in a black chest and a couple of polished wood cases. On a table swiftly erected by the crew on the rear deck they laid out an altar with cloths and bejewelled caskets of relics. Xenophontos has a drop of blood of John The Baptist and a fragment of the skull of St Stephen the first martyr, but I didn't catch if they were included. One of the young monks put the wooden cases on a table next to the bench where we were sitting. He opened them up to reveal a travelling repository of medals, crucifixes, icons, prayer ropes and other souvenirs soon to be transmuted into contact relics. I joined the crowd for chanting and hymns and browsing the memento tray and queuing up for the veneration of the relics, handing plastic bags of purchases to the presiding priest to dunk onto the reliquaries. Arfa looked on, bemused, as I took my turn, made the sign of the cross, bowed and air-kissed the caskets.

"See, woman, if you can't go to Athos, Athos will come to you," I said when I came back to the bench. She frowned.

"What are you playing at?"

"When not in Rome, do as the not-Romans do."

"You belong to the Romans."

"Imposters. The Latin mass brigade who want to bring back the ancient rituals are barking up the wrong linguistic tree. They should be lobbying for the original Greek."

"I thought you were all for it being in English."

"Don't get me started."

Our Saxon-Danish-German-Norman Macaroni dialect doesn't feel like the language of God. It's good for annual reports and maintenance manuals and text messaging but its dull sounds and cut-and-paste grammar and leaden Germanicism sucks the poetry out of worship. Like English the degenerate dog-Latin of the missal is the language of colonial administrators. It has a certain charm but doesn't compare with the cadences of Virgil and Cicero. Our God may listen in tongues but He only comes to life in the languages of His scriptures, Hebrew, Aramaic and Greek.

When everyone was catered for the monks packed up. The one in charge of the repository next to us pressed a miniature icon of the Virgin into Arfa's hand and smiled. She scrabbled in her purse for money but he put his free hand on his chest. The monks got into their boat with smiles and handshakes and their fee to speed back home in a cloud of exhaust and spray. Arfa was touched. She keeps the icon in her special box with single earrings, broken chains, her first communion rosary beads and rubber bands of various sizes.

Xenophontos has other enterprising ventures reaching out to the wider world. Apart from icons, Turkish Delight, its own label wine - the white is not at all bad - the monks market a range of pharmaceutical products, including hair restorer and haemorrhoid cream, of which I have heard good reports from pious friends in Athens.

Panteleimon

As we head towards the arsanas of Xenophontos monastery I tell Papas Depardieu about the relics brought out to the pilgrim boat.

"Do you like science fiction?" he says.

"You think relics are science fiction?"

Guffaw.

"I didn't say that," he says. "If you read science fiction you know about parallel universes. We are material creatures and spiritual creatures, we live in two worlds side by side. We bridge the gulf between them with material things."

"In an infinite universe there must be an infinite number of parallel universes, not just two," I say. "Because they all obey the same laws of physics they must be identical. If you passed from one to the other you would never know,".

"Trapped in infinity. Keep exploring my friend. Here I get off. I will look out for their salutary creams." Guffaw.

We shake hands with implausible promises to meet again in Athos or Avignon. I help take his bags down the companion to the bow. A monk waiting on the jetty picks them up and escorts him to the monastery gate.

Our ferry casts off, backs out and steers towards the last monastery before Dafni, Panteleimon, the *Russikon,* a little piece of St Petersburg. Massive buildings like barracks and tenements sprawl along the shore and up the hill, silver grey stone with aquamarine roofs setting off tumescent green onion domes speared with gilded Russian crosses, brilliant in the sun. The buildings used to get a bad press but since Russian benefactors have done them up they look elegant and imposing. We dock to disgorge a flock of Russians. The Russikon takes a hundred pilgrims a day, more on feast days.

Before the Russian Revolution of 1917 the total population of Athos was about 7,500, of whom Russians outnumbered even the Greeks. Conspiracy theorists muttered that Russia wanted to take over Athos, arms were stashed in the cellars, the monks were Tsarist soldiers. Their numbers plummeted after the Revolution and buildings were taken over by other monasteries. No arms caches were found. Since the collapse of the Soviet Union the population of Russian monks has been rising again and Russian money is pouring in to restore buildings and conspiracy theories. The relics cruise that Arfa and I took was postponed for a day as President Putin had come to venerate something other than himself.

In October 2018 rivalry and suspicion between Greeks and Russians erupted into confrontation when the Patriarch of Constantinople prised the Orthodox Church of Ukraine away from the Russian Patriarchate by granting it autocephaly, independence. The Russian church, which had about 150 million Orthodox Christians under its authority, lost a fifth of its members. It countered by breaking off ties with Constantinople. There are now two Ukrainian Orthodox churches, the Moscow-backed 'canonical' Ukrainian Orthodox Church and the Orthodox Autocephalous Church of Ukraine. It is the latest round in the perennial struggle for primacy between Moscow and Constantinople. The implications are political as much as ecclesiastical. The leader of the Russian Orthodox church, Patriarch Kirill, is an ally of Putin, whom he has described as a miracle sent from God. The split was a blow to Putin in his bid to legitimise the invasion of Eastern Ukraine while the autocephalous Church is a vehicle for western-backed Ukrainian nationalism.

The shockwaves wash up on the shores of Athos. Monasteries and monks are divided in their support. Some have welcomed delegations from the autocephalous church and let them concelebrate the liturgy. Others slam the doors on the 'schismatics'. It affects pilgrims too. Ukrainians need a certificate from the 'canonical' church in Kiev to worship in the Russian and Serbian houses where 'schismatic' pilgrims are banned. According to the Moscow patriarchate, Russian pilgrims can visit the Holy Mountain, enter churches, and venerate the relics, but they should only make confession or take communion in Panteleimon, even though it comes under Constantinople and is technically excommunicated...

... so sad.

16 DAFNI TO KARYES

The monasteries were rich pickings for pirates, a portmanteau word for raiders, thieves, warlords, crusaders, armies of many principalities and religions. Piracy was endemic until suppressed by the Pax Ottomana. But it's not polite among Greeks to mention this, much less the ejection of Catholic Franks and the reestablishment of Orthodoxy throughout the Ottoman Empire.

Is this relevant today? A notorious scourge of the Aegean in the fourteenth century was the Catalan Company of mercenaries. For two years they pillaged the monasteries of Athos. In the timeless Athonite perspective it might have happened yesterday. Until 2000 citizens of Catalonia were banned. In the monastery of Vatopedi the Catalan government paid for the conversion of a storehouse into a state-of-the-art pirate-proof treasury in reparation. It's now uncontroversial to wear a Barça shirt.

Defences were not only physical. One morning three hundred years ago the Abbot of Vatopedi was giving the keys of the front gate to the porter when a fresco of the Blessed Virgin and Child told him not to open it but drive off the pirates lurking outside. He saw the Child putting His hand over the mouth of His Mother, telling her not to protect the monks as they were sinful and deserved punishment. But the Blessed Virgin repeated the warning. The painting was cut out and is now an icon called the *Paramythia* in its own chapel, where the liturgy is celebrated in its honour every Friday.

If you doubt that the Virgin is responsible for excluding women from Athos, the wall painting of the *Antiphonetria,* the Responder, should put your mind at rest. In about AD 400 Placidia, a daughter of Emperor Theodosius, visited Vatopedi and tried to enter the katholikon from the side door. The icon spoke: 'How dare you come here, a woman, don't come any further.' And if you think this is too far back in time, indeed it happened before the monastery was built, any monk will tell you that exactly the same thing happened to a female journalist disguised as a man about thirty years ago.

My seventieth birthday present from our surgeon son Jim was our first visit to Athos. We stayed at Vatopedi. It is large and rich, home to over a hundred monks of several nationalities and host to scores of pilgrims. Beside the sea massive walls make a rough triangle enclosing a sloping courtyard of Herculean stone slabs. It feels like a fortified village in contrast with the compact fortresses of the smaller houses. Non-Orthodox are welcome in the church for services and in the refectory for meals. A highlight was veneration of the relics that include a fragment of the True Cross, a piece of the reed which the Jews gave to Christ in mockery before the Crucifixion, and the skull of St John Chrysostomos in a silver casket with a hatch on the side to show the uncorrupted ear into which the Archangel Gabriel whispered the words of his new liturgy. If they come on the right day Scots may venerate a bit of the skull of St Andrew. After the Cross the greatest treasure is what is known as the Girdle of the Virgin that she dropped down to Apostle Thomas at her Assumption into heaven as compensation for being late for her funeral. It has nothing to do with biblical corsetry but is a long belt of woven camel hair, a brown ribbon with a thread of gold running through it inserted by a grateful Byzantine empress. Half of it is now under panes of glass in a gold casket.

Why do I join in the veneration of relics? I tell myself it is out of respect to the monks who make us welcome. I live in a world of stories. I might learn something, perhaps about myself. And what's the point of coming here if I don't join in? Otherwise I'm a tourist watching the floor show.

After the veneration Father Averkios took us on a tour of the icons and frescoes, describing their wondrous origins and miracles as if they happened yesterday. As some of them have. The Girdle is a potent aid to conception for childless couples. The monks supply white ribbons that have been sanctified on the relic. The mother-hopefully-to-be ties one round her waist. The couple fast and pray and abstain from sex for a fortnight and then go at it. A young man in our party said that his sister-in-law had recently responded to the treatment and he is now an uncle. Averkios asked him to write it up for the monastery archive. You can get one of the white ribbons on the internet for around $10.

When it is replenished, oil from the lamps burning in front of the icons is bottled in little plastic vials, a potent anointment for the sick. Averkios dug in his capacious pocket and gave us one each. Jim asked for extras for the consolation of a couple of his Greek patients, whom medicine could no longer help. As the church was closing Averkios held him back. He took us to an icon of the Our Lady *Pantanassa,* Queen of All, on a column near the iconostasis, before which two monks began chanting. Averkios dug in his pocket again for a stub of pencil and a notebook. He tore out a page and told Jim to write down the names of his patients. He gave it to one of the monks who sang out the names along with others in a sheaf of similar scraps of paper. The way these monks looked at the icon, the matter-of-fact style of their chanting, gave the impression they were not praying in abstract but talking into a speaking tube directly connected to the other world. Which, from their point of view, they were.

The King's Wine

The Catalan strongroom of Vatopedi has manuscripts, icons, crucifixes and many other priceless treasures of the last thousand years. Among them is a pink and green tin that held a slice of the wedding cake of Prince Charles and Camilla. It is empty as the abbot ate the cake. Prince Charles has been coming on private visits to Vatopedi for many years. He is a celebrity among the monks and not just those of Vatopedi, as we discovered last year, when four of us were billeted at a smaller monastery for a week as part of an annual path-clearing project organised by FoMA, the Friends of Mount Athos. We got to know Father George, a useful contact as he was the cellar master. He was originally from Romania. One evening in the cool of his cellar we sat around a table with a tin of smoked fish and a jug of decent red from a demijohn, the gift of a Transylvanian well-wisher. We did not suspect that George harboured a special mission for us.

"You must know that our abbot was a young man on the ships. His name was Dimitris then. One night he was on watch in the middle of the ocean and a sailor stood next to him he had not seen before. He asked Dimitris where they were heading. Dimitris said he didn't know. 'That is where you are going' said the stranger and pointed and Dimitris saw they were heading straight for the cliffs under a high mountain. Dimitris rang the alarm bells and the captain and crew rushed out of their cabins. The mountain and the stranger had disappeared. They were in the middle of the ocean. The captain said Dimitris was dreaming or drunk and gave him many punishments. Dimitris left the ship in Patras. He went past a shop that sold religious things and saw a picture of the mountain he had seen in the middle of the ocean. It was the Holy Mountain. He came straight here and told the abbot. The abbot said St George came to him and told him to take in a young man he had saved from the sea."

"How marvellous."

"Well I never."

"Good Lord."

"It was a miracle. Saint George comes to the abbot once or twice a year to see how he is getting on and gives advice."

"Very considerate of him."

"Of course. Two years ago Saint George visited the abbot and said he must make wine for King Charles of England. You know Saint George loves England too," said George.

"Oh yes. His flag is everywhere."

"On the football shirts."

"But he is Prince Charles. Not King."

"A great country must have a King," said George.

"We have a Queen."

"I know but that is a woman. The ruler should be a man. Byzantium had two emperors. England can have a King and a Queen."

"Fair enough."

"The abbot gave me the blessing to help him make the wine for King Charles as I am in charge of the cellar and my name is George. We had a novice to help. The three of us picked the best grapes with our hands. We pressed it down here. See, there is the press. And there is the barrel. It is ready now. It is organic for the health of the King."

"Do you use sulfites?" I asked.

"Nothing," said George.

How do you stop the fermentation?"

"When wine gets to fourteen degrees it kills all the bacteria and the fermentation stops. You must taste."

George picked up a glass jug, rinsed it under the tap and took it over to a 100 litre wooden cask lying on its side with a crown chalked on the front. It had been tapped and George turned the spigot. This was not going to be pleasant. I have experience. My friend Panaghis and I made 600 litres a year in my cellar in South London with grapes from Covent Garden.

I suspected this would be as strong as sherry and tasting of dead mouse with hints of camel urine and fartleberry. George filled our glasses and invited us with a flourish to sup the royal brew. After sniffing, holding up to the light, a loyal toast to Charlie, England and Saint George, anything to put off the moment of truth, we steeled ourselves not to pucker and sipped the littlest of sips. Then swigged. Swigged again. Held out our glasses for more. It was excellent.

"You must take it to the King," said George.

"How, Father? How do we get that barrel to London? Through the customs of several countries? We can't take it on a plane. You need a shipping company."

"We have tried. They will not take it. It is not certified. You must help us. The abbot is most anxious. What will he say to Saint George? Take some bottles."

"We can't turn up at King Charles's palace with bottles of home-made wine. Monastery made, I mean. They have security. They'll want to know what's in it."

"Of course. Wicked people always wish to poison the King. We will send a letter with the seal of the abbot. When the butler opens the door of the palace you will give the wine to him and he will taste it before he gives it to the King."

He looked so expectant, so imploring. He was under pressure from his boss and his boss's boss, Saint George.

"We will take two bottles each. That's all we are allowed."

Relief and happiness flooded over George's face. He chose eight dark green bottles from a bin and gave them a good rinse. He opened a new packet of corks and dragged out a floor-standing corker. We gathered round the spigot and filled the bottles, with hearty tastes to make sure the quality was consistent. Each of us had a turn corking two bottles with photos to prove it. George found a roll of yellow masking tape and a felt-tip to make labels that he wrote out in elegant ecclesiastical script, *Abbot's Wine*. Finally we tore up cardboard boxes for packaging that we sealed with the tape.

Two months later we turned up at Clarence House, Prince Charles's official residence, to deliver the wine to his private office. Some very senior staff kindly received us and a letter of thanks signed by His Royal Highness was sent to the abbot. I hope the wine didn't go to waste.

The Athos Diet

The hermit staples at every meal are fresh or toasted bread, olives, raw onions and garlic. This is all you should eat if you want to be skinny and ninety, plus the odd apple and whatever nuts, mushrooms and herbs you find in the woods.

The cooks do an excellent job with simple ingredients. Some dishes, like the Vatopedi mixed bean soup, could be on any restaurant's menu. The food varies from monastery to monastery, depending on their national traditions. They feed between forty and two hundred twice a day, so dishes are made in big pots and big ovens. Food is put on the table while everyone is in church so it is usually tepid. This is OK for soups but a plate of cold spaghetti is less appetising. Meals are an integral part of the preceding liturgy, collective not social, eaten in silence while listening to a reading. They last about twenty minutes and there are no seconds.

Meat is never served. Dishes I have enjoyed include salads, soups, stews, savoury rice and semolina, boiled and roast potatoes, greens with garlic purée, pasta, feta, pepper and tomato fricassé, scrambled eggs. On Sundays and feast days the treat is fish, usually bony chunks of grouper boiled in a sauce, and a chocolate biscuit for pudding. On a great feast day a pastry like kataifi or baklava may be served in a separate meeting room with coffee, a social not a religious occasion.

On Monday, Wednesday, Friday and every day in Lent, Advent and other fasting periods, wine, feta, eggs and oil are off the menu. So no salad as Christians don't eat it without dressing, with the exception of Good Friday when lettuce is eaten with vinegar. When the sea swarmed with octopus, squid and cuttlefish they figured on the fasting menu as they have no blood. Today they are delicacies. Halva, made of ground sesame, honey and sometimes hazel nuts, may replace feta. Honey and tahini on stale bread is tastier than it sounds.

Wine is an integral part of the diet, not an intoxicant but a food with sacramental significance. Most monasteries make their own or bring it in from their farms outside. I can still taste a sensational breakfast white at Simonopetra.

Karyes

Back to the present. As we get close to Dafni excitement mounts. We gather our belongings and join the crowd on the companions and walkways. I am nervous, not about the strenuous walking, lack of sleep, odd meals at odd times. I hope my mind will cope with the craziness of the place without throwing up a wall of laughter as I try to unearth the strength of a faith that is an essential part of Greekness. As a bonus it would be nice to find some spirituality of my own to take away. To prepare for conversations with monks I have been rehearsing the Greek *I dianoisi mou agonizetai me tin psychi mou,* 'my intellect struggles with my soul.' Last time I tried the words came out as 'my turkey can't stand the cold' which led us down unexpected conversational byways.

At last we arrive at Dafni. The jetty leads to a waterfront with a dozen low stone buildings housing a souvenir shop, a café and the officialdom of police station, coastguard, customs and post office. Those of us going to Karyes, the capital, push to the front to make sure we get on the bus. Word gets round that it is parked a hundred yards away. We walk, trot and then run in a mob, men of all ages lugging cases and rucksacks, clerics hitching up their cassocks and holding their hats, the young and fit outstripping the rest of us. The savvy barge straight to the hold of the bus with their luggage before shoving into the panting scrum around the steps. Years of getting on Greek buses has trained my elbows and I slump into a seat, dizzy with exertion. As we set off an empty second bus arrives for the stragglers.

The first motor vehicles came to Athos in 1963 for the millennium celebration of the first monastery. Until then the only way to get around was on two legs or four. It was beneath the dignity and comfort of the Ecumenical Patriarch, King Paul, Prince Constantine and other dignitaries to ride from Dafni to Karyes on mules. A road was bulldozed and vehicles imported. It was the beginning of the end of Athos as a silent haven of spirituality and a refuge from the mechanical world. Roads proliferated, vehicles multiplied, mules died out, the paths they trod were overgrown. Before vehicles, pilgrimage was for the hardy. Now it is open to men like me, the sedentary, elderly, idle and generally unfit.

The road follows the shore past Xeropotamou monastery brooding over the bay until turning into the hills and winding up to the spine of the peninsula. At the top we look down at Karyes, the capital, a Macedonian village of some two hundred inhabitants clustered along a main street a few hundred yards long. In the middle is the bus park, the focal point of the minibuses and taxis that serve the monasteries, and a couple of mini-markets and little cafés. Pilgrims in transit mill around the stores and squat on the kerb outside. By afternoon they will disperse, leaving the place to a handful of shoppers and sweaty hikers in search of a cold beer. Arfa would be scandalised and I am mildly shocked that in one of the mini-markets I can replenish my emergency supplies with a tin of Spam.

At one end of the street is the health centre and the skete of Saint Andrew, known colloquially as the *Serai*, the Palace. It is a monumental complex on a grandiose scale with the biggest church on Athos, built by Russian monks in the middle of the nineteenth century. It might have been numbered among the monasteries were there not a statutory limit of twenty. After the Russian Revolution Greeks took it over. It is the home of a secondary boarding school in the Greek education system. The boys dress like monks and spend their weekends at monasteries.

At the other end of town is the seat of government. A stately building houses the Holy Council, to which each of the twenty monasteries appoints a representative. Four of them make up an executive committee, under a chairman, the *Protos*. Other offices house the civil governor, the fire service and the police.

The police belong to the Greek national police force. They have nine police stations on the Mountain, attached to the larger monasteries. Officers work a ten-day shift and then have ten days' leave. They say that their work is similar to policing in villages outside, with the obvious exception of incidents involving women. The population of agricultural workers and builders, drivers delivering foodstuffs and materials and tens of thousands of pilgrims, bring human frailties with them. Another task is to look for pilgrims lost on the trails. Sometimes they are unsuccessful. Bodies may lie months or years undiscovered in a ravine. This year a pilgrim was lost in the snow and his body found only in the thaw. These days the police have cars but fifty years ago they went round on mules like everyone else. There is still a police mule stationed at Great Lavra monastery, the only animal in Greece registered as a vehicle with its own number plates. According to the records it is over seventy years old. This is because, when an incumbent dies, a replacement quietly takes its place without the need for tiresome paperwork. There's a legend in the making - the Immortal Mule of Athos.

Axion Estin

The spiritual centre of Karyes is the Protaton, the church of the Protos. I pay my respects to the most celebrated of Athos's miracle-working icons, the Axion Estin, which means 'It is fitting in truth'. With the addition of 'to magnify you, the Mother of God.' they are the opening lines of the first verse of a hymn to the Virgin sung at most liturgies and other services. The Angel Gabriel in person dictated the words to a young Greek monk over a thousand years ago.

The icon is at the back of the sanctuary behind the iconostasis. There are about thirty in the queue so there is time to catch a glimpse of the only surviving frescoes of the 13th century Cretan painter Panselinos. I am usually hard put to tell the difference between one set of frescoes and another but these are exceptionally lively, helped by an unusual level of natural light from tall windows. The icon is in a shrine up a few marble steps. It is a little patch of brown in a big silver casing. Following the example of those in front I make the sign of the cross, kiss the glass, and dip a finger in the oil of one of the three sanctuary lamps hanging behind my head. The chap in front dabs it on the acne all over his face. I give it a quick smear on my forehead. I would stay and admire the frescoes at leisure but I want to see the house where the Angel Gabriel dictated the Axion Estin in 982.

It is a downhill hike but still I take precautions with elastic socks, knee bandages and trekking poles, the rambler's walking frame. It is a glorious day, porcelain sky and crystal light. You take the road out of town past the health centre helicopter pad and down a shady footpath along the high walls of the Saint Andrew skete. Two Dutchmen overtake me and after friendly greetings stride ahead. I let them go, partly for the solitude, partly to watch my elderly step on roots and rocks. The path levels out at a wooden bridge crossing an idyllic stream tumbling over rocks into a pool shaded with reeds and oleanders. You go up the steep bank on the other side and along a few hundred yards to a tumbledown two storey building fronted by a ramshackle balcony and a kitchen garden. For hundreds of years it was the home of elders and saints until disputes, schisms, natural disasters and the passing of time brought it to a state of collapse. It is being restored with the help of FoMA, the Friends of Mount Athos.

On the balcony the Dutchmen are sitting at a table with Turkish Delight and glasses of water. Father Theodore, a tall, gangly monk, well into his sixties, with the sunken cheeks and panda eyes of an ascetic, ushers me to a chair. He speaks fluent English acquired from his boyhood in Cyprus. He tells us about his morning's work unearthing a prophecy of the Ascension that a friend of his told him is in the Book of Moses. I have nothing to say to this, partly because my tongue is stuck to my palate with Turkish Delight.

Father Theodore leads us into the chapel, redolent of incense and candle wax, lit by dust-swirling beams of light from clerestory windows. We stand in front of an icon of the Mother of God holding her child and he tells us what happened in 982. A monk and his novice called Gabriel lived here. One evening the monk went to a vigil in Karyes, leaving Gabriel to say his office. Someone knocked at the front door. Gabriel opened it and found a monk who introduced himself also as Gabriel and joined him in his devotions. When they came to the hymn to the Virgin the stranger chanted a new and beautiful verse and the icon glowed with supernatural light. He taught Gabriel the words and to make sure he did not forget, wrote them with his finger on a roof tile. He left, whether on wings or by the door he came in is not recorded. The elder came back to find the stone inscribed and mortal Gabriel in shock. He took them both to the Holy Council. It declared a miracle and dispatched them both to Constantinople, where the Patriarch declared that the verse should be sung throughout Byzantium. The miraculous icon was taken to the Protaton in Karyes where it remains to this day, replaced by the copy in front of us. Alas the angelic tile has been mislaid.

As he tells the story, Father Theodore breaks into sobs and he wipes tears from his eyes. At the end of the tale he gives a big sigh, buckles at the knees and collapses full-length face-down on the flags, his arms outstretched. The three of us look at him and then at each other, wide-eyed in shock.

Red Cross training kicks in. The routine comes flooding back. Shout for a defibrillator -I can skip this; turn the patient on their back; fish in the mouth with a bent finger for dentures and other obstructions of the windpipe; watch five seconds for signs of breathing; if there are none, sit astride and press down on the sternum with the heel of one hand, the other one on top; push down hard as you can to the rhythm of 'da da da da stayin' alive, stayin' alive'; don't stop if the ribs crack, it's only the ligaments and what's a sore chest if you live; after thirty pushes kneel by their head, pinch their nose, give the kiss of life, two big puffs; get back pumping again. I lunge forward to the body as it stands up, dusts off its knees and makes three signs of the cross.

"The presence of the Virgin is so strong in here," he says.

Thank goodness I hesitated. It was a prostration not an infarction. Monks do up to a hundred of these in their cells at three in the morning before matins.

Theodore takes us behind the iconostasis to show us the exact spot, marked by indentations in the stone, where the Archangel stood when he wrote on the slate. We follow him outside to the front door where Gabriel knocked on that miraculous night. It is modern with metal bars and glass but will be restored as a replica of the original.

We go back to the table on the balcony for some tasty biscuits and a shot of the hard stuff. Our conversation meanders between the revival of Orthodoxy in the Low Countries and the current political situation in Cyprus, with particular reference to the nefarious Turk. I don't stay long. I down a litre of water for hydration, shoulder my backpack and set off in the afternoon sunshine along the path to Father Makarios's monastery.

Ancient Paths

The Jesus Prayer is the simplest and for many the most potent prayer. *(breathe in) Jesus Christ Son of God (breathe out) have mercy on me.* Monks say it over and over, like a mantra, whatever they are doing, until it becomes a part of them, like the breathing whose rhythm it follows. I find it a change from the Grand Old Duke Of York when I'm plodding the trails, the monkish equivalent of a marching chant.

The path is lined with rock rose, tree heather, strawberry tree, Spanish broom, brambles, various thorns and the persistent smilax creeper that knits the rest into impenetrable tangles and climbs trees ten metres tall. The rhythm of the Jesus Prayer sets the pace through a soundscape of raucous birdsong and distant machinery. I wish I could enjoy it more. It's been a long day and my knees hurt.

The path turns into a *kalderimi* made of massive stone slabs. A patriotic Greek may tell you that the word derives from *Kalos Dromos*, a good road. The rest of us will tell you it comes from the Turkish *kaldırım*, a pavement. Kalderimi are among the oldest man-made structures on Athos, pre-Christian some of them, following ancient routes. People walked along them long before the first monks arrived. In the middle of the fifth century BC Herodotus wrote that Athos was a great and famous mountain with six cities prosperous enough pay tribute to Athens. Acanthus, where the little port of Ierissos now stands, was wealthy enough to have a treasury at Delphi. Smaller settlements and religious sites included a temple to Artemis and probably one to Apollo. The top of the mountain had a shrine to Zeus. For centuries his statue has been rumoured to lie at the bottom of a ravine. Its other function was a signalling beacon, part of a system that could send messages throughout Anatolia and Greece. In his play Agamemnon, Aeschylus describes how news of the fall of Troy was signalled by fire and smoke from nearby Mount Ida to Athos and onwards via the mountain tops to Mycenae. Aeschylus's audience must have thought it credible.

There are still traces of a rich pagan past. In the courtyard of Koutloumousiou Monastery, high up in the wall near the main gate, is an ancient grave stele, a tombstone with the bas-relief of a seated woman dipping into a jewellery box held by her maid. It dates from around the middle of the fourth century BC. What are two pagan women doing inside the monastery? Several other monasteries have traces of a pre-Christian past in the form of sculptures and sarcophagi. Outside the refectory of the Great Lavra Monastery the porch is supported by ancient columns turned upside down to counteract their malevolent influence.

Early Christians were hostile to paganism. At the same time they acknowledged the language, ideas, arts and imagery they inherited from their predecessors. In the murals of some monasteries pre-Christian celebrities are co-opted into the Christian story. The porch of Vatopedi's main gate is adorned with Greek philosophers and the Erythraean Sibyl, a prophetess. In the refectory of Great Lavra Alexander the Great is drafted in to defeat the Persian Darius. The Byzantine artist of the murals in the church of Dochiariou shows Alexander ascending into heaven and in regal pomp with Nebuchadnezzar, Darius and Augustus.

In about 1540 the celebrated fresco painter Theophánes the Cretan depicted the Annunciation under the gables of the entrance to the refectory of Great Lavra. The Angel Gabriel on the left announces the Word to the Mother-to-be on the right. Between them is an Ancient Greek plaque of a huge human ear in high relief with the inscription "Neuris offered this to Artemis Agrotera (Artemis the Wild)." The ear was co-opted because it was thought to be the organ through which the Virgin received the Word by which she conceived. But who is that slinking away in the extreme right of the scene? With no halo, tell-tale red hair and distaff? The pagan goddess Artemis.

In the 6th century AD the Byzantine population was devastated by plague and Slav invasion. Athos was abandoned by Greeks to be repopulated by Slavs. In the 9th century the Byzantines recovered and reoccupied the peninsula, bringing in Greeks and Armenians from Asia Minor. With them came monks. They built their monasteries on the ruins of the old temples and opened up the same paths that served their predecessors a thousand years before. One of which I am walking on today.

Wine for the King

17 FATHER MAKARIOS

I first met Father Makarios in a pavilion outside his monastery on a headland overlooking the sea. The Holy Mountain blushed in the setting sun. Below us tiers of terraces dropped to the rocky shore. They were cultivated except for the nearest that had a cemetery and a bone house, a windowless stone building for storing exhumed remains. I guessed Makarios was about fifty. His expression could change instantly from cheerful to careworn to contemplative, like playing peekaboo with different faces. Mostly he looked vulnerable with sideways glances and a hesitant smile behind a bushy grey-blonde beard. Constantly fiddling with his prayer rope looked more like a nervous tic than silent prayer. I nodded to him and greeted him in Greek.

"Bless Father."

"The Lord."

"My name is John. I am from London."

He replied in English with an American accent.

"Right ho! Who do you support?"

"Birmingham City," I confessed and quickly changed the subject. "I like your boots."

They were black calfskin etched with a grape-vine motif, boots made for a Bacchanalia. I coveted them.

"I made them."

"Good Lord. I love the grapes."

"Jesus said I am the vine."

"Of course."

"My first boots were a penance for the fathers. Soon as we got the internet they wanted Crocs and Docs. I'm redundant. I make souvenirs now."

"Docs?"

"Doc Martens. They want DeWalt now. Are you Orthodox?"

"Not yet."

"Why not?"

"I have a problem with miracles."

I expected a sermon or a quote from St Paul but he smiled, looked worried, smiled.

"Many folk believe them," he said.

"I know."

"It is not obligatory."

"What? Do you believe them?"

"There's no meaning in your question. It's like asking if I believe in the moon."

"The moon isn't supernatural."

"What is supernatural? Supernatural and natural are the same."

"So I can believe what I want."

"The only true miracle you must believe is the Resurrection of Jesus Christ. If you don't believe this you are not a Christian."

"Gosh."

"You think too much. Relax. Open your heart. God brought you here. God's grace is a gift."

Sotto voce. "Does it come with a gift receipt?"

"Say again?"

"Nothing. Where are you from, Father?"

"From here."

"Before here?"

"Moldova. Do you know where that is?"

269

"East of Romania. My wife has worked in Chisinau. Famous for wine."

"Famous in Moldova anyways."

"Your English is excellent."

"I went to school in the US. Ohio State. Two years. I majored in literature."

"Not theology?"

"I was an atheist. An angel came in the night and told me to be a Christian. I fasted eighty days on bread and water. I was baptised in the Annunciation Cathedral in Columbus Ohio."

"How did you come to Athos?"

"I came back to Moldova when my mother died. She had a plate with a picture of that mountain over there. It was a message for me. There are many ways to Christ and his mother."

"I am glad you found your home."

"My home is there," he said, jerking his thumb over his shoulder to the sea. He didn't mean the sea was his home. He meant the bone house.

We talked until it was dark. What about? Everything and nothing, like talking to a stranger in a pub, sitting at the bar, sipping pints, a stream of shared consciousness. The Ohio State Buckeyes, prayer, motorcycles, the nature of love, the Pittsburgh Steelers, families, the existence of God, the Life of Brian, global warming, the meaning of life, the meaning of death. And more that I forget.

The monastery gates were closing. We stood up and exchanged little finger waggles.

"Toodle-oo," he said.

The next day after a hearty breakfast of cold spaghetti and wine I went to the souvenir shop. Makarios sat behind the till transacting with a shaven-headed Russian in a Spartak shirt. I browsed the icons and books, prayer ropes and medallions, fridge magnets and key rings, scented candles and packets of incense before settling on a mug with a picture of the monastery guaranteed dishwasher proof. I took it to the till.

"What Ho!" said Father Makarios and patted the chair beside him. He wrapped the mug and took my €10. He got up, went to a counter in the middle of the shop and brought back a little olive wood cross threaded on a leather bracelet.

"Here," he said, "This is for you. I made it. What do you see on the cross?"

I looked at it from all angles.

"Nothing."

"Very good. We like the cross empty, a sign of the resurrection. A sign of hope."

"It's lovely. How much is it?"

"It is a gift."

"Oh no. Let me pay for it."

"It is a gift. Like God's grace. Without the gift receipt."

A tubby young pilgrim in hunting camouflage brought over a black leather belt with a bronze metal buckle depicting the crucifixion. A snip at €50.

"Did you make that?" I asked when the hunter left.

"The leather. We get the buckles from China."

Another monk came in to take over the till. We left the shop together.

"Father, what can I send you from London?"

"Thanks. I have everything I need."

"Please. There must be something."

"Oh no. Well, I guess there is one thing. My favourite author is English…"

I waited at the gate while he went to his cell to write down the Jeeves and Wooster titles he already had. He came back with the list on a page torn from a note pad.

"Go with God," he said. "Toodle-pip."

Garden of the Virgin

A year later I plod the path to Makarios's monastery past fields of shimmering polytunnels. Athos is called the Garden of the Virgin - *To Perivoli Tis Panaghias*. There are two Greek words for garden. *Kipo* is the land round the house with lawns and flowers and shady places for a barbie. *Perivoli* is a more utilitarian plot away from the house for growing food, like an allotment. Beside an orchard a young monk takes photographs of men spraying pear trees. I admire his kit, the latest Canon digital and a telescopic lens. He speaks excellent English with a London accent.

"Are these for a website?"

"Could be. When we get one. The abbot gave me his blessing to record the life of the monastery for the archive."

"So who will see them?"

"Maybe nobody for a hundred years. I print them on special paper." He taps the lens and laughs. "Monks take the long view."

"Did you study photography?"

"At the London School of Printing. "

"Who do you support?"

"Spurs. I grew up in Tottenham. But I don't keep up these days."

I point at the spraying men.

"I thought everything was organic here."

"Yeah of course. The spray is our own invention. No chemicals."

"You should sell it outside."

"It's not that important."

"What is?"

"Put Saint Trifonas in the garden and give him a really good feast day. Two, rely on God - if one crop is bad he gives you more of something else. Three, weed by hand and pick off the pests."

"I'd rather take photos."

"We all join in."

A red FoMA sign with its striding pilgrim logo points steeply uphill. Trudging up with my two sticks. I get a pain in my chest and feel dizzy. My first heart attack? Should I turn back? Or is it the ribs protesting at the backpack? Is it indigestion? Only one way to find out - press on and see if it gets worse. So I do and it doesn't and twenty minutes later the pain goes away.

A barefoot young man skips past me. He has long hair, a short beard, tie dyed T-shirt and bead bracelets on his wrists. I catch him up at a wayside shrine inside the hollow trunk of a massive olive tree. Half a dozen icons seem to grow from the gnarly wood. A sign over guttered candles says not to light candles, sensible in a forest. He lights one with a cigarette lighter, makes the sign of the cross and invites me to copy him. After I've done he blows out the candles and covers the opening with a rusty piece of corrugated iron.

He trips on ahead of me and I am soon on my own again. Traffic noise gets louder. The path crosses a main road. Careful not to get run over I navigate a hundred yards of dispiriting concrete. It is not the Athos we come for but one we must get used to. Back on a woodland path I take pictures with my phone of the silver-rimmed coast, a monastery beside the sea and the marble peak of the Holy Mountain, for once without its tonsure of cloud.

A youngish monk, pink-cheeked and plump, looking the pilgrim part with a wide brimmed hat and long staff, comes uphill towards me. I smile but say nothing in case he is deep in meditation.

"Good day," he says in Greek and stops, leaning on his staff and panting. I stop too, both of us grateful for the rest.

"Good day."

"I am from Serbia, where are you from?"

"Ireland."

He breaks into English.

"Ah, Guinness. Very good."

"Our gift to the world."

"Walking is good."

"Prayer and nature together."

He slaps his pot belly.

"I do it for this. Once you get to forty…"

"Which monastery are you with?"

"I visit a friend in Hilandar."

"Have you been to Esphigmenou?"

"Of course. They are good men but crazy. Some are criminals from our wars. God forgives."

Hilandar is Serbian, the monastery furthest east on the north coast. Esphigmenou is about 3km downhill on the seashore. Esphigmenou sees itself as the guardian of authentic Christian belief, defending it against international conspiracies of freemasons, Jews, Catholics, and other enemies of Christ that it claims have infected the rest of Athos and the wider church.

"I'd like to visit the Esphigmenou pig," I say.

The monks got him last year to eat left-over food, although why they couldn't compost it like everyone else is a puzzle. He lived in a makeshift sty outside the main gate and doggedly, or piggedly, followed the monk, who looked after him. He is friendly to visitors.

"He is gone," says the Serbian weight watcher.

"What? Oh no. Was he kidnapped?"

I have PG Wodehouse on the brain. The kidnapping of the Empress of Blandings, a prize pig and the pride of Lord Emsworth, is a classic. The Emperor of Esphigmenou abducted by imposter monks, now that would be a tale.

"He was probably eaten."

"No. By the monks?"

"By the workers. Or sold. They need the money."

How sad. He was another legend in the making and should have had a more fanciful fate. But there are other things to see. Some years ago the beekeeper monk put images of the Virgin and St Nectarios into a beehive to increase the production of honey. He reported that the bees had totally covered the frames with wax except for the sacred images. He tested the bees' discernment by adding a picture of the Patriarch Bartholomew kissing the Pope. The bees ate it, leaving the others. It was judged a miracle and photographs of it hang in the guest house reception.

"I must go," says the Serbian. "God bless."

"God bless. Count the calories."

We wave our sticks politely at each other and continue on our ways. The gradient is rarely level. Downhill I use the trekking poles as bannisters to spare the knees. Up steep stretches I pace myself, twenty steps, stop, count to 5, deep breath, onwards. Most of the time the path is in the shade of unkempt forest, oak, plane, chestnut and lots of others I don't recognise. It is bathed in colour, rich blue sky between the leaves, gold dappled path, yellow broom, purple mallow, pinkish rock rose, pale honeysuckle, other blue and yellow flowers.

We cross the Ridgeway, the artery that runs along the spine of the peninsula, euphoniously known in English as the Way of The Bey, furnished with ornate Ottoman drinking fountains and shady places to rest. I stop for a break at the edge of a noisy stream cascading across the path. Unchristian thoughts of satyrs and nymphs sidle in. They were here first, after all. I lie down under a wild olive and let the sounds of Athos lull me into a nap... tanging bells, susurrating surf, walls of birdsong, wind in the trees, splashing springs and streams, frogs loud as ducks, rustlings in the undergrowth, bees, flies, beetles, insects buzzing like failing neon tubes, timeless sounds mingled with the hammering, rattling, clattering, gear-grinding of trucks, buses, pickups and vans, bulldozers, compressors, generators, mixers… the dissonance of ancient and modern.

Esphigmenou

The monks of Esphigmenou split from the Patriarch of Constantinople when he imposed the Latin Gregorian calendar to replace the Greek Julian calendar in 1923. Since then schism rears its double head at every rapprochement between Constantinople and the Vatican. In 1974 the Patriarch asked the Military Junta to evict the abbot and the elders. The government sent a gunboat to blockade the arsanas and marines to besiege the monastery. The monks locked themselves in, unfurled their famous banner Orthodoxy Or Death, and from the battlements hurled down anathemas at the besiegers.

Assets were confiscated and bank accounts frozen. The monks were condemned as trespassers and an illegal brotherhood. The other nineteen monasteries voted them off the Holy Council. Since no decisions can be taken without a full quorum the Patriarch appointed a government-in-waiting in Karyes to take its place, a virtual monastery housed in the skete of St Andrew while the real Esphigmenou lives on in limbo. Not that they would accept the analogy as limbo, like purgatory, is a Catholic invention.

In 1993 the fire of zealotry was fanned by the Vatican and the Patriarchate signing an agreement that '*the Orthodox Church along with the Papal community have the same Apostolic Succession and the same validity in their mysteries.*' In 2006 Pope Benedict visited Istanbul, where he sat on the bishop's throne during the Liturgy wearing his papal pallium and exchanged kisses with the Patriarch. This was deeply inflammatory to Esphigmenou's guardians of the true faith.

In 2013 monks threw Molotov cocktails at bailiffs come to take possession of the Esphigmenou office in Karyes. In 2017 the abbot was found guilty in absentia of "incitement" and sentenced to 20 years in prison, while other monks received 10 year sentences. There are still over a hundred monks in Esphigmenou. The banner is still there. The blockade of the main road continues but there is no shortage of supplies coming in on side tracks. The monastery pickup takes side roads to Karyes for provisions and is parked outside the town, as the number plates have been confiscated. Young men volunteer as workers and novices. There are plenty of pilgrims to welcome, although they cannot make bookings as the phone has been cut off, unless they know one of the monks' mobile numbers. Donations come in from traditionalists, Old Calendarists and Old Believers throughout the world, channeled through private bank accounts. Ever keen to dabble his fingers in troubled Greek waters the Russian Patriarch is a supporter. There is less savoury support too. Esphigmenou has become a focus for far-right nationalism. The Greek Friends of Esphigmenou Facebook page is a forum for their racist rants.

Musing on the stubborn self-belief at the heart of Greekness I brush off dead leaves and insects and plod on.

Toodle-pip

I totter into Father Makarios's monastery before vespers. I am in time to register, shower, rest, pop into church and have dinner at the non-Orthodox sitting before finding him. Slumped on a bench in the guest house reception I hand my diamonitirion to the sunken-eyed, sunken-cheeked young monk on duty. He goes away and brings back the customary restoratives, hooch, coffee and Turkish Delight, gratefully scoffed.

"Does Father Makarios still work in the gift shop?"

"Father Makarios is sleeping."

"Of course. I won't disturb him now. I'll see him after vespers."

"We buried him last month."

My first thought, to my eternal discredit, is the effort I wasted lugging his books around.

"Oh my God. What happened?" I croak, hoarse with emotion and sugary gelatine.

"He picked plums. He fell out of the tree. Thirty metres."

"Was the tree so big?"

"It is a small tree."

"Then how…

"It is on the edge of a cliff."

"He broke his neck?"

"No. He lay on the rocks twenty four hours."

"Was he alive?"

"Yes thank God. He made his confession when we found him. He died in the helicopter."

I can't think of anything more to say while the monk clears the table and leads me to a room with six beds, four of them already bagged. I lie down on a free one, sucked down into the belly of the mattress with a screech of bedsprings. Swaddled in ticking, thoughts of the grave stop me nodding off. After half an hour a monk makes his rounds of the courtyard whacking the talanton for vespers. I struggle out of the embrace of the springs and shamble to the cemetery on a terrace below the pavilion. The wrought iron gates are unlocked. There are three graves with black wooden crosses. The earth of one is still in a mound. White painted script on the cross names it Makarios, his date of birth, his date of death. He was 53 years old.

They brought him back from the hospital to his cell. They washed his face and hands, not his body. They sewed him into his habit, covered his face with his veil and put an icon of the Virgin on his chest. There was no coffin. His brothers carried him on a bier into the church for his last service and then to the cemetery where they chanted the canon of the dead as they laid him in the wormy ground.

This was not the end of Makarios's struggle for salvation. Some theologians teach that it continues after death when your soul says farewell to its body and is transported by its guardian angel along an ethereal highway to heaven through a score of toll plazas. The booths are manned by demons specialising in the different varieties of sin that damn the soul. Your angel haggles with them, offering repentance and good deeds and prayers of the living. If this isn't enough, it's the slip road to the fiery furnace. I fear I would fail at the first booth called Lies with its catalogue of empty words, dirty talk, ridicule, singing worldly songs and loud laughter. And that's before we get to sins of the flesh like gluttony and lust and unnecessary short cuts through the Marks and Spencer's lingerie section.

I push open the wooden door of the bone house. A window high in the wall, closed with mesh, floodlights a heap of skulls neat as cannonballs against one wall. The colours vary from milky coffee to dark Assam. Some have an upper denture but most are toothless. Other bones lie unsorted in open wood coffers. A few wooden boxes contain a full set of bones, the privilege of abbots and elders, their names written on their foreheads. In the middle of the floor an icon of the Virgin on a table with guttered candles waits for the next resident. In three years or so, if his bones are clean, Makarios will join his room mates.

I decide not to look for the fatal plum tree, as it is probably on the lowest terrace and my knees hurt. I sit on a wall overlooking the sea and take out my phone to search an email he sent me a couple of days before he died, in reply to mine telling him I was bringing his books. *'Thank you very, very much. You know what I think? I think that Saint Makarios showed you how I felt all these years in the Monastery: frequently snubbed by people, but always in the grace of God.'* Poor Makarios, he was so kind, cheerful and troubled. He gave you a conversation, not a sermon or quotes from St Paul. I hope his guardian angel sat with him that night on the rocks to fend off demons and dull the fear of aerial toll booths. I wonder if Jeeves and Bertie put in an appearance. When it's my turn, slipping away high on NHS opioids, it would be nice if they popped in with Stiffy Byng and Aunt Dahlia, Gussie Fink-Nottle and Chuffy Chuffnell, Tuppy Glossop and Bingo Little, Catsmeat Potter-Pirbright and other good eggs from the Drones for a spot of cheering up for the last time before the dark. Toodle-pip.

After dinner I go back to show the guest master the books and ask what I should do with them. He shrugs.

"What did you do with his things?" I ask.

"We have no things. Everything belongs to the monastery. We give them to monks that need them."

"And the books?"

He looks at the covers and frowns. They do not impress as aids to devotion.

"Ask the librarian."

The studded door of the great stone tower is open and I trudge up a circular staircase, dimly lit, towards a treasure house of medieval manuscripts, bibles, lectionaries, edicts, charters, firmans, that survived pillage, fire, peculative abbots, Edwardian manuscript looters, the ravages of worms and decay. This is as close as I get to them. On the first landing the stairs are closed off by another studded door, this one secured by a modern keypad. Opposite is a modern glass door opening into a miniature version of my kind of library with a carpet tiled floor, rows of metal shelving, the comforting smell of stale paper and old plastic. A monk sits at a desk playing solitaire on a desktop. He tears himself away to peer at me over aviator glasses from the hairiest face I have seen on the mountain, beard, eyebrows and bun merging into a luxuriant mask.

"Can I help you?" comes out in Greek from the shag.

"I was a friend of Father Makarios. I have his books."

I put them down on his desk. He looks at them without picking them up.

"Makarios had books like these," he says.

"Do you want these?"

"They are in English."

"What did you do with the others?"

"They are in Hades."

"You burn them?"

"Librarians do not burn books."

He stands up and I follow him down an aisle of shelves to the end where he points at the lowest one on the right. The lurid spines of paperbacks stand out among the sober bindings of the rest of the stacks, abandoned by pilgrims rejecting the works of Satan. I squat down and browse. Covers with voluptuous women and men with guns predominate among books in a score of languages shelved willy nilly like a charity shop. I recognise James Bond in Finnish, Dan Brown in Serbian, Fifty Shades of Grey in Greek. And there, in the innermost circle of bibliothetic hell, omnibus editions One and Two of Jeeves and Wooster. I pick them out and put them with the Three and Four I'm carrying.

"What do you do with these?"

"We send them outside."

I daren't ask where to. Recycling probably. Pulp fiction to pulped fiction. I grope for the words to save Wodehouse: joyful optimism, life enhancing generosity, glorious innocence, finest English stylist of the twentieth century, laugh-aloud funny but my Greek isn't up to it.

"These are not for Hades," is the best I can do.

"What is the topic?"

I concentrate on getting it right.

"*I chara ton lexeon,*" I hope I say, the joy of words, praying it doesn't come out as 'dawn of the lychees'.

"Ah. Philology."

"That'll do."

"Hmm. I will ask the chief librarian."

Great. I can leave with a clear conscience. Bertie Wooster might quote the Book of Proverbs:

'*Bright eyes gladden the heart; good news puts, er, jam on the scones, what Jeeves?*

'*Fat on the bones, Sir.*'

They can take their chance. I won't have to lug them around with me.

"Is this why you came to the Holy Mountain?" he asks. I surprise myself with my answer, the first time I have voiced it aloud.

"No."

18 SIMONOPETRA TO THE HOLY MOUNTAIN

I have reservations at Simonopetra and Dionysiou at the south-east end of the peninsula, two 'monasteries of the rocks' perched like seabird's eyries on pinnacles jutting out from the cliff. What possessed the founders? To get closer to God? Fear of Pirates? Imitate the hermit's vertiginous cave? It is too far to walk all the way so I decide to take the minibus to Dafni and hike the rest. It is a fasting day so I set out on a sugar high with nutty halva and dark chestnut honey with yesterday's bread.

Simonopetra is a five mile hike from Dafni along the coast road, a dirt track bulldozed out of the ancient footpath. The temperature must be over thirty degrees with no breeze and a malevolent sun. Soon hat, boots and all my clothes, including those inside my backpack, are sodden with sweat. The road is covered in thick yellow dust. I hold my breath and put my hand over my eyes and nose as trucks and SUVs barrel past, leaving sandstorms in their wake that stucco my damp clothes and turn me into a terracotta warrior. None of them stop to offer a lift. But the views are lovely. Over the indigo sea is the middle finger of the Halkidiki, Sifonia, a land of package holidays, fast food, discos and general voluptuousness, the antithesis of ascetic denial in which I slouch along with growing reluctance.

Walking helps to take the mind off poor Makarios. And off my answer to the librarian's question about why I really came here. Ahead of me through a haze of heat and dust the Holy Mountain taunts me with the hidden promise of a point to it all. My experience of Athos so far is that there is no revelation, no glimpse of the divine, no inspiration other than what you bring in yourself. You don't get spiritual enlightenment handed on a plate. You have to work hard at it with effort and sacrifice. But before this you need a kind of notion, an intuition of what you are striving for.

After an hour or so I stop to rest on a bench by a shady culvert, drink a litre of water, and eat an apple. A minibus pulls up beside me. The driver, a bearded young man, offers me a lift. I put a hand on my chest and twitch my eyebrows up and down. He's not taken in by the Levantine gesture.

"You don't have to pay," he says in English.

"Thank you. I like to walk."

"It is very hot."

"*Tama*," I say in Greek, penance. I point piously at the sky. This time he's taken in by pilgrim posing.

"God is with us," he says and drives off. I brush the dust of his wake off my half-eaten apple.

"Stupid bugger," I dis myself as I plod in the afternoon heat, regretting my vainglory, wishing I had accepted the lift. On the crest of every rise, round every bend on the sinuous track I expect to see the monastery and all I see is the next rise and the next hairpin.

At last, round a bend, perched on its rock, is Simonopetra. The joy! The soggy spring in the step! The guest house is outside the main gate, a modern remodelling of an old building, probably mule stables. The assistant guest master, a young monk with horn-rims and hipster beard, serves Turkish Delight, water, coffee and fruity raki before taking me to my room. I am billeted with two friendly Greeks, retired civil servants from Athens, sleepy Nikos, 60, and fussy, Giorgos, 65 who wears green pyjamas and takes pills out of a dosette box. They are appalled by my filth and amazed that anyone would walk when they could get a bus. I go straight to the bathroom and launder the dust off my person and all my belongings in an icy shower. I realise my mistake after every item is soaked and I have nothing dry to preserve monastic modesty but a handkerchief-sized towel. I put wet shirt and trousers back on, squelch back to the room, collapse on the bed in a stupor and fall fast asleep with grandmotherly warnings of rheumatism ringing in the mind's ear.

My room mates wake me for vespers at five. My clothes are damp but I am no more stiff and achy than usual. We go through the main gate and up a steep cobbled path under a tunnel into a courtyard bordered by the church, the refectory and the monks' quarters. Simonopetra is famous for its chanting and does not disappoint. I stay in the narthex out of politeness and join the exodus into the refectory without challenge. The meal is already set. We stand for Grace, gazing at the spectacular frescoes. At the first bell we sit down and scoff quickly in silence. If we are too slow the abbott will signal the end of the meal before we finish. The food is delicious, chick pea stew, coleslaw, creamy feta, apples. At the second bell we may drink an excellent red wine. A lector in a pulpit reads from the life of the saint of the day. Chatterboxes are hushed by a patrolling supervisor. On the third bell we stand for Grace. The monks file out and we follow, passing between the abbot at the door with a hand raised in blessing and the cooks bent double in apology for their shortcomings. We go into church for the veneration of the right hand of St. Mary Magdalene, the True Cross and other holy relics, whose provenance I do not catch.

Simonopetra has its share of miracles. The latest was in 1990. A calamitous fire started in the mountains on August 1st and threatened to engulf the monastery. The police and fire service ordered the monks to evacuate. A voice from the cross in the abbot's private chapel told him to stay put, the fire would stop at the gates on August 15th, the feast of the Virgin's Dormition. Which it did.

I go for a walk back along the road to the cave where Simeon was visited by the Mother of God and told to build his monastery and where he lived until he could move in. The first room is a chapel, lit with candles, airless and stuffy. In the far corner you can go up steps carved into the rock through a narrow entrance into the living quarters. I don't, as I have claustrophobia or rather the fear of claustrophobia. Two young Greeks, braver than me, come down the steps and we go back together. One of them has a grandmother in our village on Evia and knows our house. They are website designers, who have worked in London, and have come to the monastery to help set up a fund-raising site for America. Most of the monasteries are in debt, not least because of their obligation to give free bed and board to thousands of pilgrims a year. As more roads are built and religious tourism grows the financial burden will increase.

Back in the monastery we get espressos from a machine in the kitchenette and take them into the courtyard where they introduce me to Father Andreas, a Lebanese monk in charge of the website. He is built like a candle with a long tall body and a pointed head and a hat that comes down to his eyes and threatens to extinguish him. He speaks English with an engaging lilt. We sit and talk servers and platforms and other arcana for a while and the dark web and its perversions.

"Paedophilia is the work of the Antichrist. Yes. It is a sign of the end of the world. When I see how it infects families, schools, the churches, I wish the end of the world would come now…"

He goes on. The three of us nod. There's not a lot I can contribute. I can gossip about many things, even the internet, but shooting the breeze about the Antichrist I leave to the experts.

In the gentle light of late evening I go for a stroll around the wooden balconies, mobbed by swifts from their nests under the eaves, daring myself to look though the cracks in the floorboards to the drop beneath. I have acrophobia or rather the fear of acrophobia. Patrick Leigh Fermor has a wonderful description of the exultant bravado of Simonopetra growing out of the rock, balconied storey heaped on storey, the heart-stopping view from the fragile balconies down the sheer cliff face to the shore. I try to recapture his exuberance as he made a paper plane and threw it over the balcony, his childlike delight in seeing it hover and circle into the void until it vanished in the rocks and trees far below. I make mine out of a sheet of glossy paper I find in the self-serve kitchenette beside the refectory, an insert fallen out of a newspaper advertising skimpy beachwear, redundant information here. In my youth I was an expert on paper planes and use unforgotten skill to furnish it with broad wings, flaps and winglets. I barely let go when the wind whisks it away skywards, never to be seen again. Ah well. There's no point in recreating another's elation, I should find my own.

The bloody sun sets over a shot silk sea. Leaning on the rail I give thanks that I am here to see it. Who to? I don't know. Just thanks. Thank you. Thank you. Thank you.

Grigoriou

After a decent breakfast of savoury rice, olives, a couple of plums, a slug of fizzy new red, I fill my water bottles at the gate and set off downhill to the sea and Grigoriou. It is a steep,, rocky path full of nervousness about turning ankles. Or worse. Earlier this year a 62-year old pilgrim lost his footing on this stretch and fell ten metres to his death. The blessed tranquillity of Athos is broken by a petrol generator.

A monk supervises three workers spraying an olive orchard. The chief sprayer is drenched from head to foot. Above the racket of the motor the monk shouts redundant imperatives not to get cancer. Fortunately the path is upwind of me.

At a shady shrine to the Virgin I sit down for a rest on the pretext of admiring the view. The path divides, left to Grigoriou and right to the seaside arsanas of Simonopetra. I miss the sign and take the wrong path. After fifteen minutes the Virgin tugs at my sleeve - see how easy it is to slip into *their* vernacular. I toil back up to the shrine and find the sign. At the bottom of the path by a dry stream bed is a chapel dedicated to the Profitis Ilias we know as the Prophet Elijah. It is the first I've seen at the bottom of a mountain and not at the top and an opportunity for another sit-down.

Theologians deny that the ancient gods have been transmuted into saints. In the trade it is known as syncretism. It is surely coincidence that Ilias and the similarly named pagan sun-god Helios are both honoured with mountain-top shrines and a summer festival and are depicted riding through the sky on fiery chariots pulled by white horses. The prophet is also depicted in the wilderness being fed by ravens. Some scholars dispute the ravens tradition, saying the Hebrew word for Arab and raven is the same, but for the intonation, and that it was Arabs who brought his rations. I shall not enter this debate, except to say that he is honoured in Islam.

Leaving controversy aside I carry on uphill, easier on the knees than going down but still arduous. I fill the time on the lookout for enlightenment, inspiration, insight, prayer, peace. Not a chance. Still worrying, fretting, trivialising, vacuously concentrating on the path for stumbling blocks, all I dare hope is that the exercise will give me a good night's sleep.

Grigoriou is on an inlet nestled in mountains. A trio of pilgrims wait at the port for the fast boat to Dafni. I wave my sticks and put on a jaunty step as I pass, not to appear as knackered as I feel. A paved drive winds up through a shady colonnade and through the gates into a handsome marble courtyard with vines and a fountain. I make for the guest house, drop my things in the cloister outside and go in to slump on a velvet covered bench before my legs give way. A monk scuffs over in espadrilles. Although getting on for forty his pale face is barely camouflaged by a wispy ginger beard and there is not much of a bun at the back of his head.

"Mmm. Have you reservation?"

From his intonation and the absence of a smile I guess he is Russian-speaking. This is a Greek monastery but it is not uncommon to find monks of different nationalities.

"I'm not staying."

"Mmm. You wish to venerate icons. The church is open."

What I really wish is a glass of water and a drop of the hard stuff but I do the decent thing and slump in a misericord before the Virgin. When I come back Father Ginge welcomes me with a tray of sweet Greek coffee, a jug of water, a dish of Turkish Delight and hooch in a glass for which the description thimble would be exaggerating. I toss the glass down in one, unnecessarily as a sip would have done the job. In a flash of inspiration I remember one of the few Russian phrases that survive from the street Russian I learned in Moscow in the nineties.

"*Pirvaya kalom,*" I say, the first goes down like a stake.

Father Ginge was scuffing back to his kitchen but turns and gives me a piercing look. I smile. He goes out and comes back in again with a miniature carafe from which he refills my miniature glass.

"*vtaraya melki ptashechki*" he says, the second goes down like a little bird.

"*Na zdorovye,*" I say, cheers.

Actually there are three parts to the saying for three tots. Between the stake and the little bird is a falcon, *sokol,* but he left this one out to show I was only getting seconds not thirds. I drink the coffee, polish off the Turkish Delight and drain the water jug. I still have a stiff walk ahead of me.

The Vigil

It is 'only' three kilometres from Grigoriou to Dionysiou but there are some agonisingly steep bits. The first reward is the sight of my destination perched on its rock over the sea, a castle in a fairy story. Further on, below a waterfall in spate, looking back to Simonopetra and consoled by the thought that it is downhill from now on, I have a rare feeling of accomplishment. The steep path is unkind to the knees and there are a few uphill tests unkind to the lungs. At last the winding path to the arsanas becomes a track meandering up to the gatehouse past fruit and olive trees alive with bird song and a pale yellow cement silo proclaiming Titan.

The Dionysiou guest house is beside the church up a flight of stone steps. Holding it close to his nose, as if sniffing my credentials, a tall monk scrutinises my diamonitirion through pop-bottle lenses, the first guest-master to do so, and then his booking register, before fetching a glass of water, coffee, a single cube of Turkish Delight and no hooch. I'm too knackered to care.

"You are very fortunate. Today we have a beautiful vigil. The Nativity of the Mother of God."

"Oh good."

"It starts with Small Vespers."

"Of course."

"We eat a light meal and go back to the church."

"I am not Orthodox. May I go into the church?" I slap down the little demon on my knee whispering that I might be banned and get an early night with a clear conscience.

"We ask that you do not take communion or the *antidoron*, the blessed bread. Otherwise you are welcome to go anywhere in the church and to join the meals."

"Wonderful," says the little angel on the other knee.

"May I ask your name, Father?"

"It doesn't matter."

Father Incognito leads me out along a wide balcony, up some gruelling stairs and along a narrow corridor. It all seems new, the walls pristine white and the yellow woodwork freshly varnished. He flings open a door into a single room. What have I done to deserve this? It's the size of a ship's cabin, second class, luxurious by monastic standards with an electric socket, two clothes hooks, a firm bed, a bedside table, a switch above it so you can get into bed before turning out the light, a window with a view onto the church. I feel like a visiting bishop. There are even toilet seats and hot water in the showers.

On the wall is a copy of an icon of the Transfiguration, called the Metamorphosis in Greek. Jesus took Peter, James and John up Mount Tabor, where he shone in brilliant light and met with Moses and Elijah. From behind a cloud God said that he was well pleased with his son and they should listen to him. The Transfiguration is one of the twelve great feasts of Orthodoxy and especially important to monks, whose ultimate goal is to experience through asceticism the uncreated light of Tabor, the final stage before union with God. The church on top of the Holy Mountain is dedicated to the Metamorphosis.

After a nap, half a tin of Athonite Spam and a couple of Ibuprofen I hobble to the church in the hope of finding the oldest surviving icon in the world, the Virgin of the Salutations painted by Saint Luke, who knew her so it's from life. Two monks are preparing for the vigil. One of them breaks off from filling lamps to take me to the chapel dedicated to the icon. It is about A4 size including a wide gold frame. The image is a crusty black silhouette. The monk watches as I make three signs of the cross and air-kiss the glass. He asks if I am Orthodox. He is satisfied by *not yet/when God wills*. The other monk joins us and asks him about me. He says I am going to be baptised and I feel a fraud.

On the long wall of a covered cloister outside the refectory is a marvellous sixteenth century fresco of the Apocalypse of John in fourteen scenes, full of colour, energy and life. It is a gripping feat of imagination. Angels, demons, plagues, disasters, miracles, monsters and myths, the four famous Horsemen, the Whore of Babylon and the infamous Antichrist are swept up from histories and legends from every corner of the ancient world and lumped together in glorious mayhem until the triumph of the Lamb. I am lost in the tumult of earthquakes and raining stars in the sixth seal so do not hear Father Incognito come up behind me.

"Do you know what this is?" he asks.

"I read Revelation outside John's cave on Patmos," I say. It's a great read if you treat it like poetry and don't try to puzzle out what it means. The biggest puzzle is how it made it into the New Testament, not something you say to a monk.

"It is the truth," says Father Incognito. He nods and leaves me to contemplate the last days. Next to the Transfiguration the Apocalypse is a powerful theme on Athos as monks contemplate the end time more deeply than the rest of us.

The guest house balcony overhangs a dizzy drop to the rocky shore. I pass the rest of the afternoon in apocalyptic reverie gazing out at the sea mercurial in the late sunlight. In other circumstances time would hang heavy but here it drifts feather light.

Talanton. Talanton. Talan-talan-talanton. Five o'clock, the call for vespers hammered out on a plank. I join the troop into church and take a stall in the narthex. It is a marvel of wall painting. Floor to ceiling is dedicated to the early martyrs and some Old Testament celebrities, like Jonah in the maw of a toothy monster that looks more like a crocodile than a whale. It is an encyclopaedia of tortures depicted in gruesome detail. Asphyxiation Beheading Crucifying Dismembering Eviscerating Flaying Garrotting Hanging Impaling Jointing Kippering Lacerating Mutilating Nailing Oil (boiling in) Poisoning Quartering Racking Stoning Throwing To The Lions and much more through the alphabet of human cruelty. The labels provided by the painters are not much help unless you can read medieval ecclesiastical script but some martyrs are easy to identify: Sebastian shot by arrows, Catherine on her wheel, Peter upside-down on his cross. My martyrology falls short on the rest.

The church is packed. Four members of a motorcycle gang muscle in, big men in every direction with shaven heads and scars, their affiliation advertised in Cyrillic on bulging T-shirts. One has to be turfed out of the abbot's seat. They cannot spoil the numinous of chanting, incense, icons and frescoes alive in the light and shadow of late afternoon.

Small Vespers lives down to its name. In less than an hour we go into the refectory for the vigil meal, a dish of tepid potato soup, hard-baked bread and a handful of olives. Then back into church for the all-nighter. It starts off slowly with simple chanting from a trio of monks. A demon intrudes on my idle meditations with the Litany of the Mangas, a rebetiko song. A street-wise tough guy, a *mangas,* goes into church and prays to Almighty God to drop hash on his hookah. He asks *Theouli mou,* my little God, an affectionate pet name, to send his angels into the clouds of smoke to get high and sing him to sleep with a lullaby.

I last until half past ten, when I sneak off to my luxurious quarters. A pity to let them go to waste. Finishing off the Spam when I get into bed is an error, digestive as well as doctrinal. I toss and turn, dozing off and jerking awake. At midnight I give in and get dressed. Wide awake under a starry sky in the fresh sea breeze I slink back into the night-bathed church, lit by candles glinting on the gold and brass, otherworldly faces of the icons peering out of the dark into the candlelight. I light a candle for the living whom I love and the dead who live in me.

In the nave the massive round chandelier sheds light and shadow on the gems and precious threads of the vestments, on the filigree iconostasis, on icons clad in glittering gold and silver, on the clouds of incense swirling up to the Pantocrator in his heavenly cupola. Dark figures haunt the penumbra, made tall with hats and veils flowing down the back and shoulders. Some flit back and forth on mysterious errands with candles and lamps and saucers. Others are propped in their stalls, alert for liturgical errors, mouthing prayers, gazing rapt at an icon, meditating or dozing. New arrivals visit each icon in turn - sign of the cross, bow, kiss the glass, sign of the cross again, quickly move on. A priest, dressed in red, makes a brisk round of every corner, every icon, every person, driving away demons with his jingling censer.

Apart from the chandelier the only electric lights are fixed to the chanters' desks on either side of the nave. Three monks stand at each, one intoning the ground bass the others the melody. They bat a canon between them, stereophonic, synchronised by a prompter scuttling between them, giving them a lead, making sure they are at the right place. It is Byzantine jazz, lively, syncopated, foot-tapping, delving into a thrilling and mysterious musical world alien to the western ear. Harmony is impossible in a modal scale. You can't have the glorious multi-part wall of sound of Russian Orthodox polyphony or the western cathedral choir. Instead you have long melodic riffs migrating from mode to mode in rhythms as natural as birdsong.

A monk reaches up to the great chandelier with a staff and thrusts it swinging and turning into a *Choros*, a Dance. The effect is magical. The paintings and icons come alive, as if the church and everything in it dances.

Perched on the tipped-up seat of a misericord in the narthex, elbows on the armpit-height arms, sleeplessness, fatigue, and hunger transmute into trance. I make an effort to open myself to what I am told is the Holy Spirit. Mesmerised by the arcane business of brocaded priests framed in the proscenium of the royal doors, black-robed wraiths flitting, bowing, bent on inscrutable chores, the drone of chanted, syncopated psalms, litanies, doxologies, hymns, prayers, readings, invocations flowing through my altered consciousness, time passes unnoticed. Not once do I look at my watch.

In the darkest hour before dawn, the frescoes come to life, animated with people I love. Tortures, martyrdoms and death are replaced with figures from my deepest memories, father and mother and sister, grandparents, Arfa, our children. Out of the darkest corner steps a beautiful woman, almond eyes from an icon, a gentle smile, dressed in a cream robe and Byzantine blue cloak, the hood over rust-red hair. She comes towards me and I am filled with joy and tenderness. She slips into the misericord next to me.

"Thank you for coming," I say.

"Yes," she whispers. "I brought you here."

"Why?"

"You must climb the mountain."

"I am not worthy."

"No. You're not."

"Will you be with me?"

"I am not allowed."

"But it's your garden"

"I'm not Her. I am Harley."

"What? You're a She!"

"You think a He would put up with your blather?"

Jingling into our conversation bustles a priest exorcising demons with smoke and bells. Harley ghosts away into the flickering shadows.

The safest rule is never to trust to anything that appears to us in our dreams. For dreams are generally nothing more than images reflecting our wandering thoughts, or else they are the mockery of demons.
     St Diadochos of Photiki c.400-c.486. From the Philokalia.

from the Dionysiou Apocalypse

19 THE HOLY MOUNTAIN

The only indication of the time is the lightening of the windows, the glimmer of pearl grey through an opening door. At daybreak, the vigil segues into the holy liturgy. It lasts another two hours. At the end we queue up to leave and stoop to kiss the priest's hand. On the way out a monk serves silver cups of water from a soup tureen and sweet cake instead of bread, the *antidoron*, which I dutifully decline. The procession to the refectory is led by two monks with massive candlesticks and the magisterial abbot with his great chain, pectoral cross and gold-tipped staff. The sunlit hall is cheerful with lively frescoes and a gold-decorated lectern. The celebratory meal is a fillet of chewy fish, peppers stuffed with savoury rice, a gherkin, a nectarine and tasty red wine, fresh and sharp. A monk distributes saucers and towards the end comes round with festive *koliva*. The chap opposite me has the nerve to ask for a double helping. One is enough for me. *Koliva* is like Indian sweets, promising much and delivering less. At the end we stand up and the server comes round again with a lump of bread on its crust closely followed by a deacon with a stole and a jingling hand censer. We take a pinch of bread as it passes and make the sign of the cross, a sacramental conclusion to the night and the beginning of my ascent of the mountain.

Back in my cell I pack and armour myself for hiking. I have been three nights on Athos. My diamonitirion has expired. I could go back to Karyes for an extension from the Holy Council offices. Or I could climb the mountain now and risk a night in the open or the mercy of a guest-master. The law-abiding option would be Karyes. I suspect that when I look back on this I will think it a load of tosh brought on by fatigue, sleeplessness, disorientation and indigestion, on top of the stress of getting here on Harley, not to speak of icon kissing, incomprehensible prayers and encounters with otherworldly monks, but right now I feel inspired. The hidden goal of my journey is about to be revealed in the Metamorphosis on the summit of the Holy Mountain.

The path starts at the skete of the apocryphal Agia Anna, mother of the Virgin. It boasts one of her feet. 'Apocryphal' is technical not derogatory. Jesus's granny and her husband Joachim, the patron saint of grandpas, are not mentioned in the Bible but in the apocrypha, texts deemed untrustworthy by the earlier church. Does it matter? Mary must have had parents. According to the ever reliable FoMA guide Agia Anna is two hours away. Say three for me. So I should be there at one o'clock. If shattered after a disturbed night I will nap under a tree. From Agia Anna it is five hours to the summit but it is possible to spend the night at the *Panaghia* refuge three and a half hours away before tackling the summit at dawn. Then it is four hours back down to Agia Anna where the ferry to Dafni stops at about one o'clock. I will survive on Spam, peanuts, ibuprofen and Lockets.

A seersucker sky striped with high cirrus clouds sheds a luminous pearly light on a warm, clear and breezy morning, perfect for walking. For the first time since I got here I feel heady with purpose. The path zigzags downhill from Dionysiou to a broad dirt road along the shore to a Byzantine tower, where it turns left uphill into the terrace gardens of Agiou Pavlou monastery, huddled in the rock behind sheering walls. The mountain looms behind, an invitation and a threat. At the entrance to Agiou Pavlou I am tempted to go in, sit in the shade, gulp down tsipouro and Turkish Delight, pay my respects to the gold, frankincense and myrrh that the Three Wise Men gave to Jesus. I don't want to lose the delicious mania that keeps weariness at bay so, after a sit down on a wall and a guzzle from a convenient fountain, plod on, stalking on my sticks like a robotic quadruped.

The views are marvellous along the coast, roofs of tile and tin, rectangles and cupolas among the trees and down jumbled clefts to the rocks and surf. I concentrate on the path, counting steps, whispering the Jesus prayer, anxious not to stumble. In less than an hour the path skirts round Nea Skiti, a cluster of cells dedicated to the birth of the Virgin. Passing through iron gates feels portentous, a reminder of aerial toll-booths.

Concrete steps signal the beginning of the ascent to Agia Anna. I stop to hitch up the knee bandages and munch a handful of peanuts and press on. A drift of clouds over the sun brings welcome cool and a breath of breeze. I toil upwards for half an hour, made into an hour by stops for breath and sustenance, through another ominous tollgate of an iron gate topped with crosses. The path is steeper, alleviated by zigzags and steps. Labouring and breathless, a cool haze sneaking in from the sea is welcome. Another iron gate creaks open into rolling mist and a few hundred yards of uphill, flattening out and narrowing to the foot of an elegant rectangular bell tower. Leaning on sticks, locking my wobbly legs, I look up at the cupola melting into mizzle. It isn't sweat I've been wiping from my forehead but raindrops. I take stairs down to the right, through the main gate of of Agia Anna and onto a terrace overlooking the sea. The cliffs and surf to the west, the sheer plunge to the arsanas a thousand feet below, the coast to the east and the vista of the open sea are veiled in grizzle. The Holy Mountain that should loom over the katholikon has disappeared into the murk.

I order myself to press on but am not so stupid as to obey in the wet without waterproofs and in the fog without a compass. An elderly monk, a bare bald head peeking over a great white beard, appears and opens the church door. I accept the invitation in the hope of refreshments to follow. I drop my hat, pack and sticks inside the door and pay my respects to the icon of Agia Anna, a madonna with an adult miniature Virgin perched on her knee. Slumped in a misericord, the elation of the morning drains away into the puddle of damp beneath my aching feet. Gazing into the light of the candle I have just lit, a deeper conviction replaces it. A revelation.

I don't want to be here any more.

I am not looking at the icon. The icon is looking at me. The Virgin and her mother see through me. And through their eyes I see myself. I do not belong in this place dedicated to spirituality and prayer.

I want to be with Arfa and the rest of the family, leading busy lives with all our sins and foibles, enjoying today without fear of tomorrow, not brooding on the Last Judgement. I want to play the baglama and sing earthy songs with friends and strangers in a noisy taverna, go to the pictures, joke with women I know, admire those I don't, munch on chops and steaks, drink too much, sleep too much. I want to strive to be kind and make amends when I'm not. I don't want to live each day as if it's my last. I want to live it as if it's my first, full of wonder and hunger and immersed in love. This is where I find *Theouli Mou*.

In my world there are no miracles, only freak accidents and coincidences; no angels and demons, only hopes and fears; no heaven or hell other than what you make yourself; no sacred texts only legends and fairy tales; no lives of the saints only fictions; no faith only wishful thinking; no other reality only this one. It was inspiring and wonderful to leave behind my silly, chaotic world at the gates of Athos; to leave doubt and scepticism and reason and logic behind in tawdry bag-lady's bundles; and it will be lovely to gather them up again, stash them in Harley's vegetable crate and putter off into the future until the night takes me in.

It is ten to one. With a sigh I gather my pilgrim's hat and pack and sticks, go out into the mist, turn in the porch to make a farewell sign of the cross, mutter a thank you, and head for the main gate. I scuttle past the guest house and its temptations and take a path downhill signposted to the arsanas. Stumbling and skipping as fast as I dare in a tunnel of dripping trees, I plant the sticks together in front of me like a walking frame, a precaution against tripping and slipping on rock, rubble and mule shit, treacherous in the rain to a tired and clumsy geriatric. Calves and thighs join the knees in protest. The drizzle becomes rain. Lightning splits the sky, thunder rolls down the mountain. At last the path flattens out. I totter past stores and boathouses and a line of steaming mules to join the huddle of monks and pilgrims shuffling onto the ferry.

After a change of T-shirt, hot Nes and a cheese pie I leave the fuggy saloon and stand in the shelter of the walkway for a last look at Athos through the mist and rain. In those beautiful hills I have met kindness and hospitality among men solid in their faith and in constant striving to live up to it. Sacrifice and self-denial enhance their humanity. I am grateful they have let me into their world. It is different from mine. Their world is a shadow of reality. My world is.

Behind me the Holy Mountain has disappeared. Put it on The List. The journey goes on.

ACKNOWLEDGEMENTS

My heartfelt thanks to those who gave advice, suggestions and encouragement, especially Helen Cavadias, Robert Connor, Clare Gordon, Ellen James, John Jammes, Christopher Jones, Hilary Kyriazis, Sue Marks, Greg Marks, Hilary Marshall, Julian Marshall, Noonie Minogue, Nicos Nicolas, Jonathan Rickford, Richard Rickford, Anne Rooke, Elizabeth Walsh, Paul Watkins.

Editor Tatiana Wilde combined invaluable insights into structure and theme with meticulous attention to detail. Brilliant cover designer Andy Bridge captured the essence of the book in a single image. Annie Kovacevic patiently guided me through the digital world.

My family - Nuala, Alexander, Olivia, Damian and Ben, and their partners and children - have given me so much love and material over the years. My gratitude to them is inexpressible.

ABOUT THE AUTHOR

John Mole was born in Birmingham, England. He lives in London and Greece. He has travelled extensively through Greece, Turkey and the Middle East for business and pleasure.

His love of travel around the Aegean has resulted in several books. The best-selling travel memoir *It's All Greek To Me!* is about life in a village on Evia. The same place is the location of *The Hero of Negropont,* a novel about English Tourists exploring Ottoman Greece. *The Sultan's Organ* is a modern English version of the wonderful diary of an Elizabethan musician taking a self-playing organ and clock through the Mediterranean to Constantinople.

These and his other books are on Amazon and Kindle and in selected bookshops.

www.johnmole.com

IT'S ALL GREEK TO ME!

Sun, Sheep and Sea, Ruins, Retsina – and Real Greeks.
A love affair with Greece.

A little whitewashed house with a blue door and blue shutters on an unspoiled island in a picturesque village next to the beach with a taverna round the corner - in your dreams Moley. Welcome to a tumbledown ruin on a hillside with no road, no water, no electricity, no roof, no floor, no doors, no windows and twenty years of goat dung.

Come to our village on Evia. Meet Elpida, who cures bad backs with a raw egg and spells; Ajax the death-dealing butcher; Saint John the goat-headed saint; beautiful Eleni yearning for Düsseldorf; old man Christos, dug up on a sunny summer morning; sun-touched Dionysos dancing like an English tourist; the family saved from a watery grave and Hector their dog, a mutant specially bred to frighten little children.

Here is timeless, rural Greece - catch it before it goes.

Published by Nicholas Brealey (including Kindle)

ISBN: 9 781857 883756

THE HERO OF NEGROPONT

A travel book, a comedy, a history, a fiction.

To escape debt and summonses, rakish Lord Exford is exiled in 1788 to Constantinople with a prudish tutor and a truculent artist. They are shipwrecked on a Greek island ruled by a Turkish pasha and populated with stories of passion and delusion. Star-crossed lovers, renegades and minstrels, pirates and djinn are just some of the characters our travellers encounter. They also meet Amelia Burbage, a botanist, feminist and intrepid explorer, with her Syrian servant and an irascible camel. Befuddled by love, hashish and his classical education, Exford's tutor takes on the might of the Sultan and it is left to the wily Exford to deliver his eccentric band from an unspeakable fate.

Between Ancient Greece and Modern Greece were four centuries of Ottoman Greece. Join Lord Exford on his grand tour.

ISBN: 9 780955 756931

John Mole

THE SULTAN'S ORGAN

The diary of Thomas Dallam put into modern English

In 1598 merchants of the City of London paid for a Present to be given by Queen Elizabeth to Sultan Mehmet III of Turkey. In return they hoped to secure trading concessions and to turn the Sultan's military might on England's Spanish enemies. The Present was a carved, painted and gilded cabinet about sixteen feet high, six feet wide and five feet deep. It contained a chiming clock with jewel-encrusted moving figures combined with an automatic organ, which could play tunes on its own for six hours.

With it went Thomas Dallam, musician and organ builder. He encountered storms, volcanoes, exotic animals, foreign food, good wine, pirates, brigands, Moors, Turks, Greeks, Jews, beautiful women, barbarous men, kings and pashas, armies on the march, janissaries, eunuchs, slaves, dwarves and finally the most powerful man in the known world, the Great Turk himself.

Dallam was the first foreigner to record a glimpse into the Sultan's harem and the first to cross mainland Greece. His diary is a wonderful traveler's tale that will richly entertain and inform travellers to Greece and Turkey and fans of Elizabethan history.

ISBN: 9 780955 756924

MARTONI'S PILGRIMAGE 1394

An ordinary man. An extraordinary journey.

In 1394 Nicola Martoni made a dangerous journey from a small town in Italy to Jerusalem. He was a little, short-sighted, middle-aged provincial lawyer. He sailed through Aegean storms to Egypt, walked across the desert in high summer, climbed Mount Sinai with malaria, and finally made it to the Holy Places. Five companions died on the way.

Desperate to get home and running out of money, he wandered from island to island and across mainland Greece, braving more storms, shipwreck, pirates, mercenaries and brigands, sustained by curiosity, determination and faith in God.

It was an age of marvels and miracles, before printing and the intellectual and scientific revolutions that shape our world. His journal translated from Latin, gives us a rare insight into a medieval mind.

Join him on his journey

English translation only
ISBN 978-0-9557569-8-6

*

English and Latin Text
ISBN 978-0-9557569-9-3

John Mole